新世纪高等学校教材 | 英语语言文学系列教材

U0646569

听辨与译述

Listening Comprehension
and Summary Interpreting

总主编　常俊跃
主　编　邹德艳
副主编　刘　清　傅　琼　陈　婧　张华慧
编　者　王少爽　方　菊　赵　颖　刘春伟
　　　　高璐璐　张微微　邹存慧　姜　涵

北京师范大学出版集团
BEIJING NORMAL UNIVERSITY PUBLISHING GROUP
北京师范大学出版社

图书在版编目（CIP）数据

　听辨与译述／邹德艳主编．—北京：北京师范大学出版社，
2020.8（2024.8重印）
　新世纪高等学校教材·英语语言文学系列教材
　ISBN 978-7-303-25976-2

　Ⅰ．①听…　Ⅱ．①邹…　Ⅲ．①英语－口译－高等学校－
教材　Ⅳ．①H315.9

　中国版本图书馆CIP数据核字（2020）第124717号

图书意见反馈　　gaozhifk@bnupg.com　010–58805079

TINGBIAN YU YISHU

出版发行：北京师范大学出版社　　www.bnupg.com
　　　　　北京市西城区新街口外大街12–3号
　　　　　邮政编码：100088

印　　刷：北京虎彩文化传播有限公司
经　　销：全国新华书店
开　　本：787 mm×1092 mm　1/16
印　　张：22
字　　数：450千字
版　　次：2020年8月第1版
印　　次：2024年8月第3次印刷
定　　价：56.00元

策划编辑：周劲含　　　　　　　　责任编辑：王　蕊
美术编辑：焦　丽　李向昕　　　　装帧设计：焦　丽　李向昕
责任校对：段立超　　　　　　　　责任印制：马　洁

前　言

翻译人才是中华民族伟大复兴进程中沟通中国与世界的重要桥梁，是全面建设社会主义现代化国家新征程中不可或缺的重要力量。讲好中国故事，传播好中国声音，促进中外文明交流互鉴，助力中国开放发展和人类共同进步，我们需要为此提供人才支撑。翻译人才的培养是实现从"翻译世界"到"翻译中国"的转变，展现真实、立体、全面的中国的重要保障。自教育部2006年批准设立翻译本科专业（BTI），到2007年为培养高层次、应用型翻译人才设置翻译硕士专业（MTI），再到2014年对培养更高层次翻译人才的翻译博士专业（DTI）设置进行探讨，以及2022年DTI被列入教育部新版《研究生教育学科专业目录》，主管部门、行业协会、高等院校一直积极推动翻译专业学科发展和翻译专业人才培养。目前，我国翻译本科专业院校数量为301所，翻译硕士专业院校数量为316所，后者招生人数由2008年的约350人，发展到现在每年招生超过1万人，累计招生约9.7万人，毕业生约6.8万人（《2022中国翻译及语言服务行业发展报告》）。数量空前的翻译专门人才培养给翻译教学带来了挑战，也提出更高的要求，需要大力推进翻译教学研究。

大连外国语大学开设本科口译课程的历史已有30余年。于2005年招收英语专业高级翻译方向本科生，2010年招收翻译专业本科生。研究生层次的口译教学随着2009年大连外国语大学获批成为第二批MTI培养单位而逐渐展开。多年来，我校积累了丰富的口译教学及科研成果，获批国家、省部、市、校级口译科研立项数十项，口译课程改革获得省级教学成果奖多项，所培养学生数百人次获得国家、省、市级口译比赛的各级奖项。目前，我校已经形成了翻译本科和翻译硕士相互结合、教学和科研齐头并进的翻译人才培养体系。我校翻译专业于2019年获批为国家级一流本科专业建设点。

目前，口译课程已经成为诸多高校翻译课程设置中的必修课。市面上已出版的教材大多体现口译的专业性和职业化的特点，更适合本科高年级甚至研究生阶段的口译教学，与本科基础口译课程相配套、适用于课堂教学的扩展教材还比较缺乏。为满足本科阶段的教学需求，结合多年来的口译教学经验，我们编写了这本《听辨与译述》教材。该教材包括十五个单元，章节设计注重"听"和"述"分支技能的呼应和互动，从听辨和译述两条线平行展开训练设计，最后进阶至无笔记交替传译和对话口译的模拟实践环节。本教材适用于"听辨与译述"学期课程的教学，或者作为"交替传译"课程的辅助教材加以使用。

《听辨与译述》教材的编写体现了如下特点。

1. 听辨技能与译述技能的有机结合

本教材强调口译训练的技能性原则，按照由浅入深的先后顺序涵盖了听辨的主要技能，包括对"说明性演讲、说服性演讲、话语标记、信息结构（已知及未知信息/核心句/话题链）、多任务处理、语言预测、非语言预测、信息密度、信息冗余、记忆训练"等环节的集中训练；同时涵盖了译述的主要技能，包括对"词性转换、同义词替换、有提示演讲、断句、句法转换、详述、影子跟读、PPT演讲、主题演讲、归纳、缩减、复述"等环节的集中训练。最后进阶至无笔记交替传译和对话口译的模拟实践环节。

2. 技巧渐进与课堂操作的有机结合

本教材每个章节都从"热身练习"开始，进而结合听辨和译述相关技能的讲解和练习，之后通过"信息连线"拓展行业知识，最后通过"课后练习"巩固所学。相关练习材料的设计丰富多样，难度进阶合理，步步为营，稳扎稳打，有效辅助技巧讲解，提升训练效果。同时，练习的设计充分考虑教材的课堂应用，针对练习加入合适的课堂活动和可操作的练习指导。此外，大多数口译教材提供的练习参考答案多为笔译类译文，不能有效体现口译的即时特点及应对策略。针对这种情况，本教材提供的练习参考答案是口译场景中可以接受的译语产出，同时体现本书讲授的技巧及口译工作的特点，提升本教材的课堂适用程度和实践指导作用。

3. "信息连线"与行业知识的有机结合

本教材每个章节都设计了"信息连线"（Information Link）专栏，为学习者拓展口译行业内的相关知识。这些知识包括：口译的定义和类型、口译的认知负荷模型、交替传译与同声传译、语料的选择、口译的方向性、脱离源语语言外壳、口译中的不流利、输出自动化、口译中的视觉化、口译中的自我监控、语言转换速度、时滞/听说时差、记忆类型和遗忘曲线、视译等。了解行业重要概念，有助于加深学习者对口译的全面了解，提升学习兴趣和学习效果。

本教材的主编具备多年的口译实践、教学及研究经验，毕业于英国巴斯大学及上海外国语大学，曾赴北京大学及英国伦敦大学学院访学，主持完成国家社科基金及教育部人文社科基金口译研究课题，负责口译教学团队及创新团队项目，获得辽宁省教学成果奖一等奖2项，入选辽宁省"优秀专家""本科教学名师""百千万人才工程"百人层次人选，出版专著《口译的记忆训练——理论与实践》《口译中的话语——分析与重构》《交替传译工作记忆能力的差异研究》。本教材的编写团队具备专业口译学习、实践、教学及研究背景，具有英国巴斯大学、英国伦敦大学学院、英国埃塞克斯大学、英国贝尔法斯特女王大学、澳大利亚麦考瑞大学、北京外国语大学、上海外国语大学、厦门大学等国内外著名口译院校的学习及访学经历。团队建设的系列口译课程《交替传译》《专题口译》《口译的记忆训练》《同声传译》《口译工作坊》获选辽宁省一流本科课程，《交替传译》《同声传译》《英汉视译》入选国家高等教育智慧教育平台课程。

本教材是多年教学经验的总结，书中疏忽错漏在所难免，请读者不吝指正。

编者
2023年7月

CONTENTS

Unit 1

Informative Speech & Transfer of Part of Speech

> It's much easier to be convincing if you care about your topic. Figure out what's important to you about your message and speak from the heart.
>
> — Nicholas Boothman, English speaker,
> author of bestsellers on public speaking

Unit Goals

- To gain a general knowledge of how informative speech is organized.
- To become more flexible in summary interpreting by transferring part of speech.
- To gain a general knowledge of definition and type of interpreting.

Warm Up

Directions: Listen to the following passages and fill in the blanks with the given words. Make sure the words you fill in are both grammatically and semantically acceptable.

Task A

How can we help the millions of people (1) _____ (got up; caught up) in conflict, suffering massively in wars with no end in sight?

Civilians are pounded with (2) _____ (deadly force; daily force). Women, children and men are killed and injured, forced from their homes, (3) _____ (dispossessed; desperate) and destitute. Even hospitals and aid convoys are targeted.

No one wins these wars, everyone loses. (4) _____ (Millions; Trillions) of dollars are spent destroying societies and economies, (5) _____ (fueling; filling) cycles of mistrust and fear that can last for generations. And whole regions are (6) _____ (distabilized; destabilized) and the new threat of global terrorism (7) _____ (effects; affects) us all.

On this New Year's Day, I ask all of you to join me in making one shared New Year's resolution: Let us (8) _____ (solve; resolve) to put peace first. Let us make 2017 a year in which we all — citizens, governments, leaders — strive to overcome our differences.

From (9) _____ (solitary; solidarity) and compassion in our daily lives, to dialogue and respect across political divide. From ceasefires on the battlefield, to (10) _____ (compassion; compromise) at the negotiating table to reach political solutions.

Peace must be our goal and our guide. And all that we strive for as a human family — dignity and hope, progress and prosperity — depends on peace. But peace depends on us.

I appeal to you all to join me in committing to peace, today and every day. Let us make 2017 a year for peace.

🎧 **Task B**

The (1) _____, better known as APEC, is the most influential economic (2) _____ in the Asia-Pacific region. With 21 member economies, it accounts for nearly 50% of the world trade, and about 60% of global GDP (3) (_____). In total, APEC houses 2.8 billion people or about 40% of the world's population.

Established in 1989 in response to the growing (4) _____ of Asia-Pacific economies, APEC aims to facilitate economic growth and prosperity in the region. Over the years, it has developed various meetings, including Economic (5) _____. Ministers, delegates and technical experts gather together on different occasions, trying to find (6) _____ on doing business.

With time, APEC has become a (7) _____ of economic growth. Real GDP in the region increased from $16 trillion in 1989 to $20 trillion in 2015. (8) _____ of the Asia-Pacific witness their (9) _____ rise by 74 percent, lifting millions out of poverty and widening the middle class in a little less than two decades.

China joined the organization in 1991, and has since hosted APEC twice — the first time in 2001, in Shanghai, and in 2014, in Beijing. Economic and financial cooperation aside, APEC member economies have increasingly worked closely on issues like (10) _____

_____ as well as communication and cultural sectors.

This summit was a chance for me to engage directly with many of our partners including

(11) _____. We talked about

the need for greater cooperation on a wide range of issues, especially on the economic

(12) _____. We know that trade can have a positive impact on middle-class families and

those working hard to join it. But at the same time, we realize that it is our job to make sure that

(13) _____, and it is our duty to ensure that

(14) _____. I look forward to working closely

with my fellow leaders in the years ahead to build a better, more prosperous future for all.

‖‖‖‖‖‖‖‖‖‖‖‖ Listening Comprehension ‖‖‖‖‖‖‖‖‖‖‖‖

Skill Focus

Informative Speech（说明性演讲）

　　说明性演讲是向听众说明一个主题的演讲，主要任务是针对某个主题让听众了解更多的情况，类似于针对某个主题对听众讲一节课。我们的工作和生活中涉及很多说明性演讲，比如，说明情况、汇报工作、介绍产品等。与说服性演讲不同，说明性演讲不是要说服听众接受某个主题的好坏正误，而只是将某个主题的事实展示清楚，由听众自己做出判断或得出结论。说明性演讲最重要的目的是：自己说清楚，别人听明白。说明性演讲有很多种类，主要包括关于物体、过程、事件、概念的说明。

关于物体的说明性演讲

　　物体指有形可见的事物，可以是地方、结构、物件，比如，博物馆、熊猫、高铁等。当然，针对每个主题，我们不可能穷尽其特点和信息，需要将题目细化，比如，大英博物馆的历史、熊猫的外交角色、高铁的技术输出等。在对物体进行说明的过程中，可能会用到的说明方式包括时间顺序、空间顺序、逻辑关系等。

关于过程的说明性演讲

　　过程是一系列动作的集合，可能产出具体的结果或产品。关于过程的说明性演讲解释事物的工作过程、制作过程或者完成过程。比如，我们可以告诉听众飓风是如何形成的，如何成功设计个人简历，如何学会游泳，饺子是如何制作的等。在对过程进行说明的时候，可能要用到的说明方式包括时间顺序和逻辑关系等。

关于事件的说明性演讲

事件是发生过的或者被认为发生过的事情，比如，地震、春游、法国大革命等。我们可以告诉听众爬山需要的装备，法国大革命的过程，春游中发生的有趣的事等。在对事件进行说明的过程中，可能要用到的说明方式包括时间顺序、因果关系、逻辑关系等。

关于概念的说明性演讲

概念包括信仰、理论、创意、理念等。相比以上提及的物体、过程和事件，概念更加抽象。比如，我们可以告诉听众教育理念、电影理论、国际法、基督教等的概念。

说明性演讲需要注意的问题

1. 把讲话主题限制在一定范围内。只针对一个要点，紧扣主题，一次只谈一个话题。
2. 讲话要遵循一定的顺序。过去、现在、将来的时间顺序，由外及内、由内及外、东南西北等的空间顺序，或事物内部的逻辑顺序等。
3. 条理分明，使用数字使演讲更加井然有序，易于理解。还可以采用图片、视频音频等视听辅助材料，帮助听众更好地理解并记忆说明性演讲的主题。
4. 不要高估听众对演讲话题的了解程度，可以把讲话主题与听众熟悉的话题进行比较，尽量少用或者简化术语，使演讲的内容更加通俗化，以提升其可理解度。

说明性演讲的主题及展开

说明性演讲的主题包罗万象，从下面几个主题中找出你感兴趣的，并尝试写一篇说明性演讲稿。

1. The Biography of Your Favorite Actor 你最喜爱的演员的传记
2. How to Make a Pizza 如何做比萨饼
3. How to Read a Map 如何看地图
4. How to Cook Chinese Food 如何做中国菜
5. All About Your Favorite Vacation Spot 你最喜爱的度假胜地
6. How to Find Cheap Airline Tickets 如何找到便宜的机票
7. How to Be More Romantic 如何变得更浪漫

8. How to Improve Your Conversation Skills 如何提升你的对话技巧

9. Poverty in Mexico 墨西哥的贫困问题

10. How to Apply for a Credit Card 如何申请信用卡

下面来看两篇说明性演讲的提纲。更好地了解说明性演讲的组织方式，可以帮助译者对说明性演讲进行有效的听解和译述。

Five Principles of Peaceful Coexistence

Thesis statement: As norms of relations between nations, the five principles of peaceful coexistence have become widely recognized throughout the world.

Main Points

1. The first principle refers to mutual respect for each other's territorial integrity and sovereignty.

2. The second principle emphasizes mutual non-aggression.

3. The third principle stresses mutual non-interference in each other's internal affairs.

4. The fourth principle calls for equality and mutual benefit.

5. The fifth principle advocates peaceful coexistence.

Major Arguments for and Against Private Cars

Thesis statement: Supporters and opponents of private cars both have legitimate arguments.

Main Points

1. Supporters of private cars argue that with private cars life will become more convenient. A car allows one to move freely and with a car there is no need to wait for the bus.

2. Supporters of private cars believe that the automobile industry provides jobs for countless workers, thereby a strong boost for employment.

3. Opponents of private cars argue that automobiles give rise to the problem of poisonous emission, polluting the environment and causing harm to the health of people.

4. Opponents of private cars emphasize that private cars lead to traffic congestion so greatly that the drivers are more often frustrated by traffic jams.

Guided Practice

Task A

Directions: Skim the passage and fill in the blanks based on the information structure. Then listen to the recording and check how the combination of known and unknown information helps with the anticipation.

Welcome to the activities of Australian week — A Unique Experience of Australian Flavor. We have arranged the following activities for the five-day Australian Week. On (1) _____, the Australian (2) _____ Festival will be held to show you the Australian Food Flavor; (3) _____ is to be held on the 14th of March; On Wednesday, March the 15th, there will be an (4) _____; On March the 16th, you can enjoy the (5) _____ while on the last day, the (6) _____ will be held. We hope you will know more about Australia through "Australian Week".

Try This: _____

Please fill in the following chart with relevant information from the paragraph. Then try to rebuild the above paragraph with the help of the chart below. You may use English or Chinese in the reproduction.

Australian Week		
March the 13th	Monday	The Australian Food Festival

Task B

Directions: While listening to the following passage, please underline words or phrases that you think are important to help you rebuild the information structure of the passage.

This is the main library. This is the periodical room, mainly for current or recent periodicals. For earlier issues, there's another periodical room on the left. Over there are the audio-visual rooms. You can borrow tapes, cassettes, or film strips and listen or watch without disturbing others. Here are the typing booths. Typewriters can be rented for 25 cents an hour. Here you see the copying machines. You'll find several on almost every floor.

The Reading Room is open Monday — Friday, 9 a.m. — 6 p.m.. The Reading Room is closed for Bank Holidays and University closures. The last order for documents and books is 4:15 p.m. and materials can be used until 15 minutes prior to closing time. Anyone is welcome to visit the Reading Room. On your first visit, you will be asked to register as a reader. Please see our "Regulations and Registration" page for more information. For various reasons, access to some materials may be restricted. If you wish to consult the archives or rare books, we strongly urge you to contact us in advance, to let us know the subject of your research, and to make an appointment to view the material, which can then be made ready for you.

How do you go online at the library? It would be hard to find a library without a computer nowadays and most of libraries will provide some form of internet access, whether free or paid by time slots. You may need to use your library card for "time" on or simply purchase slots of time — ask the librarian for details. Just be sure to heed the usual copyright rules and don't download anything that is illegal because that will just get the library into trouble and could lead to restricted or no internet access. You can also access our library system online now, from your home or smartphone, to check for availability of resources, and put them on hold, or to order titles from other libraries in the same system, and many other functions that might have previously required your physical presence at the library.

Try This:

Please fill in the following blanks based on the words or phrases you have underlined. Then try to rebuild the above passage with the help of the words or phrases. You may use English or Chinese in the reproduction.

Main library

Periodical room: (1) _____ periodicals

Another on the left: (2) _____ issues

Audio-visual room: (3) _____ tapes, cassettes, or film strips

                (4) _____ without disturbing others

Typing booths: (5) _____ rented for 25 cents an hour

                (6) _____

Reading room

Open: (7) _____

Closed: (8) _____

Last order: (9) _____

Use until: (10) _____

First visit: (11) _____

Consult archives or rare books: (12) _____

Getting online at the library

Internet access: (13) _____

Library card: ask the (14) _____

Heed the copyright rules: not to (15) _____

Library system online, home or smartphone: resources

(16) _____

(17) _____

(18) _____

Task C

Directions: Listen to the recording and fill in the blanks. Pay attention to the role of the missing words and sentences, and check how the combination of both known and unknown information helps with the anticipation.

Industry

(1) _____. Industry comes from the Latin industria, which means "diligence, hard work" and the word is still used with that meaning. If you build a house in three weeks, when the same job takes everyone else three months, you're showing impressive industry.

(2) _____. For example, workers in the textile industry design, fabricate, and sell cloth; the tourist industry includes all the commercial aspects of tourism. The major source of revenue of a group or company is the indicator of its relevant industry. When a large group has multiple sources of revenue generation, it is considered to be working in different industries.

(3) _____. At the top level, industry is often classified according to the three-sector theory into sectors: primary (extractive), secondary (manufacturing), and tertiary (services).

(4) _____. This came through many successive rapid advances in technology, such as the production of steel and coal. Following the Industrial Revolution, possibly a third of the world's economic output is derived from (5) _____. Many developed countries and many developing/semi-developed countries depend significantly on (6) _____. Industries, the countries they reside in, and the economies of those countries are interlinked in a complex web of interdependence.

(7) _____. Service industries include banking, communications, wholesale and retail trade, (8) _____ _____ such as engineering, computer software development, and medicine, nonprofit economic activity, (9) _____, including defense and administration of justice, as well as other service-dominated businesses. (10) _____ _____.

Try This:

Please choose from the given industries the ones that are of manufacturing or service industries, and fill the corresponding numbers into the blanks.

Manufacturing industries such as _____ make up the manufacturing sector.

Services or service industries such as _____ make up the service sector.

1. catering (restaurants, bars, etc.)

2. aerospace (planes and space vehicles)

3. cars and automobiles

4. computer hardware (computers, printers, etc.)

5. financial services (banking, insurance, etc.)

6. healthcare (medical care)

7. leisure (sport, theme parks, etc.)

8. construction (buildings, etc.)

9. defence (arms, weapons, etc.)

10. food processing (canned, frozen foods, etc.)

11. household goods (washing machines, refrigerators, etc.)

12. media (books, newspapers, film, television, etc.)

13. pharmaceuticals (medicines, etc.)

14. textiles (cloth and clothes, etc.)

15. property/real estate (buying, selling and managing buildings)

16. retail (shops, etc.)

17. telecommunications (phone, Internet services)

18. tourism (travel and holidays)

19. power engineering and manufacturing (gas, wind turbines, etc.)

20. entertainment (TV, films etc.)

Try This:

Please fill in the blanks with appropriate words or phrases that are given below.

Here is how industry has developed in South Korea. The growth of (1) _____ was the principal stimulus to its economic development. In 1950, South Korea was a poor country, with most people living and working on the land. The government decided to (2) _____ _____, and the new (3) _____ were textiles, and (4) _____ like steel and shipbuilding. In the 1970s, South Korea turned more and more to (5) _____ like electronics, making electrical goods such as televisions cheaply. It also started producing cars. Turning to the 1980s, South Korea moved into specialized electronics. This was one of the (6) _____ of the 1990s: making specialized parts for computers and telecommunications equipment. In 1990 South Korean manufacturers planned a significant shift in future production plans toward (7) _____. In June 1989, panels of government officials, scholars, and business leaders held planning sessions on the production of such goods as new materials, mechatronics, including (8) _____, bioengineering, microelectronics, fine chemistry, and aerospace. This shift in emphasis, however, did not mean an immediate decline in heavy industries such as automobile and ship production, which had dominated the economy in the 1980s. Seoul's (9) _____ introduced modern technologies into outmoded facilities at a rapid pace, increased the production of commodities. (10) _____ analysts stated that poor export performance resulted from structural problems embedded in the nation's economy.

emerging industries 新兴产业	light industries 轻工业
industrialize 工业化；产业化	industrialists 工业家；实业家
the industrial sector 工业行业；产业领域	heavy industries 重工业
Ministry of Trade and Industry 贸易及工业部	industrial robotics 工业机器人领域
high-technology industries 高科技产业	growth industries 成长行业；增长行业

Summary Interpreting

Skill Focus

Transfer of Part of Speech（词性转换）

英语源自印欧语系，而汉语属于汉藏语系，两者在语言结构上有较大差异。无论是英译汉还是汉译英都需要从语言形式上把握原文的主旨，力图再现原文的信息和意图。翻译的目标在于让读者从译文中获得与原文读者相同的感受。从翻译原则来看，首要任务是对原文语义进行准确表达，不能随意增加、删减、歪曲原文；其次是做到通顺易懂，也就是从行文规范上保持应有的结构及逻辑关系，避免言之无物、词不达意。

在翻译过程中，词性本身往往可能是障碍，翻译时不能照搬原文的词性。翻译的目标在于实现与原文信息的等值，而非单纯追求语言形式上的完全对等。因此，在翻译实践中，突出译文信息、功能等值的同时，还要避免过于追求形式对应而忽视译文思想内容的一致性。特别是在词性转换中，要使用好词性转换的技巧，协同好翻译中英语词汇、汉语词汇的有效等值关系。词性转换是翻译的重要方法，在词性及语义规范上突出结构合理、逻辑严密，避免词不达意，还要避免形式上的过于对等而带来的译文晦涩难懂。为此，本节对英汉翻译中词性转换的具体方法进行分析，以提升译文质量，实现语言翻译的目标。

名词转为动词

1. This book is a careful study of the power struggle between the warring states.
这本书认真研究了交战各国之间的权力斗争。

2. All countries shall work hard for effective prohibition of the production and stockpiling of all chemical weapons.
世界各国都应该努力，从而有效地制止生产和储备各种化学武器。

3. We have a shortage of human resources shortage because our industries developed very quickly.
我们缺乏人力资源，因为工业发展得非常迅速。

4. It is a very different place than it was 22 years ago because of the benefit of free labor, free trade and an open market.
现在这个地方与22年前大不相同了，这得益于自由劳动力，自由贸易和开放的市场。

5. Through the face-to-face exchange, the two delegations had a better understanding of each other's intentions and capabilities.

通过面对面的沟通，两个代表团更好地了解了对方的意图和实力。

6. Careful forethought about the possible consequences would have helped them avoid all the trouble, which almost destroyed their plan completely.

事先考虑可能产生的后果，本来能够帮助他们避免所有的麻烦。这些麻烦几乎毁了整个计划。

介词短语转为动词结构

1. We will be more active in international cooperation.
我们将更积极地进行国际合作。

2. With all its disadvantages this design is considered to be one of the best.
尽管存在各种缺点，这个设计仍被认为是最佳设计之一。

3. Faced with the daunting task, the Chinese government will double its efforts with more effective measures to contain the spread of HIV/AIDS.

面对艰巨的防治任务，中国政府将进一步加强工作力度，采用更加有效的措施，坚决遏制艾滋病病毒及艾滋病的蔓延。

4. Hong Kong built its new airport in two years on reclaimed land with mostly imported labor on a budget of 200 billion dollars.

香港用两年时间，花费了两千亿美元，依靠大多数外地劳工填海建造了新机场。

5. The villagers spent a lot of human and material resources on a 10-year drive to make such an achievement.

村民们花费了大量人力物力，历经10年的奋斗，才取得了这样的成就。

6. China was looking for a way to balance rapid industrialization with the preservation of its cultural tradition.

中国当时正在寻找一条道路，在快速实现工业化的同时保护其文化传统。

Guided Practice

Directions: Interpret the following passages. Pay attention to the underlined parts and see how transfer of part of speech can help smooth your interpreting.

🎧 Task A

The dynamism of the ASEAN economies is certainly an opportunity for Europe. However, a lot of that opportunity is still potential rather than real. EU enterprises trying to trade or invest in South-East Asia still face tariff and non-tariff barriers and markets tilted against foreign service providers, especially in public procurement markets. The same is true for foreign direct investment in general. EU enterprises also find that their intellectual property rights are still too poorly protected, and the general transparency of some markets is fairly low. This requires us to formulate a free-trade agreement.

🎧 Task B

The extremely uneven development of the North and the South is the root cause of the world economic imbalance. The LDCs (Least Developed Countries) are a vulnerable group in the world economy. Medium-income countries, home to over 60% of the global poverty population, face multiple external impacts and risks. To achieve the MDGs (Millennium Development Goals) on schedule, a key element is to provide these countries with lasting financial support, and establish a new type of global development partnership that is more equitable and balanced.

🎧 Task C

Africa's development is indispensable to the development of the world economy. China calls upon the international community to take more concrete steps to support Africa's development.

First, the international community should not waver in its resolve or weaken its effort to help Africa meet the MDGs. It should honor the commitment of assistance to Africa and foster an enabling external environment of international economy, trade and finance.

Second, the international community should have a keen appreciation of African countries' pressing need for stronger capacity in adapting to climate change, and help them better meet the climate challenge in the larger context of enhancing Africa's ability for achieving sustainable development.

Third, the international community should show more understanding of the special difficulties facing Africa in addressing such global issues as food security, energy security and epidemic diseases.

|||||||||||||||||||||||||||||| **Information Link** ||||||||||||||||||||||||||||||

Definition and Types of Interpreting（口译的定义和类型）

　　口译的定义：口译是翻译活动，也是交际行为。顾名思义，"口"即口头表达，"译"即翻译，"口译"即"口头翻译"。除此之外，按照国际惯例，手语传译也是口译的一种形式。口译活动中，源语只呈现一次，不可重复；目标语在比较紧张的时间内产出，几乎没有更正和修正的机会。或者说，口译是在源语一次性表达的基础上用另一种语言呈现的一次性翻译。

　　按照口译的形式、方向、任务等不同标准，口译主要分为以下类型：一、按照口译的形式分为同声传译、交替传译、联络口译、接力口译、耳语口译、视译等，二、按照口译的方向分为单向口译和双向口译，三、按照口译的任务分为会议口译、技术口译、外事口译、商贸口译、医学口译等。

　　会议口译最基本的类型是交替传译（Consecutive Interpreting）和同声传译（Simultaneous Interpreting）。交替传译是指讲话人先讲一段话，译员快速记笔记，讲话人语停，译员根据所记笔记，通过目标语将讲话人的意思传达给听众。在交替传译中，译员可以借助笔记，但同时需要熟练掌握笔记技巧并具有较广的知识面，因此，交替传译对译员的要求较高。交替传译的译语产出时间不受限，准确率较高，因而在许多外事、接待场合应用较多，但其比同声传译较为费时。同声传译是讲话人一边讲，译员一边译。它要求译员边听边译，难度较大，译员往往需要经过专业口译院校的集中训练才可以应对同声传译的任务要求。同声传译可以分为三种类型。一、会议同传，即译员利用会场设备，在同传箱里通过耳机接收讲话人的讲话，同时通过话筒以目标语将讲话内容译给听众，并几乎与讲话人同步。这种类型的同声传译可以是无稿的，也可以是有稿的，稿子包括源语提纲、源语PPT、源语稿件或译语稿件。二、视译，即译员一边看原文讲稿，一边以目标语译出材料的内容。三、耳语同传，即不使用任何设备，译员坐在少数听众旁边为其进行耳语同声传译。

|||||||||||||||||||||| **After-class Assignment** ||||||||||||||||||||||

Directions: Listen to the following passage. Pause after each paragraph, and try to summarize the main idea of the paragraph.

Tourism and Tourism Investment

Paragraph 1

Ladies and gentlemen, the subject of today's forum is more into the discussion of tourism and tourism investment. As you all know that according to our forecast, by the year 2020, we anticipated non-stop continuous expansion of international tourism worldwide. And there is a need, ladies and gentlemen, for tourism investment almost in all subregions and almost in all subsectors, and especially in the Asia and Pacific area. For me, probably four following areas may be explored.

Paragraph 2

No. 1, the phenomenon of money-rich and time-poor is nowadays pushing the tourism product investments more into the weekend city breaks; is pushing more into short breaks and multiple travels. This is further pushing products related to spas. This is further pushing products related to shorter duration but maximization of one's experiences. So, probably this is the first area that a tourism investor would like to look at in terms of tourism products linked with money-rich and time-poor.

Paragraph 3

Secondly, in terms of transportation, the concept of LCC, the low-cost carrier, will probably be the factor that will affect our tourism industry for the next decade. And due to this, there will be increasing demands for accommodation and especially along the line of three stars and even lower. And there will be, with this concept of LCC, increasing demands for the construction of secondary airports and their related facilities. And with this concept of LCC, there will be increasing demands for the destination development, not necessarily mega cities, but in less-known areas and less-known regions and less-known cities. So in that sense, the LCC will probably change Asia in terms of expansion of three-star hotels, and in terms of reaching out to smaller townships and remote areas.

_____

_____

_____

Paragraph 4

Finally, ladies and gentlemen, what is the challenge for Asia and Pacific tourism? The way I see Asia must enrich quality. The way I see Asia and Pacific tourism must dilute quantity. Too much development, too much concrete, and too many numbers may not lead to healthy development of Asia tourism. It is us, you, the mayors, and the tourism directors who should control growth so that our tourism development will be more modest, and our tourism development will be more social, and our tourism development will be more responsible.

_____

_____

_____

Paragraph 5

Asia tourism remains still very much in the cities. It is our job, ladies and gentlemen, that we must go, go to the vast countryside in order for us to develop products relating to rural tourism, in order for us to develop products relating to low-scale and small-scale tourism projects like what they have already succeeded in France, in Ireland, in Switzerland and in Austria. Thus, our tourism industry can contribute more to the agenda of the remote area development, therefore, achieving the New Millennium Goals set forth by the United Nations.

_____

_____

_____

扫码获取本单元音频资料

Unit

2 Persuasive Speech & Synonym Replacement

If you can't communicate and talk to other people and get across your ideas, you're giving up your potential.

—Warren Buffett, American investment guru and one of the most respected businessmen in the world

Unit Goals

- To gain a general knowledge of how persuasive speech is organized.
- To become more flexible in summary interpreting by replacing synonyms.
- To gain a general knowledge of Effort Model of interpreting.

Warm Up

Directions: Listen to the following passages and fill in the blanks with the given words. Make sure the words you fill in are both grammatically and semantically acceptable.

Task A

It's great to see China stepping up to engage even more with other countries. It is greatly equipped to do so. No other country has accomplished what China has achieved in the last few decades — breaking the (1) _____ cycle of poverty and disease for hundreds of millions of people while modernizing its economy at a scale and (2) _____ speed in human history.

Although no one is expecting China to fill a gap in development aid from wealthy countries, it has made a very smart commitment to (3) _____ its commitment to African development. China has long understood that helping other countries lift themselves out of poverty creates a (4) _____ world for people everywhere.

And by encouraging investment through (5) _____

18

like the (6) _____, China is strengthening not only Africa's economic capacity, but also, over time, the markets for Chinese goods.

It's great to see President Xi's commitment to (7) _____ here in China by 2020. China did a great job of lifting millions out of poverty. But progress has been (8) _____. Forty-three million people still live in extreme poverty.

We look forward to a new partnership with China that will focus on innovative ideas to bring this number down to zero — working on (9) _____, healthcare in rural areas, and also finding ways to increase financial services for the poor.

Of course, China is not only striving to reach new (10) _____ here at home. It's using its own experience fighting poverty and disease to help other countries tackle similar challenges. A few years ago, Vice Premier Wang Yang said something that stayed with me. He said: "Africa today is our yesterday." Now, China is using the lessons it's learned to (11) _____ a new tomorrow for Africa, too.

This is a pretty incredible time to be a young person in China. Your generation's entrance into the workforce will (12) _____ with your country's rise as a center of global progress and innovation. The world's eyes are on China. And as a new generation comes of age, the world's eyes are specifically on all of you.

Task B

I want to send my best wishes to everyone in Britain, China and around the world celebrating Chinese New Year.

From the (1) _____ (fires; fairs) in Beijing, to the fireworks in Hong Kong and the parades here in London, families and (2) _____ (communications; communities) will come together and look to the year ahead — the Year of the Rooster. Our starting point is stronger than ever before. We had the (3) _____ (historical; historic) state visit of President Xi just 15 months ago. We receive more Chinese investment than any other major European country. We've got around 150,000 Chinese students studying here and the number of Chinese tourists visiting has doubled in 5 years. Meanwhile, as (4) _____ (permanent; permitted) members of the UN Security Council, our countries are working together on the most (5) _____ (pressing; impressing) global issues. This year also marks some important anniversaries: 20 years since the handover of Hong Kong to China; and 45 years of ambassadorial relations between our countries.

I want us to take this chance to build on all the ties we share — in business, diplomacy, education, tourism and culture — as we (6) _____ (forge; fog) a new role for Britain, as the most outward-looking, free-trading nation in the world. And it is an auspicious time. The Rooster — the Fire Rooster — represents so many of the characteristics we need to (7) _____ (deploy; employ) in that endeavour: openness, confidence, hard work and leadership. These aren't alien (8) _____ (concepts; conceptions) to any of us. Indeed, they are characteristics demonstrated day in, day out by the British Chinese community. This is a community that makes an enormous (9) _____ (attribution; contribution) to our society — proving that the strength and success of this country rests on (10) _____ (delicacy; dedication), diversity and a deep spirit of citizenship among our people.

So as the lanterns are lit and the dumplings are served, let me wish you and your family, wherever you are, a very happy and healthy New Year.

ⅠⅠⅠⅠⅠⅠⅠⅠⅠⅠⅠⅠ Listening Comprehension ⅠⅠⅠⅠⅠⅠⅠⅠⅠⅠⅠ

Skill Focus

Persuasive Speech（说服性演讲）

说服性演讲的主要目的是说服听众，创造、加强或者改变听众的想法和行为。与说明性演讲比起来，说服性演讲的目的是成功说服听众，改变听众的认识、看法，感召听众做出具体的行为，因此更具难度。我们的工作和生活中涉及很多说服性演讲，比如，售货员说服顾客购买产品，上级说服下级接受指示，律师说服法官被告无罪等。

说服性演讲的类型

说服性演讲包括事实性说服（fact questions），价值性说服（value questions）和决策性说服（policy questions）。事实性说服的演讲主题可能包括：伦敦的人口密度是多少、上海距离广州多远、火星上是否有智慧生物、美国的经济衰退两年内是否会有转机、新推出的一部好莱坞大片能否获得明年的奥斯卡奖。事实性说服类演讲有时可能与说明性演讲比较接近。价值性说服的演讲主题可能包括：西双版纳是中国的最佳旅游地之一、游泳是最理想的运动方式、大量摄入食盐是不健康的饮食习惯、安乐死在道义上是不可以接受的。决策性说服的演讲主题可能包括：中国的高考制度应该改革、中国大学生应为希望工程义务服务、中国的省会城市应禁止在公共场所吸烟、公司的产品营销策略应该做出提升、应该更加严格管控网络安全等。

说服性演讲需要注意的问题

1. 说服性演讲是所有演讲类型中难度最大的，因为其涉及的主题往往具有两个或者更多个观点，而演讲者的目的是要说服听众接受自己的观点。

2. 说服性演讲是需要讲话人和听众共同构建的说服及接受的过程。目标听众的自身认识和接受说服的程度都不同，演讲者的说服性演讲只能在一定范围内影响听众的认识。

3. 进行听众问卷和听众分析，在组织说服性演讲的过程中时刻考虑听众的实际情况，都有助于成功地展开说服性演讲。

4. 演讲者的专业背景如果与演讲主题很相关，那么在演讲中加入自我介绍，将有利于提升演讲的说服力。

说服性演讲的主题及展开

说服性演讲的主题包罗万象，从下面几个主题中找出你感兴趣的，并尝试写一篇说服性演讲稿。

1. Capital punishment should be abolished in all countries.

2. More measures should be taken to protect the public sites against terrorist attacks.

3. Measures should be taken to ensure that children in China's poverty stricken areas receive adequate education.

4. Colleges and universities should carry out more effective policies to deal with cheating.

5. Stricter safety standards should be applied on amusement-park facility utilization.

6. Factories causing serious air or water pollution should be closed down.

7. College English curriculum should place greater emphasis on student's communicative competence.

8. Online teaching should be given equal importance as the regular form of teaching.

9. Studying martial arts is good for mind and health.

10. Companies manufacturing guns should be held responsible for the crimes involving guns.

下面来看两篇说服性演讲的提纲。更好地了解说服性演讲的组织方式，可以帮助译者对说服性演讲进行有效的听解和译述。

Say NO to Antibacterial Chemicals in Household Products

Thesis statement: The use of antibacterial chemicals in household products is a serious problem that requires action by governments and consumers alike.

Main Points

1. Rather than making us healthier, antibacterial chemicals in household products are contributing to long-term health problems.

2. The antibacterial chemicals in household products are also creating environmental problems because they eventually end up in the water supply.

3. The government should regulate and control the use of antibacterial chemicals in household products.

4. Consumers should avoid purchasing household products that contain antibacterial chemicals.

Public Places Should Offer Free Public WiFi

Thesis statement: Access to the Internet should not be unreasonably restricted and governments have a responsibility to ensure that Internet access is widely-available, at least in public places.

Main Points

1. The Internet is becoming so important in our lives that many people consider Internet access as important as water or power supply. Some even argue that Internet access is a human right because it enables people to educate themselves and connect with other people.

2. Governments should offer free public WiFi access to everyone, as it can bridge the digital divide, which is one of the root causes of inequality and poverty in today's world.

3. Free city WiFi gives citizens, businesses and the government itself an opportunity to influence productivity and innovation. It provides incremental opportunities to drive economic development, cost reductions, job creation and heightened collaboration.

4. Governments implementing this public service have their popularity boosted

immediately. Tourists and visitors would find their trip more pleasant as free public WiFi can help them avoid expensive roaming charges.

Guided Practice

Directions: Skim the passages and fill in the blanks based on your understanding about persuasive speech. Then listen to the recording and check whether your anticipation is close to what you hear.

Passage 1

Should Cell Phones Be Banned While Driving?

(1)_____. Many believe that both lawmakers and businesses should ban the use of cell phones while driving. However, some opponents say (2) _____. Others argue that (3) _____ _____, like eating, talking with passengers, arguing with kids in the back seat, listening to music, so it makes little sense to outlaw one activity. We believe the practice should be banned based on the following reasons.

First, (4) _____, so we should ban it to save lives. Studies show that the practice of using cell phones and text-messaging devices while driving is as dangerous as drunk driving, putting drivers at a four times greater risk of a crash. (5) _____, and if the conversation is stressful your reaction time will not be as quick.

Second, many countries and cities around the world (6) _____ _____. In New York, which enacted the first ban on handheld cell phones in 2001, drivers' use of such phones went down by about 50 percent shortly after the law took effect. But this decline had dissipated substantially when measured a year later. The result was different after a similar law was enacted in Washington, D.C., where use also declined by about 50 percent and the decline was sustained a year later. More intensive enforcement in Washington could be a reason for the difference. So, (7) _____ _____ _____.

Last but not least, we believe law enforcement of all policies take time, but eventually will arouse special attention of people. We have various approaches available and good models to follow, as we have enforced (8) _____, and many others, to ensure safety on the road. Therefore, (9) _____. But we do not support laws that would permit the use of hands-free devices, because (10) _____ that those devices are any safer for drivers. In fact, hands-free-only laws tend to send the wrong message that (11) _____ . And such laws may actually do harm if drivers start using hands-free phones to make more calls and talk longer.

Passage 2

Dress Code and High Heels

(1) _____ are becoming more important in the workplace. Dress codes are often used in the workplace and there are many reasons why an employer may have one, for example workers may be asked to wear (2) _____ to communicate a corporate image and ensure that customers can easily identify them. Often an employer will introduce a dress code for (3) _____ reasons, for example health care workers may not be allowed to wear jewellery for safety reasons when around patients and certain clothing may not be allowed in factories while operating machinery.

However, an employer's dress code must not be (4) _____ in respect of the protected characteristics for age, disability, religion or belief, sex, or sexual orientation. Reports in the media have high-lighted the case of a temporary worker who was sent home without pay for refusing to wear high heels at work. Although staff can be dismissed for failing to (5) _____ _____, employers should be cautious when operating a dress code in this way. Any dress code should not be stricter, or lead to a detriment, for one gender over the other.

As to this case of high heels, all can easily imagine the (6) _____ of wearing high heels for several hours on the trot for five consecutive working days, at an incline of almost 45 degrees. And many women employees who go to glamorous events always take a spare pair of flat shoes, which they change into the moment they can fling off the heels. Apart from discomfort, what's more disturbing is that it has been reported that wearing high heels can cause (7) _____. An investigation by the University of

Aberdeen has found clear links between wearing high heels and physical damage.

Drawing a lesson from this case, it is good practice when drafting or updating a dress code for an employer to consider the reasoning behind it. (8) _____ with employees over any proposed dress code may ensure that the code is acceptable to both the organisation and employees. Once agreed it should be communicated to all employees. When setting out a policy employers should (9) _____ employees who may dress in a certain way for religious reasons. However, workers can be required not to wear certain items that could be deemed a safety risk, for example, loose clothing may be a hazard if operating machinery.

Old-fashioned stereotypes have no place in a modern organization. If companies want to prosper they should (10) _____.

Passage 3

Personal Finance Should Be Taught in School

When you stop to think about it, why was algebra a required subject in school, but learning how to manage personal finances wasn't even on the school's radar screen? Without a doubt, (1) _____. And although algebra might help getting into college, knowing the ins and outs of their personal finances can actually help students stay in college. The following reasons explain (2) _____ _____.

First, (3) _____.The assumption that all parents are capable of teaching their kids how to manage money is (4) _____. Young people need to (5) _____, as well as improve their math skills.

Second, start early for better results. Learning how to use and manage credit cards, become familiar with credit score and rating services, understand mortgage rates, know how to create a personal budget, and then live within it, are (6) _____ _____. The sooner students start learning the basics, the better. *Forbes* reported that college-related debt includes student loans, credit cards and family loans. Students need to (7) _____ _____.

Armed with the knowledge and understanding about how and why things happen in financial world gives young people the power to (8) _____, both personal and public. It also helps them to understand how personal and public finance are inexplicably intertwined, and how the actions of individuals impact on others. In this way, young people (9) _____

_____ .

Try This: _____

Please skim the following passage about personal finance, and then fill in the blanks with appropriate words or phrases that are given below.

How you manage, spend, and invest your money can have a profound impact on your life, yet very few schools teach these important skills.

Spend less money than you earn. I have an (1) _____ at my local (2) _____ of one of the big (3) _____. I have a (4) _____ for writing cheques, paying by (5) _____ and paying bills. Normally, I'm (6) _____, but sometimes I spend more money than I have in the account and I (7) _____. This is called (8) _____, which is agreed by the bank and I pay quite a high (9) _____ on it. I also have a (10) _____ or savings account for keeping money longer term. I have a (11) _____ with the same bank too. (12) _____ is very convenient. I pay off what I spend each month, so I don't pay interest. The interest rate is even higher than for overdrafts. So, the bigger the gap between your income and your spending, the better.

Always plan for the future. This doesn't just mean retirement. When a store offers to let you pay off some gadget in 6 months with no interest, you need to know you can (13) _____, or avoid that deal. Establishing an (14) _____ will allow you to deal with unexpected car repairs or medical bills. Having a (15) _____ will ensure you have income when you're unable to work anymore. Your finances should always look forward beyond the current month.

Make your money make more money: Want to know how the rich keep getting richer? It's because money can grow while you sleep, provided you save some of it. Properly invested money earns more money over time. Sometimes that's an (16) _____, but sometimes it's starting a business, or even getting an education to get a better paying job.

The most important personal finance rules don't change, though there will always be newer, better tools to (17) _____. However, spending less than you earn will always be beneficial. Investing your money will always be better than doing nothing with it. And planning for the future will always be better than (18) _____.

account 账户	overdraft 透支；透支额
debit card 借记卡	branch （银行）分支机构
living from paycheck to paycheck 月光族	high-street banks 高街银行；商业大街（High Street）上的银行，提供便民服务，也被称为零售银行
in the black 盈余	pay it off 还清（债务）
current account 活期账户	retirement plan 退休金计划
credit card 信用卡	emergency fund 应急基金
go into the red 负债	deposit account 存款账户
investment account 投资账户	manage your money 管理资金

Summary Interpreting

Skill Focus

Synonym Replacement（同义词替换）

　　笔译中较少用多种方式表达同一个意思。笔译往往要求译者通过多方比较和鉴别，找到一种最为恰当的表达。在口译中，这种"精雕细琢"与其即时工作性质是相冲突的。在口译训练中，尤其要避免养成字对字、句对句的口译习惯。口译实践的首要目的和原则是促成交际双方的交流与沟通，这就要求译员在短时间内完成对源语核心信息的有效传递。"字字对译"或"逐句对应"并非口译实践的常态，"信息对等"和"功能等效"才是评价口译质量的首选因素。

译员可以通过同义词练习进行词汇的联想和积累。有了更多的选择之后，译员就不至于面临"无米之炊"的窘境。比如，汉语"建立"就有很多英语译法，create, construct, establish, build, set up, work up, frame, found等。译员首先要做到能够使用任意译法完成口译。在这个阶段之后，才需要考虑分辨各个表达法之间的细小差别，进而有能力选择更加契合的一个。这样练习的好处是培养译员在口译中的灵活应变能力，同时可以判断不同译语之间的优劣，从而提高自己的口译能力。

例如，"改善"可以翻译为improve, upgrade, perfect, better, enhance等。包含"改善"意思的句子如下所示。

1. 工作人员说，他们想要帮助商家理解怎样改善自己的设计。

The researchers say they want to help businesses understand how to improve their designs.

2. 尽管存在缺陷，但这一历史性举措或类似的措施，将极大地改善美国的健康安全。

For all its flaws, this historic measure, or something like it, would greatly better health security in the US.

This historic measure has its flaws, but measures like this would greatly better health security in the US.

例如，"目的"可以译为so as to、in order to、with the object of、to achieve (goals)、for the purpose of、with the aim of等。包含"目的"意思的句子如下所示。

1. 企业参加展览会的最终目的是为了向该地区推销产品。

The ultimate goal/aim/purpose of an enterprise participating in an exhibition is to market its products in the area.

2. 广告是指向大众传递视觉或口头信息的一系列活动，其目的在于让大众了解并购买其产品或服务。

Advertising includes those activities by which visual or oral messages are delivered to the public for the purpose of (with the aim of) informing them and influencing them to buy merchandise or services.

Advertising includes those activities by which visual or oral messages are delivered to the public, the aim of which is to inform them and influence them to buy merchandise or services.

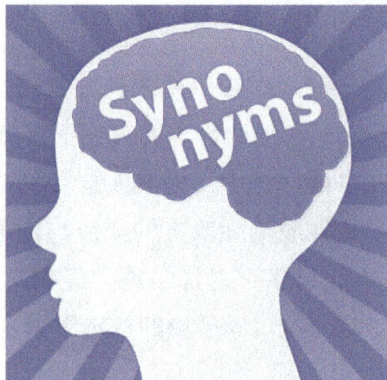

3．大多数的国家设立了阻止农产品贸易的障碍，目的是保护农民或者消费者。

Most countries had erected barriers to trade of agricultural products so as to (in order to, to) protect either their farmers or their consumers.

4．一些发展中国家已经采取措施强迫跨国公司和当地的投资者结成伙伴，目的是牢牢地控制某些有战略意义的重要行业和产品。

Some developing countries have taken measures to compel multinationals to enter in partnership with local investors in order to gain firm control over some of their important industries and products that may bear strategic significance for the host countries.

上面这个句子较长、较复杂，还可以采用综合拆句的方法对它进行重构。

Some developing countries have taken measure to compel multinationals to enter in partnership with local investors. The purpose is to gain firm control over some of their important industries and products, as these industries and products are strategically significant (for the host countries).

综上所述，词汇的灵活使用往往也连带着句式的变化，而句式的变化也对词和词组的使用形式提出不同的要求，二者紧密联系、不可分割。

Guided Practice

Directions: Read the passages and fill in the blanks with words or phrases that are both grammatically and semantically acceptable. Then listen to the recording and fill in the blanks with what you hear. You may sight interpret the passages, and check whether your alternatives are close in meaning to what you hear, and whether the differences between the two affect the interpreting of the main idea.

Passage 1

"Busy" has become a word packed with meaning in social (1) _____, it has become as common as a response as "fine" to the question "How are you". (2) _____ it might be but are you telling people what you really want to when you use this word? And is it really (3) _____ to be telling yourself you are "busy"? Human beings spend (4) _____ _____ on things they, (5) _____, believe are important. That doesn't mean you like everything you do. If you believe making other people happy is important, you will (6) _____ your time and energy on activities that meet that (7) _____.

We all need time to recharge. To (8) _____ healthy and (9) _____ stress building up, most people need to take a 15 minutes (10) _____ every 90 minutes or so, if not we risk stress hormones (11) _____ in our bodies, making us frazzled and potentially impacting your health. Plan to take (12) _____ breaks during the day, go for a little walk, read a bit and take time to eat lunch. The little breaks all (13) _____ a much more (14) _____ experience of life and the little rests actually make you more (15) _____ as your brain gets a (16) _____ .

Passage 2

We are constantly being bombarded with good advice on how to stay healthy and live longer by eating (1) _____ and taking (2) _____ . However, there are other ways to keep your (3) _____ in good condition and one is to keep a pet.

(4) _____ have shown that forging a relationship with (5) _____ can have benefits both physical and psychological. Interacting regularly with a pet can (6) _____ blood pressure and (7) _____ anxiety. A Cambridge University study showed that (8) _____ reported fewer headaches, coughs and colds. Also, according to the Pet Health Council, stroking a dog or cat can reduce the heart rate, thereby helping to lower blood pressure.

Also, (9) _____ tend to get more exercise from regular walking. It's amazing how much better we all feel for a daily stroll and evidence shows that even just 20 (10) _____ exercise a day (11) _____ illness and (12) _____ life expectancy in most people. By developing a connection with a pet, whether it be a dog, cat, snake or rabbit, (13) _____ with your pet can provide you with a reason for appreciating life and connecting with others. This can be especially (14) _____ for older people who can be socially (15) _____ or struggle with finding a sense of purpose. (16) _____ , can have, as we are constantly reminded, a very damaging effect on quality of life as we age.

Passage 3

Dementia is a general term for a (1) _____ in mental ability severe enough to

(2) _____ daily life. Memory loss is an example. (3) _____ is the most common type of dementia. (4) _____ is caused by damage to brain cells. This (5) _____ interferes with the ability of (6) _____ to communicate with each other. When brain cells cannot communicate normally, thinking, behavior and feelings can be (7) _____. Different types of dementia are associated with particular types of (8) _____ in particular regions of the brain. For example, in Alzheimer's disease, high levels of certain proteins inside and outside brain cells make it hard for (9) _____to stay healthy and to communicate with (10) _____.

Dementia is the biggest health and social care (11) _____ facing society today. Someone develops the condition every three minutes and too many are facing it alone. Because (12) _____ of dementia is so poor, people with dementia often are misunderstood, marginalised and isolated and that means that they're (13) _____ likely to be able to live (14) _____ in their own communities. As part of a long-term commitment to help more individuals, (15) _____ become dementia-friendly, Alzheimer's Society has set an ambitious target of creating four million Dementia Friends by 2020.

When most people hear the word dementia, they think of (16) _____. And it does often start by affecting the short-term memory. Someone with dementia might repeat themselves and have problems (17) _____ things that happened recently. But dementia can also (18) _____ the way people think, speak, perceive things, feel and behave. Other common (19) _____ include: difficulties concentrating, (20) _____ planning and thinking things through, (21) _____ with familiar daily tasks, like following a recipe or using a bank card, (22) _____ with language and communication, for example (23) _____ remembering the right word or keeping up with a conversation, (24) _____ judging distances (even though eyesight is fine), mood changes and (25) _____ controlling emotions. For example, someone might get unusually sad, frightened, angry, easily upset, or lose their self-confidence and become withdrawn. (26) _____ of dementia gradually get worse over time. How quickly this happens varies from person to person, and some people stay (27) _____ for years.

IIIIIIIIIIIIIIIIIIIIIIIIIIIIIIIIIIIII **Information Link** IIIIIIIIIIIIIIIIIIIIIIIIIIIIIIIIIIIII

Effort Model of Interpreting（口译的认知负荷模型）

"口译的认知负荷模型"是由著名口译学专家丹尼尔·吉尔（Daniel Gile）基于"认知负荷模型"构建的。起初，吉尔在口译现场发现了一种现象：即使是熟练掌握工作语言、知识面丰富且经过专业口译训练的译员，在口译现场也会陷入捉襟见肘的困境。由此看来，口译中除了语言、知识和口译技巧，还需要另外一种"认知资源"。他认为这种"认知资源"是有一定限度的。在口译过程中，如果译员不能有效地将这种"认知资源"分配在源语听辨理解、目标语表达以及工作记忆之间，或者由于口译任务本身难度过高而导致"资源短缺"，就会使译员陷入困境。在此基础上，吉尔于1995年构建了"口译的认知负荷模型"，主要包括交替传译和同声传译的"认知负荷模型"。

1. "同声传译的认知负荷模型"：SI= L+M+P+C (Listening and analysis+ Short-term memory + Speech production + Coordination)，也就是，同声传译=听与分析+短时记忆+言语表达+协同。

2. "交替传译的认知负荷模型"：第一阶段：CI = L+N+M+C (Listening analysis+Note-taking+Short-term memory+Coordination)，也就是，交替传译（第一阶段）=听与分析+笔记+短时记忆+协同；第二阶段：CI = Rem+Read+P (Remembering+Note-reading+Production)，也就是，交替传译（第二阶段）=记忆+读笔记+产出。

"口译的认知负荷模型"完整并详细地呈现了口译过程。该模型提出后，在国内外的口译研究中常被用作解释性的理论工具，并在口译教学中被用作教学实践的理论基础。实际上，这个模型虽然在理论解释和实践应用中显示了合理性，但至今未经过充分的实证检验。

IIIIIIIIIIIIIIIIIIIIIIIIIIII **After-class Assignment** IIIIIIIIIIIIIIIIIIIIIIIIIIII

Directions: Listen to the following passage. Pause after each paragraph, and try to summarize the main idea of that paragraph.

GM Food

Paragraph 1

GMOs are one of the most controversial areas of science. Genetic engineering is used in many fields. Even though medical applications like GMO insulin are widely accepted, the debate heats up when it comes to food and agriculture. Why is that? Why is the same thing treated so differently? Let's try to get to the bottom of this and explore the facts, the fears, and the future of GMOs.

_____

_____

_____

Paragraph 2

Humans have been genetically modifying plants and animals for thousands of years. Maybe a few of your crops had very good yields. Maybe one of your wolves was especially loyal. So you did the smart thing, and bred the plants and animals that had traits beneficial to you. Traits suggest an expression of genes. So with each generation, those genes got more pronounced.

_____

_____

_____

Paragraph 3

After thousands of years, almost every single plant and animal around us is vastly different from its pre-domesticated state. If humans have been changing genes for millennia, what makes a so-called "Genetically Modified Organism", or GMO, different? Selective breeding is basically hoping for lucky hits. Genetic engineering eliminates this factor. We can choose the traits we want — make fruit grow bigger, immune to pests, and so on. So, why are people concerned about them? Is food that comes from GM crops different to food from non-GM crops?

_____

_____

_____

Paragraph 4

This question has been a major concern from the very beginning. GM plants that are destined to be eaten are checked for possible dangers, and the results are evaluated by multiple agencies. After more than 30 years and thousands of studies, the science is in. Eating GMO plants is no more risky than their non-GMO equivalent. But don't just take our word for it, sources for this and other claims are in the video description. That's one of the most fundamental problems with the GMO debate. Much of the criticism of this technology is actually criticism of modern agriculture and the business practice of the huge corporations that control our food supply. This criticism is not only valid, it's also important. We need to change agriculture to a more sustainable model. GMOs as a technology are actually an ally and not an enemy in that fight, helping to save and protect nature and minimize our impact on the environment.

_____

_____

_____

Paragraph 5

Scientists are working on GMOs that could improve our diet — plants that produce more or different nutrients, like fruit with higher antioxidant levels that help to fight diseases or rice with additional vitamins. On a larger scale, we're trying to engineer plants more resilient to climate change — plants that can better adapt to erratic weather and adversarial conditions, making them resistant to droughts or floods.

_____

_____

Paragraph 6

GMOs could also not only reduce agriculture's impact on the environment, but actively help to protect it. We could even modify plants to become super-effective carbon collectors, like the American chestnut tree, to mitigate and actually reverse climate change. With the tools we have today, our imagination is the limit.

_____

_____

_____

Paragraph 7

The world eats 11 million pounds of food every day. A UN estimate suggests we'll need 70% more by 2050. We could grow that food by clearing more and more forests to create fields and pastures and by using more pesticides. Or we find a way to do it on the land we've got right now, with more effective methods like GM crops. Intensifying farming instead of expanding it means GMOs could become the new organic.

_____

_____

_____

Paragraph 8

In a nutshell, GMOs have the potential to not only drastically change agriculture but to also dampen the effects of our own irresponsible behaviour. GMOs could be our most powerful weapon to save our biosphere.

_____

_____

_____

扫码获取本单元音频资料

Unit

3 Semantic Marker & Speech with Cues

> The ultimate aim of utterance comprehension is to identify the pragmatic meaning of utterance as well as its semantic meaning.
>
> — Anonymous

Unit Goals

- To gain a general knowledge of how the information structure of a text can be built with the help of semantic markers.
- To become more flexible in summary interpreting by using speech with cues.
- To gain a general knowledge of directionality of interpreting.

Warm Up

Directions: Listen to the following passages and fill in the blanks with words or sentences. Make sure the words and sentences you fill in are both grammatically and semantically acceptable.

Task A

100, 000 people in Britain alone live with HIV and 6,000 people are (1) _____ the condition every single year. That's why the 1st of December, (2) _____, really matters. It is an opportunity for everyone to stand alongside all those people living with HIV and AIDS, and all those people who are family members and loved ones of those living with HIV, to say that the (3) _____ surrounding HIV is something we must absolutely challenge and stand up to make sure that people living with HIV (4) _____ _____ and to the right medical treatment, the right care, and the right support and the same opportunities as everybody else.

Of course, around the world, HIV and AIDS are hugely (5) _____ — massive problems, particularly in large areas of Africa. We must stand (6) _____, too, to fight against the tragic disease that (7) _____ so many lives every year. 1st of December matters. Chances are standing in (8) _____ with one another to stand against HIV and AIDS and standing in favor of all those people who live with those conditions.

🎧 Task B

For me personally, it was a gradual (1) _____(waking; awakening) over many years through work I've been privileged to witness with (2) _____ (vulnerable; valuable) young people — the homeless, the (3) _____ (employed; unemployed), those who are unable to (4) _____ (fill; fulfil) their potential. It was their openness about their mental health, their anxiety issues, and their honesty about not coping that made me realise that (5) _____ (pure mental health; poor mental health) was a major issue in our society. And it was an issue that needed (6) _____ (dressing; addressing) if we were to attempt to solve many other problems that trouble us.

I know what I have just said may sound obvious to you — of course, poor mental health underpins many other problems. But to me — as it still is for many, many people — mental health is the great (7) _____ (tatoo; taboo).

If you were anxious, it's because you were weak. If you couldn't cope with whatever life threw at you, it's because you were (8) _____ (feeling; failing). Successful, strong people don't suffer like that, do they? But of course — we all do. It's just that few of us speak about it.

But I got interested in mental health for another reason. The suicide rate among young men in this country is an (9) _____ (appalling; appealing) stain on our society. Suicide is the biggest killer of men under 40 in this country. Not cancer, not knife crime, not road deaths — suicide. If one of these other issues took so many young lives, there would be a national (10) _____ (outcry; out-try). But there has only ever been silence. And this has to stop. This silence is killing good people.

I learned from experts that the most important thing that needed to happen was to (11) _____ (normally; normalize) mental health — to get people comfortable with the subject and to talk about it. Simple as that. At the moment, on average, it takes a sufferer ten

years to admit to a problem. This means that what often starts as a fairly (12) _____
(minor; miner) issue becomes something serious and medical after the time. Silence can kill, but talking can lead to help and support.

IIIIIIIIIIIIIIIIII **Listening Comprehension** IIIIIIIIIIIIIIIII

Skill Focus

Discourse Marker（话语标记）

话语标记是实现话语连贯性的重要因素。话语标记作为衔接手段反映的是作者/说话者的思维模式，在译文中反映的是译者的思维模式，而把这两种思维模式联系到一起的则是译者的准确理解和等效表达。语言信息的获取和记忆是口译的重要环节。译员有效获取源语的信息，并有效地将其加以记忆和存储，能够保障其译语的产出，有助于提高口译的效率。译语话语的连贯性和逻辑性对口译的质量至关重要，而话语标记虽是语言表层成分，但却能够增强话语深层的连贯性和逻辑性，因而在译语话语构建中发挥着重要的作用。

话语标记对话语的展开和理解具有重要作用，是口译听解中不可忽视的环节。在口译训练中，可以专门针对这一部分进行训练。同时，在交替传译训练加入笔记之后，口译源语中的话语标记依然是笔记中应该加以格外重视的元素。

美国学者弗雷泽（Fraser）根据语用功能的不同，把话语标记分成四类。

1．对比性标记语（contrastive markers），如though…but, contrary to, however, on the other hand, whereas, in comparison; in contrast, yet, still等。

2．阐发性标记语（elaborative markers），如and, in addition, moreover, what is more, for another thing, furthermore。

3．推导性标记语（inferential markers），如as a consequence, as a result, so then, therefore, because of, accordingly, all things considered等。

4．主题变化标记语（topic change marker），如by the way, incidentally, speaking of, just to update you, to return to my point, back to the original point等。

对话语标记在听力理解中作用，学者们进行了研究，考得龙（Chaudron）和理查兹（Richards）的实验表明，宏观标记语有助于听力理解，而微观标记语的作用则不明显；弗劳尔迪（Flowerdew）等人的实验也表明语义标记有助于听力理解。杨承淑认为，这类词汇的数量虽然有限，但出现的频度却非常高，担负前后句子之间的信息与逻辑的转折功能。因此，无论从传讯功能或频用程度来考量，都值得在口译课程中特别加重话语学习的分量。

勒博布（Lebauber）将话语标记称为"重要的线索词"，它们是说话者有效组织自己的语言，并借助语言表达思想、观点和意图的重要工具，他认为这样的线索词可以具备如下功能：

引出话题（clues to topic introduction），

提出话语结构（clues to organization），

引出结论（clues to conclusion），

指出以下为重复信息（clues to repetition），

引出解释或例证（clues to exemplification），

指出以下为偏题信息（clues to tangential information）。

总的来说，加工过的信息更加容易记忆并被复述出来，而有意识地记忆"话语的衔接词"和"重要线索词"，有助于听者更好地把握讲者的话语含义。多数情况下，这些词是意思的引领者。换句话说，正是因为有了这些词，它们衔接的上下文才可以很顺利地被回忆或复述出来。

下面这篇文章的主题为教育，从高等教育大众化到学习型社会，再到终身学习。文章的展开和概念的联系采用了若干话语推进的标记语，请关注粗体部分的表达法，结合这些表达法，再对全篇进行主旨口译。

First of all, I'd like to take this opportunity to thank Guangdong University of Foreign Studies to give me this opportunity to share my views with you about making higher education more accessible to the public. I just want to share some of my views here. The topic is really good, **because** to make higher education more accessible to the public, which I would think, that is to make society to become a learning society.	首先， 感谢主办方（广外）让我来谈主题（高等教育更加大众化）。 这个主题非常好， **因为，** 它意味着成就学习型社会。

Traditionally the full-time education is considered to be the only proper way of getting quality education. This type of formal education is well accepted by all people and students and they have taken this path as their formal way of getting higher education in life. **As** full-time education is normally funded by the government which usually has limited resources for education, and **so** students have to compete for limited places in universities. **And therefore** usually there is a constraint in supply of human resources in the society.	一直以来， 全日制教育都被认为是获得高质量教育的最好方式，被人们和学生们广为接受。 因为， 全日制教育由政府出资，教育资源有限， 所以， 学生们不得不竞争有限资源， 因此， 社会上经常出现人力资源短缺。
As you know, we now live in a rapidly changing world in terms of technological, economic, political and social transformation. **And** the overall direction of change is toward an increasingly knowledge-based society. This change means that the cycle of knowledge-and-skill renewal is shortening. **So as a result**, the formal education received during the early part of one's life is inadequate to support our career development throughout our working career and beyond. **So** the implication of this development is that "lifelong learning" will become a central feature of our lives and a necessity for everyone to keep up with the escalating pace of change — in the family, at the workplace, in the community and in the worldwide society.	我们都知道， 当今社会变化迅速，体现在技术、经济、政治、社会等多方面， 而 变化主要方向是更加以知识为基础的社会，也就是知识技术更新更加迅速。 因而， 人生早期接受的正式教育不足以支撑事业发展， 所以， 终身学习就成为我们生活的中心特征，使得我们能跟上家庭、工作、社会甚至世界变化的节奏。
In order for both individuals and organizations to constantly upgrade themselves with the latest knowledge and skills **so as to** adapt, compete and excel in the highly competitive and globalized economy, higher education **therefore** should be made more accessible to the public.	为了， 个人和组织都可更新知识技能， 以 在高度竞争的全球化经济中，适应、竞争并脱颖而出， 因而， 高等教育应该更加大众化。

Guided Practice

Try This: ————————————————————————

Please fill in the blanks with discourse markers and other information that fit the context. Then compare what you put in the blanks with the answers given, and interpret the sentences with all the necessary information provided.

1. Globalisation is not a zero sum game. If we manage things properly, _____ win the arguments for free trade, _____ find a way to better regulation, we can both grow together. But _____.

2. Some say that "to succeed in this world, we need to become more like India, or China, or Brazil". But _____: we need to become more like us, the real us, hard-working, pioneering, independent, creative, adaptable, optimistic, can-do.

3. So let's reject the pessimism. Let's bring on the can-do _____. Let's summon the energy and the appetite to fight for a better future for our country.

4. The global economy has transformed in recent years. It _____ take companies decades to become global giants: _____ it can take a couple of years. When you step off the plane in Delhi or Shanghai or Lagos, you can feel the energy, the hunger, the drive to succeed.

5. So we set a clear target: to return net migration to 1990s levels when even though we had an open economy, proper immigration controls meant immigration was in the tens of thousands, not _____.

6. And we set to work on it immediately, with a clear plan to tackle non-EU migration in a targeted way while continuing to permit companies to _____ and allowing universities to _____.

7. Put simply: China has reemerged as a great global power. Now people can react to this in one of two ways. They can see China's rise as a threat, or they can see it as an _____. They can protect their markets from China, or _____. They can try and shut China out, or _____, to a new place at the top table of global affairs.

8. There has been a change of Government in Britain and a change of Prime Minister. But on this vital point there is absolute _____ between my government and the

governments of _____ and _____. We want a strong relationship with China. Strong on _____. Strong on _____. Strong on _____.

9. So I want to make the positive case for the world to see China's rise as an opportunity not a _____. But China needs to help us to make that argument, to demonstrate that as your economy grows, so do our shared interests, and our _____ responsibilities.

10. We share an interest in China's integration into the world economy, which is essential for China's development. _____ in an international system governed by rules and norms. And _____ in effective cooperative governance, including for the world economy. Also, _____ in fighting protectionism and in a coordinated rebalancing between surplus and deficit countries. These interests, those responsibilities are both economic and _____.

Try This:

Fill in the blanks with the corresponding letters of the suitable answers. Please check how the filled-in answers help build the information structure. Then read the questions and answers, and ask your partners to interpret.

Task A

Question: The Chinese government says we will set up the GDP target around 7.5 percent this year. Do you think we can achieve the target? And what is the challenge behind that?

Answer: Well, economy is a very complex thing, and nobody can predict (1) _____. You could ask a hundred greatest economists in the world, and (2) _____. So, (3) _____ to create expectations that the growth rate will be exactly 7.5. Given all the difficulties that exist at present time, it's possible that (4) _____ will come up during the year, and there would be (5) _____. So, (6) _____. But, as I say, the world is a complex thing and things might tip (7) _____. Therefore, the growth rate might (8) _____. There are many forces acting and cannot be predicted, or (9) _____.

A. come out higher

B. in favor of China

C. more bad news

D. it doesn't make sense

E. cannot be identified

F. the growth rate could end up being less than 7

G. they would have the estimates all over the place

H. what growth rate it is going to be

I. some undershooting of the target

🎧 Task B

Question: We have had a great deal in the last few months how deceit has caused the problems that we are now facing globally. Are you being totally honest with the people of the world to say that there has been genuine agreement here when we know there have been a number of splits among the G20, and also there is a one-size-fits-all agreement for twenty countries who are at different points in the economic cycle and different points in the global recession as well?

Answer: Isn't that what is remarkable, that you can have countries that would never even have sat round the table a few years ago coming round a table and coming to agreement? The reason (1) _____ is that unlike a few years ago when you could run national financial systems without thinking about what was happening in the rest of the world, every bank affects every other bank, and a bad bank in one country (2) _____. That is (3) _____, so that (4) _____ that are global; we have that (5) _____ that is necessary; we have (6) _____ coming together so that we know what is happening not just in one continent but (7) _____.

I believe people will be encouraged by the fact that (8) _____ and many countries from Asia, Latin America, Brazil, and Argentina, Mexico, Africa, South Africa, and the African Union, and the European countries, Russia as well, and of course the United States of America, we have all been able to come together in a way (9) _____ to decide quite detailed proposals that will (10) _____ for a long time. I must say, I have been proposing some of these for (11) _____. We have achieved more in (12) _____ as a result of people coming to terms with the need for change in the international financial system.

A. ten years

B. cross-border regulation

C. we could never have done even a year or two ago

D. ten weeks

E. affects good banks in every country

F. China and India and Japan

G. all continents

H. the international regulators

I. why we have to come together

J. reshape the global financial system

K. we've got to meet together and come to agreement

L. we have rules and supervision on financial institutions

Task C

Question: Prime Minister, do you think financial boom and bust is inevitable?

Answer: I think we have seen how a global financial system can (1) _____ when what happens in one bank that is entangled with many banks, then creates almost a (2) _____ right across the world. We have been dealing in the last 50 years with (3) _____. The crises that most countries are faced are when inflation gets out of control, you have to raise interests, but the cost of (4) _____ is you push businesses out of existence and people lose their jobs.

The problem now is not inflation. In fact, inflation is (5) _____ in most economies. The problem is a global (6) _____. The banking system froze up. The problem is that we are now finding banks are so entangled internationally with each other that you've got to have (7) _____ governing the system, you have to have rules that are worldwide, and you can't just deal with one national regulatory system; you have to have a form of (8) _____ that can deal with the flows of capital around the world. If the banking system can freeze up, we've got to be able to (9) _____ to deal with that. That is why we have put in place (10) _____, the new funds that will enable countries that cannot afford to restructure their banks to do so, and of course also (11) _____ that banks will have to agree to (12) _____ in the future.

A. principles

B. very low

C. raising interest rates

D. inflation crises

E. power cut

F. financial failure

G. go wrong

H. the rules for pay and for behavior and for standards

I. take action immediately

J. in every country of the world

K. global supervision

L. the restructuring of banks

|||||||||||||||||||||||| Summary Interpreting ||||||||||||||||||||||||

Skill Focus

Speech with Cues（有提示演讲）

美国著名人际关系学大师戴尔·卡耐基曾经说过，演讲是人人都有的一种潜在的能力。公共演讲能力是口译中一项非常重要的能力，而口译中的公共演讲与一般情况下的公共演讲有相同点，也有区别。二者都经过组织架构和有声产出两个阶段，但是，前者不需要自主构思，只需重述源语的内容。不需自主构思看似是口译的优势，但是反过来看，正因为有了源语这个框架作为参照，如果处理不好，则这个框架就可能成为表达的桎梏。从这个意义上看，我们就更加容易理解"翻译是戴着镣铐跳舞"这句话。本节介绍的有提示演讲练习可以帮助同学们提升"在框架下自我产出"的能力，为之后的口译学习打下良好的表达基础。

无声电影配音：同学们在学习小组内分配不同的角色，根据电影画面的提示内容，为无声电影配音。在时间有限的情况下，同学们尽量产出逻辑清晰、可以理解的语言。这样的练习可以训练同学们更好地将输入的信息进行视觉化。

有提示即兴演讲：同学们根据互不相关的词汇进行演讲，比如"交通堵塞—国际会议—绿化—明星"，需要将所给词汇加入演讲并保持演讲的合理性和流畅性。训练难度可以通过控制所给词汇的难度和数量来加以调节。此外，依次展示词汇或控制展示速度，也可以作为控制难度的重要方式。

单词表自由演讲：与有提示即兴演讲相似，单词表自由演讲基于事先提供的单词表。同学们需要在演讲中将单词表的词汇全部囊括，不要求按照单词出现的顺序进行自由演讲。之后，可以比较同学们根据同一单词表所做的自由演讲之间是否存在巨大差异，还可以要求其他同学进行同语或他语复述。

积极输出练习：这个练习要求同学们阅读报纸杂志，收听广播电视（母语及外语，尤其是外语），同时记录下新的、不熟悉的或者对自己来说转换不够快速有效的词汇，并熟悉这些词汇使用的上下文，尝试利用这些词汇组词成篇，进行积极输出。这样的练习不仅有助于提升词汇量，更重要的是可以提升对于多种专题话语的熟悉度和整体理解能力。

输出填空练习：选择适合的文本材料，在所选材料的重要语义或句法节点留出空白，同学们对材料进行输出的同时，自行填充空白。在训练中，可以采用阅读填空的方式，在阅读材料（母语或外语）上留出空白，同学们边朗读边填空；也可以采用跟读填空的方式，边听边跟读，同时在视听材料的空白处自由产出适合的缺失信息。

Guided Practice

Directions: Please read aloud Task A and Task B. While reading, try to fill in the blanks with words or expressions that you think most fit the context. Then listen to the recording and check whether what you put in is acceptable. When you have everything filled in, please read the passage one paragraph after another, and ask your partner to interpret the paragraphs into Chinese.

Task A

The Accommodations Industry

A hotel is (1) _____. In a hotel, the traveler can rest and has access to food and drink, either on the premises or nearby. The hotel may also offer facilities for recreation, such as (2) _____. In many cases, the hotel also provides (3) _____, which nowadays is the automobile. All of these services are designed to accommodate the traveler, so the hotel business is often referred to as (4) _____.

Travel and hotels have always been closely related. Now the airplane has extended the distances that people could travel in a short period. The airplane has made many places available for development as resorts, including places (5) _____. A resort is a place (6) _____. It may offer (7) _____ _____, or features that are entirely man-made like Disneyland in California.

All hotels do not serve the same clientele. In fact, it is possible to place hotels in four broad categories. (8) _____ is the commercial hotel, which provides services essentially for transients, many of them (9) _____. Many city hotels and diversely located motels fall into this group. (10) _____ is resort hotels. Located in vacation areas, they often provide recreational facilities of their own as well. (11) _____ aims its services largely at the convention trade, which refers to meetings, held regularly or irregularly, of various business or professional groups. At present, it has become trendy for resort hotels to attract this kind of business. (12) _____ is resident hotels. People who do not wish to keep house themselves can rent accommodations on a seasonal basis or even permanently in many hotels. Not firm distinction exists between the different kinds of hotels. In large cities that are also tourist centers, one hotel may offer all types of service.

Task B

Genetically Modified Food and Labeling

In the USA, GM foods are not treated any differently to natural foods. Therefore, (1) _____.
In contrast, in the EU, (2) _____.There are legal regulations that make sure foodstuffs are specifically labeled when detectable levels of DNA and/or protein derived from genetic modification are present. Food producers and retailers have to include the phrase (3) _____ or (4) _____, as appropriate, on the label. A similar legal requirement exists in Australia.

There are problems with labeling however. There is no single test that can be used to detect all types of GM material. Also, there is no international agreement relating to the labeling of GM foods. Even the countries that require labeling do not have the same rules. For example, (5) _____
_____. Nor is there any agreement on how the GM foods should be analyzed.

There has been considerable debate over the issue of labeling. Food manufacturers claim that (6) _____. For example, pure starch from GM maize is identical to starch from non-GM maize. When some foods are processed the DNA is broken down or removed so it is impossible to test (7) _____

_____. Opposing this view are the consumers who (8) _____.
Many consumers are not concerned that GM ingredients may be used in foods, but they would like clear, unambiguous labeling to help them make informed choices. They may decide that (9) _____. Either way, they want to have the information in order to (10) _____.

Directions: Please organize a speech by using the words and expressions listed in their given order in Task C and Task D. Try to make your speech logical and smooth. Then listen to the original speech and find the differences between your speech and the original.

Task C

How to Chair a Meeting

organised and authoritative

a good timekeeper

agenda complete, distributed, discussed

participant make points

a break at the mid-point

Task D

Corporate Social Responsibility

Ericsson

mobile phone

economic globalization and liberalization

environmental issues

corporate failures

stakeholders

shareholders

investors

communities

regulators

employees

customers

‖‖‖‖‖‖‖‖‖‖‖‖‖‖‖‖‖‖‖‖‖ **Information Link** ‖‖‖‖‖‖‖‖‖‖‖‖‖‖‖‖‖‖‖

Consecutive Interpreting and Simultaneous Interpreting（交替传译与同声传译）

作为会议口译的两种主要形式，交替传译和同声传译之间的差异是不言自明的：前者边听边记笔记，然后再翻译，译语总在源语后；后者边听边翻译，译语与源语几乎同步，有时还会出现经过预测，译语先于源语的情况。作为不同的口译模式，交替传译与同声传译在使用范围、译语与源语时差、译员运用记忆能力的方式、技术手段和工具、译语质量评估指标等诸多方面都存在较大差异。

实际上，从技能习得的角度，交替传译和同声传译都要求学习者具备较好的双语水平、记忆能力、反应速度、应变策略。对交替传译和同声传译异同的探讨，更多集中于它们之间的差异，二者的相似点少有提及。实际上，如果基于交替传译和同声传译的基本过程（参看本书第2单元的口译认知负荷模型）来看，二者并不是格格不入、截然分开的。

一方面，同声传译需要译员具备快速的双语反应能力和信息预测、调整、补足的技巧。可以说，同声传译是几乎不需笔记的"超短迷你交替传译"。另一方面，研究发现，交替传译的信息输入和信息输出之间有一个中间地带，也就是在交替传译的第一环节存在并行翻译过程（Parallel Translation）。在并行翻译的过程中，不仅仅存在信息处理，部分信息输出已经在这个阶段完成了，比如，概念的理解和译语的转换等。也就是说，交替传译译员在开口翻译之前已经在头脑中进行了语言和概念的转换，即与同声传译相似的信息听辨、理解、存储甚至转换。可以说，针对每个语段，交替传译译员在开口之前已经做过一遍"同声传译"了。

释意理论的创始人塞莱斯科维奇（Seleskovitch）在其早年著作中提到，口译中最重要的是理解。交替传译中的理解主要发生在信息输入阶段。在这个阶段，译员的头脑中发生了复杂的运作，是难以看清和解释的"黑盒子"。信息输出阶段也可能对前一阶段的理解进行补充甚至重构，但更多是进行验证和夯实，并通过记忆对其进行保持和回溯。然而，在信息输出阶段，受到了话语产出的抑制和影响，理解的保持及记忆的回溯本身就是难点。

因此，交替传译译员在听取源语的过程中，不论是否记笔记，都要在头脑中对信息进行处理及转换。而这种处理和转换的有效程度，直接影响交替传译的最终效果。译员在有限的脑力和精力范围内，信息输入阶段信息转换越有效，则产出阶段越从容；

反之，信息输入阶段信息转换不够有效，则产出阶段的总体任务压力加大，译语质量也会大打折扣，而译语不流利现象正是大脑努力思索，甚至思索也不得其解的直接表现。

综合来看，基于交替传译和同声传译相互交织的关系，可以在口译训练中将这两种口译模式的训练方法交叉使用。在传统口译教学中，交替传译教学往往先于同声传译。那么，如何把同声传译的技能训练融入交替传译教学中，有效提升交替传译"并行翻译过程"中的信息转换速度和程度，进而有效提升交替传译总体表现呢？

首先，同声传译中的双语快速转换练习可以融入交替传译教学中，以辅助学习者在交替传译的"并行翻译过程"中更快、更好地进行双语转换，为其交替传译的产出阶段做更好的准备和铺垫。

其次，可以在交替传译教学中引入源语信息结构分析、新信息选择等练习方法，训练学习者在有限时间内更大程度地进行主动分析，把握信息主干，增强源语输入阶段的信息处理程度，进而增强译语产出的质量和效率。

此外，同声传译教学中的顺句驱动练习可以融入交替传译教学中，使学习者更好地了解并适应"脱离源语语言外壳"的理念。具体来说，视译训练，特别是限时视译训练可以提升学习者的信息转换速度和程度。与此类似，学习者可以针对语段文本选择关键词，并根据关键词进行自我产出。这样做的目的是让学习者认识到，口译是基于意义的自我表达：对源语的有效理解+译员自身的公共演讲能力=较好的口译效果。

|||||||||||||||||||||||| After-class Assignment ||||||||||||||||||||||||

Directions: Listen to the following passage. Pause after each paragraph, and try to summarize the main idea of that paragraph. Pay attention to the discourse markers in the context, and see how they help with the comprehension of the passage.

Bacteria

Paragraph 1

Trillions of bacteria, viruses, and fungi live on or inside of us, and maintaining a good, balanced relationship with them is to our advantage. Together, they form a rich ecosystem that performs a variety of functions in our bodies. The bacteria in our guts can break down food the body can't digest, produce important nutrients, regulate the immune system, and protect against harmful germs.

_____

_____

_____

Paragraph 2

We don't yet have the blueprint for exactly which good bacteria a robust gut needs, but we do know that it's important for a healthy microbiome to have a variety of bacterial species. Many factors affect our microbiomes, including our environment, medications like antibiotics, and even whether we were delivered naturally or not.

_____

_____

_____

Paragraph 3

Diet, too, is emerging as one of the leading influences on the health of our guts. And while we can't control all these factors, we can manipulate the balance of our microbes by paying attention to what we eat.

_____

_____

_____

Paragraph 4

Dietary fiber from foods like fruits, vegetables, nuts, and whole grains is the best fuel for gut bacteria. When bacteria digest fiber, they produce short chain fatty acids that nourish the gut barrier, improve immune function, and can help prevent inflammation, which reduces the risk of cancer. And the more fiber you ingest, the more fiber-digesting bacteria colonize your gut.

_____

_____

_____

Paragraph 5

So what goes wrong with our gut bacteria when we eat low-fiber processed foods? Lower fiber means less fuel for the gut bacteria, essentially starving them until they die off. This results in less diversity and hungry bacteria.

_____

_____

_____

Paragraph 6

We also know that specific foods can affect gut bacteria. In one recent microbiome study, scientists found that fruits, vegetables, tea, coffee, red wine, and dark chocolate were correlated with increased bacterial diversity. These foods contain polyphenols, which are naturally occurring antioxidant compounds. On the other hand, foods high in dietary fat, like whole milk and sugar-sweetened sodas, were correlated with decreased diversity.

_____

_____

_____

Paragraph 7

How food is prepared also matters. Minimally processed, fresh foods generally have more fiber and provide better fuel. So lightly steamed, sautéed, or raw vegetables are typically more beneficial than fried dishes.

_____

_____

_____

Paragraph 8

These are just general guidelines. More research is needed before we fully understand exactly how any of these foods interact with our microbiomes. We see positive correlations, but the insides of our guts are difficult places to make direct observations. For instance, we don't currently know whether these foods are directly responsible for the changes in diversity, or if something more complicated is happening.

_____

_____

_____

Paragraph 9

While we're only beginning to explore the vast wilderness inside our guts, we already have a glimpse of how crucial our microbiomes are for digestive health. The great news is we have the power to fire up the bacteria in our bellies. Fill up on fibers, fresh and fermented foods, and you can trust your gut to keep you going strong.

_____

_____

_____

扫码获取本单元音频资料

4 Information Structure I & Segmentation

A text cannot be translated if it has not first been analyzed. The most common translation mistakes are due to a lack of analysis.

— Gerardo Vázquez-Ayora, Spanish translator

Unit Goals

- To gain a general knowledge of how the information structure of a text can be built with the help of both known and unknown information.
- To become more flexible in summary interpreting by applying the tactic of segmentation.
- To gain a general knowledge of principles in selecting training materials of interpreting.

Warm Up

Directions: Listen to the following passages and fill in the blanks with words or sentences. Make sure the words and sentences you fill in are both grammatically and semantically acceptable.

Task A

It is impossible not to re-state how urgent it is that we move towards a "circular economy", particularly when considering ways to (1) _____ (dress; address) the seemingly unending flow of plastic into our oceans which we've had today. We already know the extent of the damage that this is having on marine life today, and if current trends continue, the (2) _____ (implications; impressions) for the viability of the ocean ecosystem, on which humankind relies so heavily, are stark indeed. And given the tremendous opportunity that a transition to a circular economy offers, both towards improving the health of our oceans, as well as to businesses, surely it would be wise to move ahead with its implementation with a degree of considerable

(3) _____ (urgency; emergency).

One critical part, as I see it, of the transition towards a circular economy, particularly in relation to plastics, is that of (4) _____ (innovation; renovation) and the need to rethink the way we design products. This would entail moving from a model that encourages a buy, use, throw-away (5) _____ (vitality; mentality), to one that facilitates reuse, recovery and (6) _____ (generation; regeneration). We do need to consider, from the very beginning, the second, third and, indeed, fourth life of the products we use in everyday life.

I appreciate that this is easier to say than do, so I was particularly interested to hear the key findings from the design workshop held in various locations across London this week. As some of you know, I have always been a great believer in the "seeing is believing" idea, so I very much hope that your field visits left you feeling inspired to create new (7) _____ (resolutions; solutions) within your organizations that are supported by your senior executives, many of whom — I am very grateful to see — are around the table today. And given how critical the design (8) _____ (face; phase) of a product's life is to its later environmental impact, I can hardly overstate how important this work is and I know that my company stands ready to help continue to (9) _____ (facilitate; facility) these conversations.

Whilst solutions do seem to be at hand, we are only likely to succeed if there is considerable, concerted and collaborative action into the future by all involved. Therefore, I am much encouraged by the willingness of the (10) _____ (business; businesses) round this table to collaborate. Such collaboration between and within different industry sectors is absolutely fundamental if we are to find innovative solutions to rapid decarbonization, an essential part of which will come from a redesign of the plastic supply chain. The implementation of these solutions will inevitably require great leadership, as well as a determination to take very practical and ambitious action.

Task B

A British study has found that B vitamins can reduce brain shrinkage in older people with mild memory loss. It (1) _____ that B vitamins caused an average ⅓ (2) _____ in brain shrinkage among adults who had trouble remembering. David Smith was a leader of the study. He (3) _____ the use of the vitamins as simple and safe. He also said researchers do not yet know if B vitamins could (4) _____ or slow Alzheimer's disease.

Vitamins are important for good health. These (5) _____ organic substances help to carry out chemical changes within cells. If we do not get enough of the vitamins we need in our food, we are at risk of developing (6) _____ diseases. Some shrinkage of the brain is thought to happen normally as people grow older. Yet studies have shown a (7) _____ between a larger shrinkage and Alzheimer's disease.

(8) _____.
They say half of these people develop serious loss of their mental ability, as in Alzheimer's disease. (9) _____

_____.

Prof. Smith had a warning for older adult worried about memory loss. He said they should talk to their doctors before starting to take the vitamins. He added that the vitamins could speed the growth of some cancers. (10) _____

_____. That was true whether or not the people took the vitamins.

ⅢⅢⅢⅢⅢⅢⅢⅢⅢ Listening Comprehension ⅢⅢⅢⅢⅢⅢⅢⅢⅢ

Skill Focus

Information Structure: Known and Unknown Information（信息结构：已知及未知信息）

在语言学意义上，信息是由新旧交替产生的。信息结构指把语言组织成信息单位的结构，而每个信息单位都是由已知信息和新信息组织而成的。一般来说，新旧信息在信息结构中的位置是：已知信息在前，新信息在后，前一句的新信息又可以成为下一句的已知信息。这是符合听话人心理认知过程的最理想的信息处理方式。

在话语发展中，新信息是必不可少的，否则会因为已知信息过多而使话语变得乏味；而新信息过多也是不可取的，这样会加大话语的理解难度，甚至使其变得不能理解。新信息是发话人要受话人格外留心的信息，它可能以前没有被提到过，或不可预测，或需要强调。这一点对话语理解特别重要。如果能够准确快速地分辨新旧信息，则可通过跟进信息结构的新信息部分，在听解高速不可复听的口语表达过程中，赢得时间，更好更快地把握话语的要旨。

新信息往往不可预测，如果我们可以对话语中的已知信息更加敏感，尽量做到不受其干扰，则新信息自然会凸显出来，变得更加清晰可辨。那么，已知信息在话语中的显现方式主要有哪些呢?

语言层面上的已知信息

我们可以通过一定的语法形式对其附带的已知信息加以判断。英语话语信息结构中，常用于表达已知信息的语法形式主要有以下几种。

1. 带定冠词的名词短语

I bought a new shirt yesterday. The shirt is very cheap.

2. 上下义词

I bought some flowers yesterday. The roses are very beautiful.

3. 前指某一个名词的代词

What were the children doing? They were playing football.

4. 外指的代词

(Sag produces a cleaver and prepares to hack off his left hand.) He never actually does it.

5. 替代动词

Her sister studies in Beijing. So does she.

请看下面的段落。

The right nutrition is absolutely vital for good health, and in terms of the right nutrition it means a very varied and balanced diet. There are three main food groups: protein, carbohydrate and fat. It is very important to make sure that you have a blend of each of those different nutrients because they each play a very different role, and an important role, for the various bodily functions. If you don't get enough of one of them, then there will be a knock-on effect, which may ultimately lead to some kind of health problem. If you get too many of one, the same kind of thing can happen. So it's very important to make sure you're having a good balance of all three.（阴影部分是同义语反复；下划线部分通过两个方面的说明，得出balance的结论，是通过已知信息可以推导出的结论。）

这段话简洁一点的说法是：The right nutrition is vital for good health, and it means varied and balanced diet. Protein, carbohydrate and fat are the three main food groups, which are important for various bodily functions. Having insufficient or too many of the nutrients will both lead to health problems. Therefore, a balance of them is recommended.

主题知识中的已知信息

是否在话语中已经被提及，并不是判断已知信息的唯一标准。在框架（scenario）的概念中，已知信息是被语言激活的那一部分。例如，如果建立一个"教室"的框架，则"学生"就应被看作已知信息，因为他们是这一框架的一部分。已知信息也包括受话人从背景知识中推导出的信息。

虽然口译的主题千差万别，所需知识包罗万象，给人无从下手的感觉，但是我们应培养自己对多种知识的好奇心和学习兴趣。一旦所听话语中的主题知识是我们熟悉的，那么已知信息的比例就会增加。对译员来说，口译话语中已知信息的比例越大，话语听解的难度越小，越有助于我们高质量地完成口译任务。我们来看下面的例子。

Two managers of a restaurant in central China's Hubei Province have been arrested by police on suspicion of adding parts of the opium poppy plant to dishes, authorities said Friday.

According to the Procuratorate of Hanyang District, Wuhan City, the local food and drug administration detected main ingredients of poppy seeds including papaverine and narcotine from dishes of a restaurant during routine tests in March.

The two managers of this restaurant allegedly added poppy seeds to dressings of its stewed pots for the purpose of improving taste of dishes and keeping customers coming back for more, said police investigation.

Adding poppy seeds containing morphine to food is prohibited by law. Doctors say they contain only a small amount of alkaloid, but long-term consumption will lead to addiction, damage to the nervous system and induce chronic intoxication.

在这篇关于"不良饭店在饭菜中添加罂粟壳"的报道中，第一段就点出了主题。如果我们平时接触过相关知识，可以迅速在"restaurant"和"poppy seeds"这两个关键词之间建立联系，也就可以预测下面可能会说到的问题：为什么会这么做（增加回头客牟取暴利）、这么做有什么危害（对食客的身体有害）、应该如何应对这种做法（立法监察）等。语篇中其他段落确实涉及了这些问题，只不过展开的顺序可能不同，提及的细节也可能不一样。然而，一旦主题的"框架"确定下来，之后反复听到的"restaurant"和"poppy seeds"等关键词就可以一步步夯实我们对主题的预测。即便我们不能在听到第一段的时候就搭建起"框架"，之后出现的关键词也会帮助我们理清思路，一点点构建出全篇的主题。由此可见，主题知识可以更大程度上作为已知信息，帮助我们更好地理解语篇。

Guided Practice

Directions: Skim the passages and fill in the blanks based on the information structure. Listen to the recording and check how the combination of known and unknown information helps with the anticipation.

Task A

The Importance of Keeping a Good Mood

In such a quick-fixed society today, keeping a good mood is of great importance for the following two reasons.

(1) _____

_____. It is written in a Chinese traditional medical book that various negative (2) _____ will have a bad influence on various parts of your body. For example, if one easily gets angry, he is likely to have his (3) _____ hurt. If one is gloomy for a long time, his kidneys are easily hurt. If you keep a good mood, you would have a (4) _____ chance to suffer them.

(5) _____

_____. If you keep (6) _____ when you greet and treat your relatives, friends, and colleagues, for example, smiling to them, they may hardly take offence on you, (7) _____ may they respond to your passion with coldness. As a result, you will be in a better term with people around you and feel much happier yourself.

(8) _____, (9) _____ does have such kind of magical power under whatever circumstances and it is worth (10) _____.

> **Try This:** _____
>
> Please rebuild the above passage with the help of the chart provided.
> You may use English or Chinese in the reproduction.

Task B

The Harm of Foreign Fast Food

Nowadays, foreign fast foods like KFC and McDonald's are criticized as "junk food", which I think is a quite reasonable attitude.

The first harm fast foods may bring us is that frequent consumption will lead to unbalanced nutrition. Some experts investigate that most fast foods are (1) _____ calorie, fat and salt, but (2) _____ food fiber, minerals and vitamins, (3) _____ for the development of children's brain. That is why children who enjoy fast foods are fatter than others, and (4) _____ they are more likely to be slower in intelligent activities, less concentrated on their study and (5) _____ to get anxious. What is more serious is that a (6) _____ will decrease children's immunity.

Secondly, fast foods lead to BPA pollution. (7) _____ is a poisonous chemical contained in the packet paper of (8) _____ like sandwich and fried chicken. It not only disturbs people's endocrine, but also pollutes the environment.

fast food
unbalanced nutrition
BPA pollution

Due to the above serious (9) _____ foreign snacks may do to our health, we strongly suggest rediscovering our traditional and (10) _____ dieting, mainly in the form of crop, vegetable and less fat.

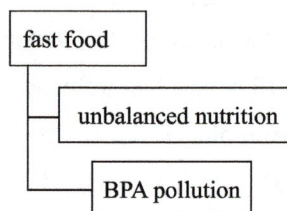

Try This: ——————————————————————————————
Please rebuild the above passage with the help of the chart provided. You may use English or Chinese in the reproduction.

Vocabulary

calorie	卡路里	immunity	免疫力
fiber	纤维	chemical	化学制品
mineral	矿物质	packet paper	包装纸
vitamin	维生素	endocrine	内分泌

Task C

Drinking Bottled Water

There are a few things that are just not right with drinking bottled water.

(1) _____ is the bottle itself is made from plastic. Did you know that most (2) _____ are made from petroleum? Yes, you heard me right. One of the biggest consumers of oil is (3) _____ itself.

(4) _____ that I find wrong about bottled water is its price. When compared

to tap water the cost is more than 500% higher. The same money you spend on one gallon of (5) _____ can get you roughly 500 gallons of (6) _____. Of course it all depends on where you live and what your water company charges.

If you are a (7) _____ drinker here are some things you can do today to help. For one go to WalMart or Kmart or whatever and purchase a reusable plastic sport drink bottle. Then while at the store purchase a pure water filter that either attaches to the faucet itself or the water supply line. Then when you want some fresh (8) _____ turn your sink faucet on and fill up your reusable plastic bottle and immediately you have clean, filtered (9) _____.

If the average person drinks just one bottle of water per week, with 302 million Americans in the country, it would reduce the use of over 15 million petroleum-based (10) _____ bottles. That is huge savings on the need for oil, reduced landfill space, and of course savings in your wallet. Make the change today away from (11) _____ and toward the more economical and environmentally correct option of (12) _____ bottles and (13) _____ or in the Chinese case, (14) _____.

Vocabulary

petroleum	石油	pure water filter	纯净水过滤器
tap water	自来水	sink faucet	水槽水龙头
WalMart or Kmart	沃尔玛或凯马特（超市品牌）	water supply line	供水管道
gallon	加仑（容量单位）	landfill	垃圾填埋场

Try This:

Please rebuild the above passage with the help of the chart below. You may use English or Chinese in the reproduction.

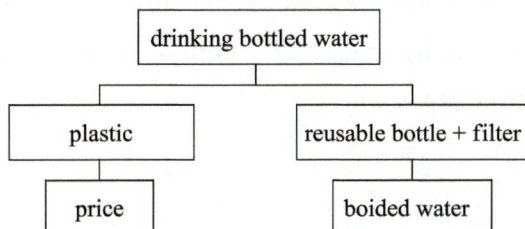

🎧 **Task D**

Three Things a Country Can Do

Every country has to accommodate the emerging changes around the world. So if you look at what countries can do, they can really only do three things for their citizens to make them more competitive going forward.

One of the things they can do is the reason you are here in this university. They can provide a good education, and generally standard of living goes directly with the (1) _____, so the higher the (2) _____ within the country, the greater the opportunity for standard of living, the greater the opportunity for economic competitiveness. So providing an (3) _____ to the whole citizenry really is important.

(4) _____.
Research and development creates ideas for the future. And (5) _____ create new products, new services, new companies. So we need to invest in research and development and just as the (6) _____ in any country is directly related to the education level of the workforce, we find the standard of living and the economic competitiveness of any country is usually related to its (7) _____. And obviously China has recognized both of these characteristics with a great emphasis on education in the last decade. And the more recent emphasis on increasing and expanding the research and development.

The third thing that any country can do is in fact to create an environment that allows smart people to come together with smart ideas, generated from research and development and create new products, new companies, new services, new economic growth. And increasingly we see this sort of entrepreneurial spirit here in China. My company happens to be the largest high-tech venture capital investor in the world. And increasingly we see more and more (8) _____ made here in China. Ten years ago those investment were predominantly made in (9) _____. Now only 50% of those investments are made in the United States. About 50% are made here in (10) _____, especially China.

So those are the three things that every country can do, education, research and development and setting the environment.

Vocabulary

accommodate	适应，调整
research and development (R&D)	研发
entrepreneurial spirit	企业家精神
venture capital	风险投资
predominant	占主导地位的

Try This:

Please rebuild the above passage with the help of the chart below. You may use English or Chinese in the reproduction.

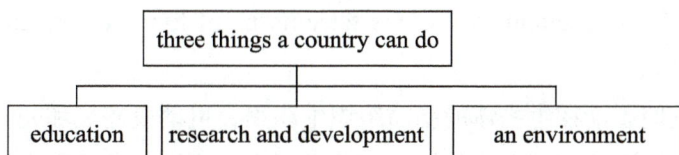

```
          ┌─────────────────────────────────┐
          │  three things a country can do  │
          └─────────────────────────────────┘
            │              │              │
   ┌───────────┐  ┌─────────────────────────┐  ┌──────────────────┐
   │ education │  │ research and development │  │  an environment  │
   └───────────┘  └─────────────────────────┘  └──────────────────┘
```

IIIIIIIIIIIIIIIIIIIIIIIIII Summary Interpreting IIIIIIIIIIIIIIIIIIIIIIIIII

Skill Focus

Segmentation（断句）

"断句"是按照意群将句子进行切分处理的一种技巧。断句可以称得上是口译中最重要的技巧，特别是当源语句子过长或较为繁复时，断句显得尤为重要。正是依靠恰到好处的断句，译员才能游刃有余地应对潮水般涌来的信息，并结合其他技巧，最终流畅地完成口译。

断句的目的不是简单地切分句子，而是更好地把句子顺承接续下去。如果只是把句子切割成一截一截的零碎信息而不加任何处理，然后一股脑地抛给听众，译文质量势必十分糟糕。因此，译员应做到断得恰到好处，接得迅速自然。断句的标准是断而不散，零而不碎，自然衔接。句子切断的单位在多数情况下应该是意群，而不是单词。断句应该适度，断得太急太短会使信息破碎，也给"连接"带来更大的挑战，因此断句要把握好节奏和尺度。

63

实际上，断句技巧也有几点缺憾：断句后句子的紧凑度或多或少会有所下降，如果打的"补丁"过多过密的话，也会让译语冗长零散。因此，断句时应把握好意群。某些情况下，断句会改变句子语义的重心，口译时应该通过补足或调整语气弥补这一缺点。

以单词作为断句的单位是不可取的，以意群或类意群断句更为合理。在真实口译的过程中，译员并没有时间仔细思考、分辨，更多的是凭借平时积累的经验和一些基本的"信号"把握意群或类意群，更好地完成断句和顺句驱动，确保口译顺利进行。当然，这些"信号"并非金科玉律。在口译过程中，译员要灵活变通，既学会利用这些"信号"进行断句，同时也不要囿于其中而被束缚手脚。以下例析给出断句可能采用的方式。请注意，断句不是必要的，而是为了流利顺畅产出译语才采用的一种方式，需要灵活应用。

1. 介词结构

例：They gradually accumulate / in the fatty tissue of living organisms, / and can cause cancer and birth defect.

笔译译文：它们逐渐在生物体的脂肪组织中积聚，可诱发癌症和先天缺陷。

口译译文：它们逐渐积聚在生物体的脂肪组织中，可诱发癌症和先天缺陷。

例：This meeting marks a new chapter / in the history of Stockholm Convention.

笔译译文：这一会议开启了斯德哥尔摩公约历史上的崭新篇章。

口译译文：这一会议标志着崭新的一章，在斯德哥尔摩公约历史上的新篇章。

2. 不定式结构

例：It is equally important / to make progress / on all aspects of the scope of the convention.

笔译译文：公约的各个方面都要取得进展，这一点同样重要。

口译译文：同样重要的是，要取得进展，公约的所有方面都要有所进展。

例：We must not allow ourselves / to deviate from our obligations / to honor the dignity of human life, / to protect individual freedom / and to protect the independence of a fair judicial process.

笔译译文：我们决不允许自己背离尊重人类生命尊严、捍卫个人自由以及保护公平司法程序独立性的承诺。

口译译文：我们决不允许自己背离承诺，也就是尊重人类生命尊严、捍卫个人自由和保护公平司法程序独立性的承诺。

3．分词结构

例：During the second review / of the UN Global Counter-Terrorism Strategy / in September, Member States adopted a new resolution / reaffirming their support for the Strategy.

笔译译文：9月对联合国全球反恐战略的第二次审议中，各成员国通过了一份新决议，重申了他们对这一战略的支持。

口译译文：第二次审议联合国反恐战略的工作在9月进行，期间各成员国通过了一份新决议，重申他们都支持这一战略。

例：One in every six people / on earth / wake up each morning / not knowing / whether they will have enough to eat.

笔译译文：地球上六分之一的人口每天早上醒来时，不知道自己是否有足够的食物。

口译译文：六分之一地球上的人口每天早上醒来时，不知道自己是否有足够的食物。

4．从句结构

例：It is not acceptable that / one in seven young people leaves school / without finishing upper secondary education / and only one in three young adults attains tertiary education.

笔译译文：七分之一的年轻人没有完成高中教育便离开学校，只有三分之一的年轻人接受高等教育，这些数字都让人无法接受。

口译译文：令人难以接受的是，七分之一的年轻人辍学，没有完成高中教育，而只有三分之一的年轻人接受了高等教育。

例：If my primary objective is / to make them / as effective and user-friendly as possible, / I intend also to support more directly actions / which would strengthen the interaction / between universities and the world of work.

笔译译文：如果我的主要目标是使它们尽可能地有效和便于使用，那么我还打算更直接地支持那些能增进大学和职场之间互动的活动。

口译译文：如果我的主要目标是使它们有效、便于使用，达到最佳效果，那么我还打算更直接地支持一些活动，以增进大学和职场间的互动。

Guided Practice

Directions: Divide the sentences into smaller segments by using the techniques illustrated above and then interpret the sentences. You may interpret to your partner first and then ask him/her to comment on your performance.

1. I welcome this opportunity to present the Commission's latest annual report on the progress made by EU Member States towards our joint European objectives in education and training.

2. Let me conclude by once more calling on Member States to maintain or even increase education budgets, despite the restraints imposed by the economic crisis.

3. This is why Education has been placed at the centre of the Europe 2020 strategy, the strategy put forward by the European Union to face the challenges ahead and develop a smart, inclusive and green society.

4. I am convinced that this report will help Member States target better resources towards those sectors within education that need it most.

5. They must be willing to cooperate with higher education institutions on a long-term basis by helping the development of new curricula or offering more places for internships for instance.

6. E-commerce holds particular appeal in straitened times as it enables people to compare prices / across retailers quickly and easily. Buyers can sometimes avoid local sales taxes online, and shipping is often free.

7. From the World Economic Forum, Switzerland tops the latest competitiveness ranking, best known for its annual economic forum in Davos (a Swiss ski resort). It is closely followed by Singapore. Finland has piped Sweden to third place. Of the big emerging economies, China remains on top, with Brazil moving up.

8. The Japanese spend half as much on health care as do Americans, but still they live longer. Life expectancy has risen from 52 in 1945 to 83 today. Many give credit to their cheap and universal health insurance system. The country boasts one of the lowest infant mortality rates in the world. Yet Japanese health-care costs are a mere 8.5% of GDP.

9. Given its history of innovation, the healthcare sector has been reluctant to embrace information technology (IT). Whereas every other big industry has computerized since the 1980s, doctors in most parts of the world still work mainly with pen and paper.

10. Twenty five years ago I came to Hong Kong as a student. The year was 1985. Deng Xiaoping and Margaret Thatcher had recently signed the historic Joint Declaration. The remarkable story of the successful handover of Hong Kong and the great progress Hong Kong has continued to make is an example to the world of what can be achieved when two countries cooperate in confidence and with mutual respect... Since then, China has changed almost beyond recognition. China's National Anthem famously calls on the people of China to stand up... Today

the Chinese people are not just standing up in their own country. They are standing up in the world. No longer can people talk about the global economy without including the country that has grown on average ten percent a year for three decades. No longer can we talk about trade without the country that is now the world's largest exporter and third largest importer. And no longer can we debate energy security or climate change without the country that is one of the world's biggest consumers of energy. China is on course to reclaim its position as the world's biggest economy, the position it has held for 18 of the last 20 centuries, and an achievement of which the Chinese people are justly proud. Put simply: China has re-emerged as a great global power.

Vocabulary

commission	委员会
EU Member State	欧盟成员国
joint objective	共同目标
budget	预算
inclusive	包容的
higher education institution	高等教育机构
curricula	课程
internship	实习
e-commerce	电子商务
retailer	零售商
sale tax	营业税
World Economic Forum	世界经济论坛
infant mortality rate	新生儿死亡率
information technology	信息技术
Margaret Thatcher	玛格丽特·撒切尔
Joint Declaration	联合声明
National Anthem	国歌

Information Link

Selection of Training Materials（语料的选择）

"听辨与译述"是口译的准备性课程，在"听"的过程中对信息进行分析和识别，并在"述"的过程中对信息进行回溯和概说。"听辨与译述"的练习语料应贴近口译任务中的常见语料。

口译活动主题繁杂、形式多样，其语料特点很难界定。但一般来说，口译过程中的诸多"输入变量"对口译任务具有重要影响，会使口译任务变得困难。因此，"听辨与译述"的练习语料应控制其"输入变量"，循序渐进地进行口译的准备性训练，为之后的正式口译课程打好"听"与"说"的基础。值得关注的口译语料"输入变量"包括主题、速度、信息密度、句法复杂程度、词汇难度等。

首先，主题熟悉度是保障口译顺利进行的必要条件。对不熟悉的主题需要有"认知知识"或"世界知识"的补充，这也是口译学习及实践过程中一直需要提升的部分。在"听辨与译述"练习语料的选择上，应注意控制主题难度，或对主题知识进行适当补充之后再进行练习。

其次，语料的速度也是影响口译效果的重要因素。较为舒适的源语语速为100~120词/分钟，过快的语速可能加大口译信息输入难度，导致译员出现更多错译和漏译，直接影响口译产出质量。口译信息输入和输出阶段的难度都会加大，导致译员出现更多错译和漏译。因此，新闻报道类语料不适合被选为"听辨与译述"的训练材料。

最后，信息密度（information density）、句法复杂度（syntactic complexity）、词汇难度（lexical difficulty）都是衡量语料难度的重要指标。这三项指标中，书面语高于口语，书面语的科技文本数值最高。因此，"听辨与译述"的练习语料适合选用接近口语的材料或以上三项指标较低的书面语。

After-class Assignment

Directions: Listen to the following passage. Pause after each paragraph, and try to summarize the main idea of that paragraph. Pay attention to both known and unknown information in the context, and see how the combination of the two helps build the information structure.

Back Pain

Paragraph 1

Bad backs are one of the most common health problems today, affecting people in all walks of life. The most recent available figures show that about a quarter of a million people are incapacitated with back pain every day. And many sufferers don't know the causes or the solution to their problem.

_____

_____

Paragraph 2

The majority of our patients at the clinic tend to be women. They are especially vulnerable because of pregnancy but also because of osteoporosis, which I personally believe to be the major cause of problems for women. I have many women patients who say they have completely given up exercise because the pain makes them so miserable. But of course that starts up a vicious circle. Bed rest, giving up exercise and pain killers is traditional responses to back pain but, although there are many excellent drugs on the market, at our clinic we are beginning to realize the unique benefits of relaxation therapy. Other specialists in the field make a strong case for certain types of exercise, but in our experience they are easily mishandled and can lead to more harm than good.

_____

_____

_____

Paragraph 3

Now, let's look at some of the reasons why back pain is developing into such a unique menace. In general, the body is pretty good at self-repair. A strain or a blow to a limb, though painful at the time, generally resolves itself. But the body's response to back injury can be very counter-productive. When pain strikes, we attempt to keep the back as immobile as possible, which makes the muscles tense up. Research shows that they often go into spasm, which causes further twisting of the spine. A vicious circle is underway.

_____

_____

_____

Paragraph 4

The second mistake we often make when stricken with extreme back pain is to go to bed and stay there. Although at the clinic we recognize that a short rest in bed can be helpful...up to two days...any longer makes your back muscles become weaker and unable to hold up to spine.

Then pain therefore becomes worse.

_____

_____

_____

Paragraph 5

Another problem is being overweight. Anyone a stone or more overweight who already has back pain is not doing himself any favors: though it won't actually set it off in the first place, the weight will increase the strain and make things worse. The British diet could be partially to blame for the increase in back pain: over the last several decades the average weight of men has risen by 11 lbs and of women by 9 lbs. So much for the causes and aggravations of pain. But what can we do to help?

_____

_____

_____

Paragraph 6

There are many ways in which simple day-to-day care can make all the difference. The first point to watch of course is weight. If you are overweight, a diet will make all the difference.

_____

_____

_____

Paragraph 7

Also, studies have shown that just one hour sitting in a slouched position can strain ligaments in the back which can take months to heal. At the clinic we have come to the conclusion that the major cause of the problem is not with the design of chairs, as some have suggested, but in the way we sit in them. It can be useful to get special orthopaedic chairs, but remember the most important improvement should be in our posture.

_____

_____

_____

Paragraph 8

Another enemy of your back is, of course, your beds. If your bed doesn't give enough support, back muscles and ligaments work all night trying to correct spinal alignment, so you wake up with a tired aching back. Try out an orthopaedic mattress or a spring slatted bed. Research shows that both can be beneficial for certain types of back pain.

_____

_____

_____

Paragraph 9

Another hazard for your back are the shock waves which travel up your spine when you walk, known as heel strike. A real find for our patients has been the shock-absorbing shoe insert. A cheap but very effective solution. And you might be better off avoiding shoes with heels higher than 1.5 inches. Though absolutely flat shoes can be a solution for some, others find their posture suffers.

_____

_____

_____

Paragraph 10

Finally, a word about the state-of-the-art relief, the TENS machine, a small battery-powered gadget which delivers subliminal electrical pulses to the skin. Our experience indicates that your money is better spent on the more old-fashioned remedies.

_____

_____

_____

扫码获取本单元音频资料

Unit 5

Information Structure II & Syntactic Transformation

> The relationships between words can be transferred from linguistic forms to the corresponding kernel sentences; the key to translation lies in the translation of meaning.
>
> — Eugene A. Nida, American linguist

Unit Goals

- To gain a general knowledge of how analysis of kernel sentences can help build up the information structure, and ultimately facilitate the comprehension of texts.
- To become more flexible in summary interpreting by applying the technique of syntactic transformation.
- To gain a general knowledge of deverbalization in interpreting.

Warm Up

Directions: Listen to the following passages and choose the best answer for each question.

Task A

1. Microsoft's shares are devalued drastically owing to _____.

   A. fierce competition from rivals   B. its involvement in a lawsuit

   C. the court rulings   D. the decrease in sales volume

2. According to the passage, which of the following is now the second biggest company in the United States?

   A. General Electric.   B. Intel.

   C. Cisco Systems.   D. GE Capital Services.

Task B

1. This passage is most probably _____.

    A. a review of Milton's *Paradise Lost*

    B. an introduction of what *Paradise Lost* is about

    C. a depiction of the cruelness of the British ruler

    D. part of an introduction to English literature

2. According to the passage, Milton _____.

    A. describes Satan as a Puritan

    B. doesn't believe in God

    C. is satisfied with the British ruler

    D. calls on people to fight against the dictator

3. In the poem, Satan is described as _____.

    A. an evil person   B. contrary to what is depicted in the *Bible*

    C. a stupid ghost   D. selfish and cruel devil

4. According to this passage, *Paradise Lost* is written for the purpose of _____.

    A. praising God for the creation of the world

    B. criticizing the cruelness of British ruler

    C. changing people's unfavourable impression of Satan

    D. expressing his support for the fight of Satan

Task C

1. What is the main purpose of the passage?

    A. To outline contrasting types of economic systems.

    B. To explain the science of economics.

    C. To argue for the superiority of one economic system.

    D. To compare barter and money exchange markets.

2. According to the passage, a barter economy can lead to _____.

    A. rapid speed of transactions   B. misunderstandings

    C. inflation   D. difficulties for the trader

Listening Comprehension

Information Structure: Kernel Sentence（信息结构：核心句）

核心句翻译策略旨在分析复杂句的深层结构，找到最深层简单句的施动者及受动者，分析每个核心句之间的逻辑关系，并对核心句加以转换、重构和检验，完成翻译。通过采用核心句翻译策略，可以减少口译实践过程中由于句式复杂而产生的对原文的误解，使译文更加准确、流畅。

核心句翻译策略由美国著名语言学家、翻译家尤金·奈达提出。奈达认为，译文应达到与原文"最切近的自然对等"。为使译文减少模糊、更加清晰，奈达提出核心句翻译策略。他认为，翻译中源语向目的语的转换，是在深层结构层面上进行的。译者必须通过逆向转换法（back-transformation）分析出源语表层结构背后的深层结构，再将源语的深层结构转换成目的语的深层结构，最后重组为符合目的语语法规则和表达习惯的表层结构。

为了分析深层结构，奈达采用核心句指代英语句法中最基本的深层结构，其特征是主动语态的简单陈述句句式，在句法上不可再分。奈达基于词的四大语义范畴，即物体（object）、活动（event）、抽象（abstract）、关系（relational），将英语句法的深层结构归纳为7个核心句。

（1）John ran quickly.（任何表人或物体的名词都可以做主语。）

（2）John hit Bill.（任何施事都可以对受事施加行为。）

（3）John gave Bill a ball.（任何施事都可以实施"给"的动作。）

（4）John is in the house.（画线部分可以替换为任何其他介词短语。）

（5）John is sick.（画线部分可以替换为描述主语特征的任何形容词。）

（6）John is a boy.（主语是画线部分所指概念中的一员。）

（7）John is my father.（主语与画线部分所指相同，反之亦然。）

对复杂句中出现的系列核心句，应先找到复杂句中最基本的词汇、词组，辨别其性质是动作的施动者，还是受动者，并对它们之间的关系加以说明。奈达的核心句翻译策略为翻译实践和翻译研究提供了新的模式，促进了翻译的具体化，对结构复杂的英语长句汉译具有较好的理论指导意义。在英语长句汉译的过程中，先找出源语句子的核心句，并转换成目的语的核心句，再按照汉语的句法结构，组织排列其他信息，从而摆脱英语长句复杂的表层结构的束缚，得出理想的译文。

例1

原文：I was inspired by those who came, like Dr. Rajan, who helped start the School Health Programme, and produced the original version of the Child's Health Booklet, which we still use today.

（1）I was inspired by those who came, like Dr. Rajan. (Those who came, like Dr. Rajan, inspired me.)

（2）Those who came, like Dr. Rajan, helped start the School Health Programme.

（3）Those who came, like Dr. Rajan, produced the original version of the Child's Health Booklet.

（4）We still use the original version of the Child's Health Booklet today.

下面是上面四个核心句的中文译文。

（1）来到这里的人们，比如拉詹博士，激励了我。

（2）（他们）帮助启动了"学校健康计划"。

（3）（他们）制作了第一版《儿童健康手册》。

（4）我们至今仍在使用这个版本。

译文：来到这里的人们，比如拉詹博士，激励了我。他们帮助启动了"学校健康计划"，制作了第一版《儿童健康手册》，我们至今仍在使用这个版本。

例2

原文：Singapore must always be a place where everyone can feel proud of what they do, where you are respected for your contributions and your character and anyone can improve his life if he works hard and everyone can hope for a better future.

（1）Singapore must always be such a place.

（2）(In this place), everyone can feel proud of what they do.

（3）(In this place), you are respected for your contribution and your character. (People respect you because of your contribution and your character.)

（4）(In this place), anyone can improve his life if he works hard.

（5）(In this place), everyone can hope for a better future.

下面是上面五个核心句的中文译文。

（1）新加坡是这样一个地方。

（2）（在这里）每个人都对自己所做的事情感到自豪。

（3）（在这里）每个人都因为自己的贡献和品质受到尊重（人们因为你的贡献和品质而尊重你）。

（4）（在这里）任何人只要努力工作就可以提升生活质量。

（5）（在这里）每个人都可以憧憬更美好的未来。

译文：新加坡应该是这样一个地方，每个人都对自己所做的事情感到自豪，每个人都因为自己的贡献和品质受到尊重，任何人只要努力工作就可以提升生活质量，每个人都可以憧憬更美好的未来。

例3

原文：In spite of the more and more economic and technical achievements and progress we have made, we can't afford to be optimistic, faced wtih the fact that ecological loss is unprecedented, which is demonstrated by the increasingly severe desertification, shrinking resources of fresh water, unbearable scales of air pollution, acid rain and chemical residues in food, etc.

（1）We have made more and more economic and technical achievements and progress.

（2）(But), we can't afford to be optimistic.

（3）(Because), we face unprecedented ecological loss.

（4）(We face) increasingly severe desertification.

（5）(We face) shrinking resources of fresh water.

（6）(We face) unbearable scales of air pollution, acid rain and chemical residues in food.

下面是上面六个核心句的中文译文。

（1）我们在经济和技术上取得了越来越多的成就和进步。

（2）（但是）我们依然不能乐观。

（3）（因为）我们面临前所未有的生态损失。

（4）（我们面临）土地沙漠化越来越严重。

（5）（我们面临）淡水资源越来越匮乏。

（6）（我们面临）空气污染、酸雨、食物中的农药残留越来越让人无法忍受。

顺译译文：我们在经济和技术上取得了越来越多的成就和进步，但是我们依然不能乐观，因为我们面临前所未有的生态损失：土地沙漠化越来越严重；淡水资源越来越匮乏；空气污染、酸雨、食物中的农药残留越来越让人无法忍受。

调整译文：尽管我们在经济和技术上取得了越来越多的成就和进步，然而我们的生态环境遭受的毁坏却是前所未有的。诸如土地沙漠化程度越来越严重，淡水资源越来越匮乏，空气污染、酸雨和食物中农药残留已经让我们无法忍受，所有这一切都让我们无法乐观。

Guided Practice

Try This:

Divide each of the sentences into smaller kernel segments by using the techniques illustrated in this section and interpret the sentences.

1. This pollution results mainly from the coal powered factories in developing countries, which produce inexpensive goods for North American and European consumers.

_____

_____

2. This type of pollution reduces the amount of land suitable for agricultural production and contributes to global food shortages.

_____

_____

3. Dumping of industrial and domestic waste produces much of the world's soil pollution, though natural disasters can also add to the problem.

_____

_____

4. People whose diet contains a high percentage of trans fats are at risk for heart disease and stroke.

_____

_____

5. This concerns many health professionals who point out that many cancers take at least ten years to develop.

_____

_____

Directions: Listen to the recording and fill in the blanks with what you hear.

Task A

Body Language

When we communicate with others, we express our thoughts and feelings not only through the words we choose, but also through our (1) _____. In fact, many communications experts believe that far more information is communicated (2) _____ (without words) than (3) _____ (with words). "Body language" is an important part of non-verbal communication. Body language includes many different aspects of our every day physical behaviour: (4) _____ _____ are some of the most basic.

Sometimes, cultural differences in appropriate body language can cause (5) _____ _____ too. For example, there are definite cultural differences in how much (6) _____ should be kept between two people who are speaking together. If you are used to people keeping their distance, you will feel very uncomfortable, and probably move away repeatedly, if someone keeps trying to stand closer to you at a party! We call this the "(7) _____". Another common example of misunderstanding is the use of a smile. In some Asian cultures, a smile can show (8) _____ _____. However, smiling back at a teacher who is unhappy with you, or a stranger whose foot you accidentally stepped upon is probably not a good idea in most English speaking cultures! Also, you should not assume that nodding your head means "yes" or that shaking your head means "no" or vice versa. Yes, you can even get that wrong, with (9) ____ _____.

Just as you should not allow a fear of making language mistakes prevent you from speaking, you should not be (10) _____ _____. Most people will understand that people from different cultures may not always use body language in the same ways. All the same, it's definitely (11) _____ to learn as much as possible about the body language of a new culture, and to use (12) _____ to avoid making any mistakes.

Try This: _____

Please rebuild the above passage with the help of the chart below.
You may use English or Chinese in the reproduction.

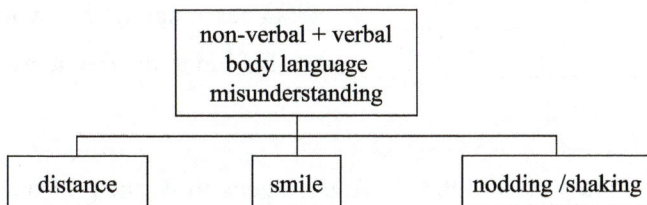

```
          ┌─────────────────────┐
          │  non-verbal + verbal │
          │    body language    │
          │   misunderstanding  │
          └─────────────────────┘
         ┌──────────┼──────────┐
    ┌─────────┐ ┌────────┐ ┌────────────────┐
    │ distance│ │ smile  │ │ nodding /shaking│
    └─────────┘ └────────┘ └────────────────┘
```

Task B

Water, Air and Soil Contamination

Pollution is an (1) _____ for people throughout the world. One university study suggests that pollutants in the water, air, and soil cause up to 40% of the (2) _____ in the world's population. The majority of these deaths occur in developing countries.

The (3) _____ (WHO) estimates that 1.1 billion people have (4) _____

Vocabulary	
contamination	污染
pollutant	污染物
premature death	过早死亡
infectious disease	传染病
pesticide	杀虫剂
food supply	食品供应
ecosystem	生态系统
domestic waste	生活垃圾
natural disaster	自然灾害

to clean water. Approximately 80% of infectious diseases in the world are caused by contaminated water. Water in many (5) _____ is contaminated with toxic chemicals. In many of these regions the water that is used for drinking, cooking, and washing is the same water that is used for dumping (6) _____.

Air pollution is a growing problem throughout the world. This pollution results mainly from the (7) _____ in developing countries, which produce inexpensive goods for North American and European consumers. Air pollution is also a concern in many wealthy countries. Those who live and work in urban centres such as Los Angeles or Toronto experience many warm days beneath a layer of (8) _____.

Soil pollution is also a major concern, both in (9) _____.
Pollutants such as metals and pesticides (10) _____ the earth's soil and contaminate
the food supply. Soil pollution causes major health risks to entire ecosystems. This type of
pollution reduces the amount of (11) _____
and contributes to (12) _____. Dumping of
(13) _____ produces much of the world's soil pollution,
though (14) _____ can also add to the problem.

Try This: ————————————————————————————
Please rebuild the above passage with the help of the chart below.
You may use English or Chinese in the reproduction.

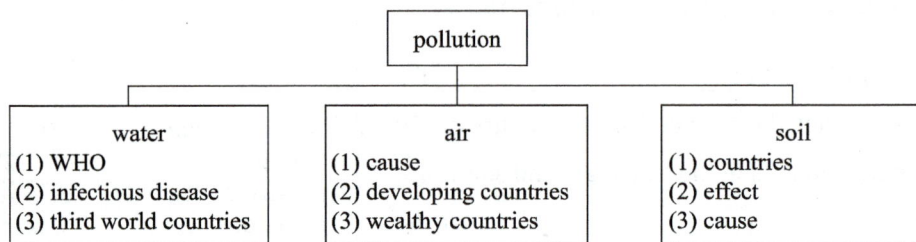

```
                        ┌─────────────┐
                        │  pollution  │
                        └─────────────┘
          ┌──────────────────┼──────────────────┐
┌──────────────────┐ ┌──────────────────┐ ┌──────────────────┐
│      water        │ │       air        │ │       soil       │
│(1) WHO            │ │(1) cause         │ │(1) countries     │
│(2) infectious     │ │(2) developing    │ │(2) effect        │
│    disease        │ │    countries     │ │(3) cause         │
│(3) third world    │ │(3) wealthy       │ │                  │
│    countries      │ │    countries     │ │                  │
└──────────────────┘ └──────────────────┘ └──────────────────┘
```

Task C

Trans Fats

Does your mouth water when you think of potato chips, donuts, and pie? Many people
prefer (1) _____ to healthy food because they develop a taste for it. Processed,
baked, and fried foods typically contain a high amount of trans fats.

Trans fat is a (2) _____ type of oil. It is made by adding hydrogen to liquid oil.
Food companies and restaurants like to use trans fat oil because it is (3) _____
and makes food like crackers and baked goods last longer. It also improves the taste of food.
Trans fats became very popular in the second half of the 20th century. This is around the time
when butter got a bad name. People were told to use (4) _____ instead
because it was made from trans fats.

Trans fat raises the bad cholesterol in your body and lowers the (5) _____ that the body needs. Fatty foods do more than cause obesity. Trans fats build up in the body and (6) _____ blood flow to the heart. People whose diet contains a high percentage of trans fats are at risk for heart disease and stroke.

Today doctors know how dangerous these processed foods are. In countries such as the US and Canada there are new government restrictions on food production. Food and beverage makers have to attach a (7) _____ label to their products. These list (8) _____ and detail (9) _____ including the amount of trans fats in a product. New York City banned trans fats from all restaurants. Even fast food chains such as McDonalds are being forced to change their recipes. In Europe, food manufacturers have started using (10) _____ at the consumers' request.

We all need some fat in our diet. There are three different types of fats: saturated fats, trans fats, and (11) _____. Doctors recommend that we get most of our fatty calories from unsaturated fats. Neither butter nor margarine fit in this category. (12) _____ are a good way to avoid eating fatty foods that are dangerous for your health. Another way is to avoid eating out. When shopping for groceries, buy the majority of your goods in the fresh food aisles.

Vocabulary

trans fat	反式脂肪酸	restriction	限制
hydrogen	氢	ingredient	原料
margarine	人造黄油	manufacturer	制造商
cholesterol	胆固醇	labeling system	标识制度
obesity	肥胖症	unsaturated fat	不饱和脂肪

Try This: ─────────────────────────────

Please rebuild the above passage by answering the following questions. You may use the expressions from the passage or your own words.

1. What is trans fat?

_____

2. Why is trans fat used in food production?

_____

3. When and why did trans fat become popular?

_____

4. What harm does trans fat do to our health?

_____

5. What measures are taken in different countries to restrict trans fat?

_____

6. What are the three types of fats? Which one is recommended?

_____

🎧 Task D

Mobile Phones

Is talking on a mobile phone hazardous to your health? It is difficult to know for sure. Some research suggests that heavy users of mobile phones are at a greater risk of developing brain tumours. However, many other studies suggest there are no links between (1) _____ and (2) _____.

The main problem with the current research is that mobile phones have only been popular since the 1990s. As a result, it is (3) _____ _____. This concerns many health professionals who point out that many cancers take at least ten years to develop. Another concern about these studies is that (4) _____ _____.

Over three billion people use mobile phones on a daily basis, and many talk for more than an hour a day. (5) _____. While both rely on electromagnetic radiation, the radio waves in mobile phones are lower in radio frequency (RF). Microwave ovens have enough RF to cook food and are therefore known to be dangerous to human tissues. However, the concern is that (6) _____ _____. It seems logical that holding a heat source near your brain for a long period of time is a potential health hazard.

Some researchers believe that (7) _____ _____, including laptops, cordless phones, and gaming consoles. Organizations that are concerned about the effects of Electromagnetic Radiation (EMR) suggest replacing all cordless devices with wired ones. They say that many cordless phones emit dangerous levels of EMR even when they are not in use. They even suggest keeping electronic devices, such as computers and alarm clocks (8) _____, or at least (9) _____

_____.

A growing number of health professionals worldwide are recommending that mobile phone users err on the side of caution until more definitive studies can be conducted. They recommend that adults (10) _____ and that children and teens, whose brain tissues are still developing, (11) _____

_____. Concerned medical experts use the example of (12) _____ to illustrate the potential risks. Many years ago, people smoked freely and were not concerned about the effects of cigarettes on their health. Today, people know that cigarettes cause (13) _____, though it is still unknown exactly how or why. Some doctors fear that the same thing will happen with devices such as mobile phones.

Vocabulary

brain tumour	脑瘤	laptop	便携电脑
radio frequency	无线电频率	cordless phone	无绳电话
human tissue	人体组织	gaming console	游戏机
health hazard	健康危害	Electromagnetic Radiation	电磁辐射

Try This: _____

Please choose the best answer for each question.

---

1. According to the text, do mobiles phones lead to brain tumours?

    A. Yes, definitely.

    B. There is no link.

    C. Too early to say.

2. The text mentions the 1990s because this was when _____.

    A. the mobile was invented

    B. cancer was linked to mobiles

    C. mobile phones became popular

3. Why does the passage mention microwave ovens?

    A. They also use EMR.

    B. They cause brain tumours.

    C. They will soon be wireless.

4. Which of the following is NOT mentioned in the passage?

    A. Video game consoles.

    B. Televisions.

    C. Wireless phones.

5. How is mobile phone use compared to tobacco use in this passage?

    A. Both cause brain tumours.

    B. Both need long-term studies.

    C. They are equally hazardous.

IIIIIIIIIIIIIIIIIIIIIIIIII Summary Interpreting IIIIIIIIIIIIIIIIIIIIIIIIII

Skill Focus

Syntactic Transformation（句法转换）

转换生成语法理论认为，人类的语言虽然千差万别，但只是表层结构不同。在深层结构层面上，各种语言之间是相似的。语言与语言之间在深层结构层面上的相似性构成了翻译的基础，翻译是从源语的表层结构到源语的深层结构，再经译语的深层结构到译语的表层结构的过程。简单来说，是将复杂的信息简单化，再用衔接方式加以调整。

诺兰（Nolan）在《口译：技巧与操练》一书中，通过举例说明：多种表达和组织方式用于同一段源语，译语在效果上没有巨大差别。换句话说，即便在同一种语言中，语言外壳也有多种可以接受的模式。这实际上体现了释意理论"脱离源语语言外壳"的理念。

汉、英两种语言在句法上有较大差异。主要体现在英语句子长，结构严谨，以结构体现逻辑关系，被动语态相对较多；汉语短句较多，结构较松散，逻辑关系通过语序、语气、语意等体现，无主语句子多，同义重复多，被动语态少。在口译中，应通过词性转换、正反变通、句子结构调整等方法进行句法转换。通过句法转换，译员可以在把握源语主要观点和概念的基础上，尽量采用灵活的方式对源语进行重组。这样的理念需要通过由浅入深的练习逐步渗透。下面我们从词、句、段的层面进行举例说明。

例1

He learns things very slowly.

He is a slow learner.

例2

Tourism earns a lot of foreign exchange for Spain.

Tourism is a big foreign exchange earner for Spain.

例3

The overwhelming happiness over the good news left me speechless.

I was too happy to say anything when I heard the good news.

例4

He didn't go to sleep until his mother came back.

He went to sleep only after his mother came back.

After his mother came back, he went to sleep.

例5

Excitement made me free from pain for an instant.

I was too excited to feel any pain for the moment.

例6

Only by eliminating corruption and bureaucracy can we establish a clean, small and efficient government.

We must get rid of corruption and bureaucracy before we are able to establish a clean, small and efficient government.

In order to establish a clean, small and efficient government, we must get rid of corruption and bureaucracy.

例7

The book he wrote 20 years ago has always been his boast and pride.

He has always boasted about and felt proud of the book he wrote 20 years ago.

He wrote a book 20 years ago. This book has always been his boast and pride.

He wrote a book 20 years ago. He has always felt proud of the book.

例8

The boom in the airline industry that began about 30 years ago resulted in a corresponding boom in hotel industry.

The airline industry started to boom about 30 years ago. This boom brought about a similar boom in hotel construction.

例9

For all its flaws, this historic measure, or something like it, would greatly better health security in the US.

This historic measure has its flaws, but measures like this would greatly better health security in the US.

例10

Advertising includes those activities by which visual or oral messages are delivered to the public for the purpose of (with the aim of) informing them and influencing them to buy merchandise or services.

Advertising includes those activities by which visual or oral messages are delivered to the public, the aim of which is to inform them and influence them to buy merchandise or services.

综上所述，对词汇的灵活使用往往连带着句式的变化，而句式的变化也对词和词组的使用形式提出不同的要求，二者紧密联系，不可分割。我们可以针对同一源语句子，采用不同的句子成分开头，"强迫"自己按照所给的开头继续句子的组织，完成源语主要意思的表达。经过这样的训练，我们可以逐渐意识到，同样的意思可以借由不同的方式表达出来，流利的，较少重复和修改的表达才是口译中最需要的。

Guided Practice

Directions: Try to reconstruct the given sentences by using different syntactic structures, and then interpret the sentences. You may also ask your partner to interpret the sentences when you finish reconstructing them.

🎧 Task A

1. The project is making very slow progress due to his lack of cooperation.

_____

_____

_____

2. Whoever wants to join the spring outing should sign up and pay the expenses before Friday.

_____

_____

_____

3. I think the dress in the shop is still too expensive even if we get a discount.

_____

_____

_____

4. If by any chance you want to cancel the trip, please give us at least one month's written notice.

_____

_____

_____

5. I'm afraid it is unlikely for him to agree to such a request.

_____

_____

_____

6. Analysis of the questionnaire responses revealed a number of female/male differences.

_____

_____

_____

Task B

Directions: Reconstruct the following sentences by using the given subjects, and then interpret the sentences. You may also ask your partner to interpret the sentences when you finish reconstructing them.

1. Researchers tested more than 46,000 adults 20 years old or older in 14 provinces and municipalities between 2013 and 2014.

Researchers _____

_____ .

Researchers _____
_____ .

Between 2013 and 2014, _____
_____ .

A survey _____
_____ .

A survey _____
_____ .

2. China's booming economy has led to major dietary changes, as people indulge in high calorie diets and get less exercise, leading to a rise in obesity.

China's booming economy _____
_____ .
_____ .

China's economic development _____
_____ .
_____ .

China's economy _____
_____ .
_____ .

The economic development of China _____
_____ .
_____ .

3. Some developing countries have taken measures to compel multinationals to enter in partnership with local investors in order to gain firm control over some of their important industries and products that may bear strategic significance for the host countries.

Measures _____
_____ .
_____ .

In some developing countries, _____
_____ .
_____ .

4. As New Zealand's most populous city, Auckland's diversity of industries—manufacturing, services, finance, entertainment and education; along with its variety of ethnic background, make Auckland both a reflection of New Zealand and a window on the wider world.

Auckland _____

_____ .

_____

In New Zealand, _____

_____ .

_____

5. My government's plans for education include: training more teachers, building more schools, providing more scholarships, helping families in rural areas lacking schools, publishing affordable textbooks, and improving educational television programs.

To improve education, _____

_____ .

_____

My government's education plans _____

_____ .

_____

6. Jane swerved in the road to avoid hitting the deer. As the car veered off the road, Jane couldn't help thinking this day may be her last. Her thoughts flashed to her children and her spouse. The car hit the tree with a sickening crunch, and Jane blacked out. However, she awoke within a few seconds, bruised and sore, but alive.

Jane saw a deer in the road, _____

_____ .

_____

While out driving, _____

_____ .

_____

Information Link

Directionality of Interpreting（口译的方向性）

在面对面的跨文化、跨语言交际活动中，译员的任务是在讲话人之间进行双向口译，双向口译是典型的"对话口译"。虽然会议中比较常用单向口译，但有时候译员也会被要求做一些提问、回答之类的双向口译。

国际会议译员协会（International Association of Conference Interpreters，AIIC）根据译员对语言的掌握情况，对译员的语言进行了分类区分：A语言（母语，主动习得的语言）、B语言（主动习得的语言，相当于母语）、C语言（被动习得的语言，即外语）。传统上，西方会议上采用从B或C语言译到A语言，即B/C到A的口译（B/C-to-A Interpreting），而A到B的口译（A-to-B Interpreting）也叫反向口译，在国际组织的同声传译中并不被广泛应用。

一般情况下，口译的方向性有两种：正向口译（B/C到A的口译，即将母语以外的其他语言转换成母语）和反向口译（A到B的口译，即将母语转换成其他语言）。此外，还有一种口译方式也与口译的方向性有关，即接力口译（relay interpreting）。当译员的语言能力不能完成直接口译时，就会采用这种口译，即通过第三种语言进行的间接口译，这种口译至少需要两个译员参与（一个译员的译语是另一个译员的源语）。比如，译员甲将讲话人的A语译成B语，再由译员乙将B语译成C语传递给听话人。

After-class Assignment

Directions: Listen to the following passage. Pause after each paragraph, and try to summarize the main idea of that paragraph. Pay attention to the kernel sentences, and see how the sentences help build the information structure.

Learn English the Hollywood Way

Paragraph 1

Having trouble learning English? Do it like the stars! Many of Hollywood's finest non-native speaking actors have had to learn English fast after realising that they were destined for movie stardom stateside. With this need to master fluent English to seize the opportunities of fame and fortune that Hollywood offers, it is no surprise that they have the inside scoop on some of the most efficient tricks to mastering English quickly.

_____

_____

_____

Paragraph 2

Watching films. Before Charlize Theron was in the movies herself, she would watch hundreds of them, and used this method to learn English the fast way. Charlize, who is originally from South Africa, spoke mostly in her native language of Afrikaans until the age of 19 when she learnt fluent English and headed for Hollywood. She became fluent in English at around 19 years old and has stated that watching American TV shows and movies was vital. Watching films and TV is an extremely good way to learn English, for a number of reasons.

_____

_____

_____

Paragraph 3

Foreign language films are often accompanied by subtitles. This is very useful as it is easier to read a new language than it is to understand it in free flowing speech. By listening to the spoken version and associating it with the subtitles, it is easier to create a link between the sound of the word and its written form. TV shows and movies also help people to learn current terms and slang, as this is not taught in classrooms. This is particularly helpful for actors, who must often play characters with a rough street background.

_____

_____

_____

Paragraph 4

Language tandem is often used when people must learn a language rapidly and is a tactic that Mexican actress Salma Hayek utilized when she moved to Hollywood early in her career. Language tandem is when two people meet up regularly so as they can each practice the language they wish to learn. For example, a French person who has just started to learn English could meet with an English person who has just begun to talk French. This will usually involve half of the conversation being in French and the other half in English so as both parties are given a chance to practice their non-native language.

_____

_____

_____

Paragraph 5

By far the fastest way to learn a new language is to go to the country and surround yourself with native speakers. Many people, including Hollywood's elite, have found this to be the best method. For actors in particular, the need to use authentic sounding slang means that immersing themselves in the language is the only way. Actors have often talked about spending days in character, perhaps speaking and moving the same way they expect their characters to. This practical approach is far more effective than any other method.

_____

_____

_____

Paragraph 6

"Method acting" is the label for a group of techniques widely used by Hollywood actors in order to better immerse themselves in a character role they are working on. Typically, when using "method acting" techniques, an actor will continue to portray their character role outside of actual filming. Quite simply, they become their character 24 hours a day, thinking and behaving like them. This technique can be utilized for English language learning also. By imagining yourself as a native speaker and going about your day using only English and not your native tongue you can rapidly increase your progression.

_____

_____

_____

Paragraph 7

Many actors in Hollywood hire accent consultants who work with them to help them master the correct diction for the role they are playing. Whilst that is not an option for most of us, we can benefit by watching films, interviews and listening to radio that is representative of the accent we are trying to adopt. Youtube can be a great resource for this.

_____

_____

_____

Paragraph 8

Speaking is an integral part of the role of an actor and we can find a lot of useful ideas and inspiration from the language methods adopted by Hollywood. Try adopting some of these tactics to your everyday use of English and you could see a measured improvement in your command of the language.

_____

_____

_____

扫码获取本单元音频资料

Unit 6 Information Structure III & Elaboration

A translator ought to endeavor not only to say what his author has said, but to say it as he has said it.

— John Conington, English scholar and translator

Unit Goals

- To gain a general knowledge of how analysis of topic chains help build up the information structure, and ultimately facilitate the comprehension of texts.
- To become more flexible in summary interpreting by applying the technique of elaboration.
- To know what deverbalization in interpreting is and how applicable it is to interpreting practice.

Warm Up

Directions: Listen to the following passages and fill in the blanks with words or sentences. Make sure the words and sentences you fill in are both grammatically and semantically acceptable.

Task A

International Women's Day

This International Women's Day, we focus on our work on enhancing women's economic (1) _____ (empowerment; impoverishment).

I'm honoured and privileged to be a spokesperson for the cause of women and girls. I've become a staunch (2) _____ (advocation; advocate) for women's rights, empowerment, and gender equality for years, and I look forward to helping fulfil our commitment to (3) _____ (advancing; advance) gender equality and women's empowerment through our combined effort.

Promoting women's economic empowerment is one of the main (4) _____ (pillars; pillers) of our governmental strategy. This supports our other priorities of (5) _____ (enhencing; enhancing) women's voice in decision-making, leadership and peace-building; and ending violence against women and girls.

(6) _____ (Genuinely; Generally) sustainable, prosperous and peaceful societies will only become a reality when women and girls have full and equal share in economic life.

The importance of women's economic empowerment is also recognised in the (7) _____ (team; theme) of this year's UN Commission on the Status of Women.

While more women than ever are entering the workforce and participating in many sectors of the global economy, they still often face (8) _____ (exploration; exploitation) and discrimination. We must therefore find smarter and better ways to work together in (9) _____ (overturning; overlooking) these barriers.

I will work tirelessly and bring meaningful change to the (10) _____ (qualities; quality) of lives of women and girls in our Indo-Asia Pacific region and around the world.

🎧 Task B

Cholesterol and Heart Attack

The American Heart Association and other groups have said for many years that people could reduce the chance of suffering a heart attack by (1) _____ _____. These include such foods as (2) _____. The Heart Association noted a number of studies which show that nations where people eat a lot of high cholesterol foods have a higher number of (3) _____.

However, the new report disagrees. It was made by the (4) _____ _____. The new report by a team of 15 scientists said there is (5) _____ cholesterol in food directly to heart disease. It noted seven major studies involving people whose diet was changed to include only foods low in cholesterol. The studies found only a very small reduction in the number of (6) _____ and there was no reduction in the number of (7) _____.

Other studies have shown similar results. They found that a change to low cholesterol foods will have only a minor effect on (8) _____ and only a minor effect on (9) _____.

Medical scientists hope that two huge new studies may (10) _____ _____. The tests are designed to learn if (11) _____ or (12) _____, or both, can reduce the amount of the substance in the blood and reduce the chance of a heart attack. The two new studies will be finished in the next year or two.

The new Academy of Sciences report also discussed other possible links between food and disease. The scientists, in general, are deeply concerned about some of the recent advice given about food. They noted that a number of (13) _____ _____ have advised that people can prevent heart disease, cancer and other sicknesses by changing the kinds of foods they eat. The new report said there is often (14) _____ to support such advice. In fact, the scientists said such ideas often produce only (15) _____ or (16) _____.

⫼⫼⫼⫼⫼⫼⫼⫼⫼⫼⫼⫼ Listening Comprehension ⫼⫼⫼⫼⫼⫼⫼⫼⫼⫼⫼⫼⫼

Skill Focus

Information Structure: Topic Chain（信息结构：话题链）

话题是会话中谈论的事情，其基本话语功能是"相关性"（aboutness）。话题链是共享话题的系列语句，把握话题链有助于提升受话人对语篇的理解。实验发现，如果受试者在阅读某个篇章前，事先被告知关于这个篇章的话题，则受试者对篇章的理解会更快捷和准确。

在语篇连贯的探讨中，传统的连贯方式包括衔接和词汇等。实际上，话题概念线索也可以构建连贯语篇，促成语篇的理解。话题作为一个语篇成分，可以通过话题之间的语义关联满足语篇连贯的外部和内部条件，实现语篇的连贯。这种语篇属性可以通过多种语言手段表现，在实现语篇连贯的功能中发挥不同的作用。

在篇章中，话题的语义可以横向和纵向发展，形成不同长短和级别的话题链。请看下面的例子，体会话题链如何实现话题展开和语篇连贯。

例1：The UN is divided into six <u>major groups</u>. <u>Each group</u> has an important job to do within the UN system. <u>They</u> are the General Assembly, Security Council, Secretariat, Economic and Social Council, International Court of Justice, and Trusteeship Council.

例2：Education is crucial to <u>your child's</u> development and as a parent you'll want to ensure <u>your young ones</u> attend the best learning facilities on offer.

例3：All <u>retirement housing</u> should be secure. <u>Some</u> are gated communities or have CCTV and/or equip each property with a telecom answering entry system. <u>Some villages</u> have 24-hour care staff while <u>others</u> have a warden on duty only during the day.

例4：<u>Burning fireworks</u> was once the most typical custom on the Spring Festival. People thought the <u>spluttering sound</u> could help drive away evil spirits. However, <u>such an activity</u> was completely or partially forbidden in big cities once the government took security, noise and pollution factors into consideration. As a replacement, some buy <u>tapes with firework sound</u> to listen to.

例5：There are 60 million <u>Mexican</u> living in poverty, and 20 million of them living in extreme poverty. Most of the time, garbage is their food, and some days, they don't even eat anything. This critical situation in <u>Mexico</u> is caused by individual, geographical and political factors. Nobody likes to see poor children eating out of garbage cans. Unless <u>the government</u> works on the causes of the poverty, the problem is going to get worse.

从以上例子中，我们可以发现，话题的展开依赖不同的语言变体和组织模式。提升对话题及话题链的敏感程度和理解能力，可以帮助译员在听解过程中更快地分辨不同层次的话题布局，为译语的产出做充分准备。

Guided Practice

🎧 Task A

Directions: Skim the paragraphs and fill in the blanks with words or phrases given below. Then listen to the recording and check whether your choices are correct and how the message is organized with the help of the topic chain.

Paragraph 1

Have you been watching Animal Rescue Live which was on Channel 4 every night last week and, if (1)_____ , did you recognize the (2)_____ which opened the show? Yes, (3)_____ with one eye which has both (4)_____ to be seen on the series was the wonderful (5)_____. (6)_____ waited four years for a home, and, now, not only has (7)_____ got a fantastic home of (8)_____ own but also the moment (9)_____ passed from the care of the National Animal Welfare Trust (NAWT) to (10)_____ new owners was recorded by a television film crew and has been shown several times during (11)_____.

Max	He
Animal Rescue Live	his (twice)
he (twice)	so
dog	the bridle Staffie
the first and the last animal	

Paragraph 2

The school holidays are an exciting time for children. It means time enjoying lovely holiday lie-ins, afternoon naps, and sometimes late nights, hugely affecting both parents' and children's (1)_____. Routine is key to children (2)_____ and feeling ready for (3)_____. The sooner you begin to reintroduce a (4)_____ after several weeks of (5)_____, the sooner all the family can fall back into a healthy (6)_____. Research has shown that having a (7)_____ enter our eyes before we go to sleep tells our brains we want to be awake. An hour or so before the children go to bed, rule out any (8)_____; this means no (9)_____. The bedroom should be a (10)_____-free environment.

body clocks	technology
constant stream of light	TV, tablets or mobile phones
irregularity	blue light
sleeping pattern	bed at a suitable time
waking up refreshed	sleeping rhythm

Paragraph 3

During 2001, the residents of California in the USA discovered what it would be like to live in a world where electricity was in short supply. The state suffered from periods of time when (1)_____ could not keep up with (2)_____ and entire districts had to survive without (3)_____ for many hours. The Californian crisis was caused by a change in the way the (4)_____ sold

(5)_____ , but it was a very good illustration of how (6)_____
people have become on a regular (7)_____. One of the
immediate effects of this crisis was that many Californians turned to (8)_____
_____ that would give them (9)_____ from the
(10)_____ who had traditionally provided their (11)_____. Many families
rushed out and purchased solar panels to provide their homes with electricity and hot water.
The supply of (12)_____ will also eventually run out. Estimated of how long
(13)_____ will last are uncertain, as new deposits are being found all the time.
However, most experts agree that (14)_____ will probably last between 30 and 50
years, while coal may last a couple of hundred years.

power companies (twice)	the supply
alternative energy sources	dependent
oil and gas	electricity
these fuels	energy (twice)
fossil fuels	independence
the demand	supply of electricity

Task B

Directions: Listen to the recording and while listening, take notes on important points. Then complete the blank-filling task.

Passage 1

Getting Things Done

(1) _____ chronically avoid difficult tasks and deliberately look for distractions, and they (2) _____ until the last minute.

They argue that they perform better under (3) _____, but more often than not that's their way of justifying putting things off, which actually reflects our struggle with (4) _____.

Those who get things done do not have (5) _____ in that, but they have (6) _____
_____.

If you want to pick up the tips to be more organized, try those that are the most (7) _____, (8) _____, or (9) _____, then you may be able to have "(10) _____ accomplishments" that others admire.

First, learn to say no, otherwise it's much harder to keep the (11) _____ down. But in saying no, you may sound helpful by giving (12) _____ or suggesting (13) _____.

Second, (14) _____ the finished thing. You may give yourself a (15) _____ or a (16) _____ once you finish the whole task, or at the end of each smaller chunk of the task if the task is a long one.

Third, (17) _____ your workload. It's always quicker to do things that belong to the same (18) _____ because you have the same (19) _____ to hand, and your mind doesn't have to make so many leaps. Even you can (20) _____ some of those tasks.

Everyone can get more done if they decide to make it happen, and that includes you. Stick with it, and you'll find that not only are you achieving far more, you're also making less effort and your life is more relaxed.

Passage 2

Walking

Traditionally well-known cardiovascular exercises:

(1) _____; (2) _____; (3) _____.

And current recommendations suggest adults make time for at least (4) _____ minutes of moderate to vigorous physical activity and it can make them active, lose weight and become healthier.

The best time of day to walk? Many prefer (5) _____ while others prefer (6) _____.

The good amount of time to walk? About (7) _____ minutes, or at least (8) _____ steps each day, or 10 minutes of (9) _____.

Fast walking is also called (10) _____ or (11) _____. Ways for individuals to tell if they are walking quickly enough for physical benefits are (12) _____, (13) _____, and (14) _____.

In Europe, (15) _____ Walking is popular. It started in (16) _____ in the (17) _____. It wasn't until the 1980s however that this kind of walking began to catch on as a general (18) _____. Advocates of this kind of walking point to evidence which suggests that it burns up more (19) _____ than ordinary walking and that the (20) _____ enable people to work the upper body at the same time as the legs.

As well as the physical benefits of walking, there's another side to the sport that is equally important, and that's the opportunity of meeting other people. The regular sessions are the perfect opportunity to share and discuss anything and everything — almost like walking therapy. Walking is such a sociable activity. Of course people can do it on their own too, but the benefits of spending time with others exercising outdoors are huge.

‖‖‖‖‖‖‖‖‖‖‖‖‖‖ Summary Interpreting ‖‖‖‖‖‖‖‖‖‖‖‖‖‖

Skill Focus

Elaboration（详述）

口译中训练译员"说话"的能力非常重要。跟自由演讲不同，口译训练中的"说话"需要受限于话题。针对给定的话题，按照不同的方式和要求进行详述，可以有效提升口译中"说话"的能力。这个过程调动译员对于给定话题的知识储备水平、语篇组织能力、任务认知水平、自我监控能力等。

比如，针对"学校的一天"，我们可以仅仅说"挺好的"，也可以详细讲述一下更多内容，包括学习内容、老师同学们、体育活动、午休时间等。还比如，针对"现代科技的利与弊"，我们不仅可以说出现代科技带来便捷和进步等诸多显而易见的"利"，还能列出更多为人忽略的"问题"：对人类健康具有潜在的危害，带来了更多的污染，增加了电子垃圾，压缩了自然交流的空间和可能，加速了数字鸿沟，更加边缘化了社会弱势群体等。

此外，我们可以针对任何大的或者小的观点，展开进行详述，可以规定所讲的句子数量，也可以规定所用时间。比如，"现代科技增加了电子垃圾（electronic waste, e-waste or e-scrap）"，我们可以说：1. 电子产品不断降价，功能推陈出新，使其使用周期缩短，淘汰速度更快，导致电子垃圾急速增长。2. 电子垃圾中的大量重金属等有毒有害元素很难降解，对人类健康和环境都产生严重影响。3. 电子垃圾的循环利用在发达国家好于发展中国家。4. 电子垃圾的循环利用技术的发展和更新远远跟不上电子垃圾产生的速度和数量。

经过这样的详述训练，译员可以扩展主题知识，开拓思维，有效组织语言，流利表

101

述观点。口译活动中，译员必须首先自身可以成功进行公共演讲，这样在为讲话人进行口译时，才能更好跟上讲话人的思路，有效进行口译。同时，如果能够灵活运用详述的能力，译员可以在口译产出中根据场景和语言组织的需要，对译语进行或长或短，或丰富或简短的控制，以提升译语的流利和流畅程度。

下面我们来看详述练习的英文例子：

原文：Courses of study should emphasize the traditional skills of engineering, as the number of American engineering graduates with these skills has fallen when compared to the number coming from other countries.

详述1：Experts have expressed their concerns regarding the current state of American engineering education. They note that the number of students focusing on traditional areas of engineering has decreased while the number interested in the high-technology end of the field has increased. We should also notice that other industrial nations produce far more traditionally-trained engineers than we do, therefore we believe we have fallen seriously behind.

详述2：America has changed dramatically during recent years. The number of graduates in traditional engineering disciplines such as mechanical, civil, electrical, chemical, and aeronautical engineering declined. Also, most of the premier American universities' engineering curricula now concentrate on and encourage largely the study of engineering science. As a result, there are declining offerings in engineering subjects dealing with infrastructure, the environment, and related issues, and greater concentration on high technology subjects, largely supporting increasingly complex scientific developments. While the latter is important, it should not be at the expense of more traditional engineering. Rapidly developing economies such as China and India, as well as other industrial countries in Europe and Asia, continue to encourage and advance the teaching of engineering. Both China and India, respectively, graduate six and eight times as many traditional engineers as does the United States. Other industrial countries at minimum maintain their output, while America suffers an increasingly serious decline in the number of engineering graduates and a lack of well-educated engineers.

需要注意的是，详述是提升扩展思维习惯和提升流畅表达的练习方式，并不是口译的常态或者既定目标，口译的译语表达还应以达意、简练为好。

Guided Practice

Task A

Directions: Elaborate on the following sentences based on the main idea and what you know about the topics. You may try to extend the sentences to short or long paragraphs, making the task more demanding and rewarding.

Sentence 1

Britain can help Chinese companies succeed in their investment in Europe and their global research, as we are the leading location of international business, with strong ICT community and R&D capabilities.

Sentence 2

London plans to help rough sleepers on public transport, by providing funds to reconnect these people with family and friends.

Sentence 3

Once you're assigned a task to someone, don't under any circumstances do it yourself, or else you'll end up doing all the chores yourself and losing your credibility.

Task B

Directions: Listen to the passages to understand the gist. Try to retell the passages with the help of the keywords given below. You may use English or Chinese in your reproduction.

Passage 1

Conflict Management

Conflict
  behind computer screens
  no face-to-face communication
Conflict at work

staff morale, staff performance, customer confidence

Four types of conflict management style

1. Avoider

2. Controller

3. Accommodator

4. Collaborator

Conflict

    predictable

    collaborative

    proactive

Passage 2

Moving into Retirement

Population aging: 2 billion/60 or older (WHO)

Countries face: health-care costs/pension cost ↑

                workforce/fertility rate ↓

        solutions: retirement age ↑

                pension benefits ↓

                elderly care spending ↑

Elderly care: retirement village popular

Retirement villages

    developed in US

    housing schemes

    activities (no restriction, active life)

Retirement care in China

    one-child policy (UN: 500m/60 or older; 2050)

    demographic opportunity

Retirement solution

    luxury high-end communities

        (good service such as... higher price...)

        (affordable care needed)

    traditional idea

Information Link

Deverbalization（脱离源语语言外壳）

"脱离源语语言外壳"是巴黎"释意理论"学派的理论核心。根据该理论，口译过程中，在话语理解和译语再表达之间，"意义"会"脱离"语言的具体表达形式独立存在。

我们都知道，口头陈述转瞬即逝。我们可以记住听到的内容，却几乎记不住陈述时使用的词语。事实上，讲话使用的有声符号逐渐消失，而听者（译员）保持了非语言形式的记忆，即处于意识状态的思想或提到的事实。译员之所以能够记住意义的各种细微差别，并自如完整地将其用其他语言表达出来，是因为启用了一项基本能力，即在词语消失时记住并理解了内容。译员摆脱了原来的语言形式，翻译的是篇章，而不仅仅是语言。篇章（文章或讲话）描述的是事实、环境、思想、感情等。简单的语言符号转换不足以表达篇章意义，后者需要脱离语言外壳，对篇章进行分析，将语言知识与百科知识相结合。

"脱离源语语言外壳"现象涉及从源语信息储存到译语表达过渡的某种中间状态，是译员译语表达的基础之一。译员在口译工作时，特别是在对源语进行加工的过程中，会使用语言以外的其他诸多载体，这就完完全全脱离了"语言"这一思维的工具。口译中的"脱离源语语言外壳"现象其实是译员在双语转换之前对源语语言所代表的信息进行某种"还原"的过程。它在巴黎"释意理论"中已经构成了口译的一个主要程序。"脱离源语语言外壳"现象在口译过程中十分常见，并且十分自然。

"脱离源语语言外壳"的主张对口译实践及口译教学的贡献在于：首先，该主张为不可译现象提供了适用的方案；其次，该主张推翻了"口译就是语言代码转换"的看法，有助于消除译语产出中的"翻译腔"；最后，该主张有效区分教学口译与口译教学，教学口译强化语言技能，口译教学注重口译技能。该主张推动了口译的职业化和专业化发展，是把基础理论研究的成果用于指导口译教学实践的典范。

After-class Assignment

Directions: Listen to the following passage. Pause after each paragraph, and try to summarize the main idea of that paragraph. Pay attention to the topic chains, and see how they help build the information structure.

Distance Learning

Paragraph 1

I suppose I've done over half my studies remotely by distance learning. For some people, it's the ideal way to go, but there are a lot of pros and cons. It depends to a large extent on each individual whether it works best for them.

_____

_____

_____

Paragraph 2

For a start, you should never underestimate the commitment and self-discipline you need to study on your own. Usually you get some support in your learning from the college, but it's never the same as attending class, meeting your teacher face to face and interacting with other students. Though when you don't have the money or time to go for full-time education, or the course or college you want to go to is too far away, then it can be a practical solution.

_____

_____

_____

Paragraph 3

My advice to students who want to study by distance learning is to set goals, set a timetable and keep to this as far as possible. Studying on your own often requires quite a lot of stamina and it should become second nature — and as pleasurable as possible. So leaving things to the last minute and juggling with all the other demands on your time have to be kept to a minimum. If you don't have the luxury of having time and space to yourself at home, then maybe you could do like I did, go to your office early or stay late to study, so that family life doesn't get in the way of your studies.

_____

_____

_____

Paragraph 4

Some subjects are easier than others to learn in this way. Learning a language is not always as easy as subjects that rely less on interacting with others. Here it is useful to have contact with a teacher. Languages have that unique feature which depends on interaction between people. That said though, there's still a lot you can do from a distance too (like being an active member on a forum of like-minded people).

_____

_____

_____

Paragraph 5

Self-discipline is essential as there's no one immediately on hand to push you. Not having classmates to discuss and share problems with can be a disadvantage too, depending on the course, and costs, you might be assigned a tutor responsible for giving you work, but this will vary from course to course. One distance learning course I did much more recently was very good in this way, with an assigned tutor giving me lots of very useful feedback almost instantly. The continuous contact meant I was very motivated to complete the assignments efficiently and on time. In the middle of this course I was sent to work for six months abroad and whilst this was a bit of a disruption to my routine, I was still able to continue as it doesn't matter where you are. Personally, I think it's best not to let it drag on over too long a period of time, as then motivation can drop.

_____

_____

_____

Paragraph 6

Usually juggling work, home and study, along with good time management is the key to success. When studying a distance learning masters' degree over two years, I used to dedicate at least one whole day at the weekend every week plus time every day during the week to keep on top of the work I need to do. I got into a routine of going to my office very early before my colleagues came in. I'd go through course material an hour or so before starting work. Then time was taken at the weekends to research and complete the many assignments that came with the course. One day per year we were expected to spend the whole day with our classmates and meet the tutors at the college, which was located outside of London, not very far from where I was living. Not having to travel to class was a definite advantage and saved a lot of time and expense. I think some students kept much more in contact with each other than I did, though I actually preferred studying independently. Of course this means you don't get much of a chance to discuss or compare notes with the other students, and there's no social side to learning. If you can keep in contact with fellow distance-learning students, this might help. I suppose this depends how much you like social networking.

_____

_____

_____

Paragraph 7

Depending on the course though, it can be a huge undertaking. It can be very lonely. Though full-time, my first masters' degree was in fact a full-time course, it was totally by research and I used to see my tutor for an hour every fortnight. The rest of the time was spent pored over documents and conducting research on a very specific area of history in a city several hours' drive from the university where I was studying. There were no classes, no one else was studying the area I was looking at and I used to generally get up every morning at the same time, go to the library and work all day. I did this for twelve months. It was distant in the sense I was on my own, away from any classroom, though I was in the lucky position of having all my time free to study. Most distant learning courses, however, are not as simple as this.

_____

_____

_____

扫码获取本单元音频资料

Unit 7

Multi-tasking I & Shadowing

> Presentation competence is more obvious in consecutive interpreting, in which the focus lies on public speaking skills, eye contact and appropriate nonverbal and paraverbal communication.
>
> — Dörte Andres, German interpreting researcher

Unit Goals

- To gain a general knowledge of how multi-tasking practice simulates the process of interpreting.
- To maintain the listening comprehension performance while doing multi-tasking practice.
- To become more articulate while doing shadowing.
- To know what disfluency in interpreting is and how to avoid it.

Warm Up

Directions: Listen to the following passages and fill in the blanks with words or sentences. Make sure the words and sentences you fill in are both grammatically and semantically acceptable.

Task A

Stages in Analyzing a Problem

(1) _____. Sometimes they try to remember a solution from (2) _____. They often accept the opinions or ideas of other people. Other times they begin to (3) _____ _____; they try to find a solution by trial and error. However, when all these methods fail, the person with a problem has to start analyzing. There are (4) _____ _____.

First the person must (5) _____ that there is a problem. For example, Sam's bicycle is broken, and he cannot ride it to class as he usually does. Sam must see that there is a problem with his bicycle.

Next the thinker must (6) _____ the problem. Before Sam can repair his bicycle, he must find the reason why it does not work. For instance, he must determine if the problem is with (7) _____. He must make his problem more specific.

Now the person must look for information that will make the problem clearer and lead to (8) _____. For instance, suppose Sam decided that his bike does not work because there is something wrong with the gear wheels. At this time, he can look in (9) _____ _____. He can talk to his friends at the bike shop. He can look at his gears carefully. After studying the problem, the person should have several (10) _____ for a possible solution. Take Sam as an illustration. His suggestions might be: (11) _____ _____.

Eventually one suggestion seems to be the solution to the problem. Sometimes the final idea comes very suddenly because (12) _____ _____. Sam, for example, suddenly sees that there is (13) _____ between the gear wheels. He immediately realizes the solution to his problem: he must clean the gear wheels.

Finally the solution is tested. Sam cleans the gear wheels and finds that afterwards his bicycle works perfectly. In short, he has solved the problem.

🎧 Task B

Gender Equality

When we talk about the (1) _____ (statement; treatment) of women, I had a very interesting discussion with the Mayor of Shanghai during lunch right before I came, and he (2) _____ (informed; reformed) me that in many professions now here in China, there are actually more women (3) _____ (scrolled; enrolled) in college than there are men, and that they are doing very well. I think that is an excellent indicator of (4) _____ (progression; progress), because it turns out that if you look at development around the world, one of the best indicators of whether or not a country does well is how well it educates its girls and how it treats its women. And countries that are

(5) _____ (typing into; tapping into) the talents and the energy of women and giving them educations typically do better economically than countries that don't.

One of the key obstacles women face is a (6)_____ (tack; lack) of education. In many countries, education is granted only to men, denying women of their right to knowledge and leaving them in the continuing (7) _____ (cycle; circle) of mistreatment, violence, and poverty. But when women are provided with education, they're better equipped to make decisions for themselves, to (8) _____ (attain; obtain) employment, and to gain new (9) _____ (prospectives; perspectives) about gender (10) _____ (equality; inequality) and basic human rights.

So, now, obviously different cultures may have different attitudes about the relationship between men and women, but I think it is the view of the United States that it is important for us to (11) _____ (affirm; confirm) the rights of women all around the world. And if we see certain societies in which women are (12) _____ (suppressed; oppressed), or they are not getting opportunities, or there is (13) _____ (virance; violence) towards women, we will speak out.

Now, there may be some people who disagree with us, and we can have a dialogue about that. But we think it's important, nevertheless, to be true to our (14) _____ (ideals; ideas) and our values. And we, and when we do so, though, we will always do so with the (15) _____ (humanity; humility) and understanding that we are not perfect and that we still have much progress to make. If you talk to women in America, they will tell you that there are still men who have a lot of (16) _____ (fashioned; old-fashioned) ideas about the role of women in society.

And so we don't (17) _____ (claim; blame) that we have solved all these problems, but we do think that it's important for us to speak out on (18) _____ (half; behalf) of these universal ideals and these universal values.

IIIIIIIIIIIIIIIIII Listening Comprehension IIIIIIIIIIIIIIIIII

Skill Focus

Multi-tasking I（多任务处理1）

多任务处理最初指计算机同时运行两个或多个程序的能力。比如，计算机可以同时下载文件和浏览网页。同样，计算机使用者也可以进行多任务处理，比如，我们可以同时在一个窗口查询信息而在另外一个窗口与网友聊天。现实生活中，我们很多时候都可以自如地进行多任务处理，比如：

一边打电话，一边记下信息；

一边看报纸，一边吃早餐；

一边听音乐，一边工作；

一边做饭，一边与家人聊天。

以上提及的多任务处理一般属于两种情况：一种情况是我们可以在两个或多个任务中自由快速地转换，另一种情况是多个任务中的一个或几个几乎不需要花费太多的注意力。

口译是多任务处理的典型认知活动。口译的难点是需要成功地克服对源语信息的预测、理解、记忆、转换和目的语的计划、组织、表达、监听与修正，同步说出目的语等多重任务间的交织、重叠和干扰给大脑造成的能量短缺和注意力分配困难，使听和说并行不悖。在训练中要使受训者能在多个任务之间自由、快速地转换，或者通过训练使其中某些任务的处理达到自动化的程度，进而可以有效地将注意力分配给更加复杂的任务，保障并提升口译质量。

Guided Practice

🎧 Task A

Directions: Summarize the main idea of the four missing paragraphs while listening to the recording. Then try to fill in the blanks with the given subtitles that fit them.

How to Fight Your Fitness Fears

Many people feel uncertain or fearful about stepping into a gym. Feeling inept or embarrassed in front of other people isn't something that any of us enjoy and it's usually the fear of this that keeps us from trying new things. We've all had that similar feeling; your self-confidence drains and the feelings of insecurity start to take hold. But don't let that stop you from exercising! Here are some top tips on how to drop the gym anxiety and make exercise something you really want to do.

Tip 1: _____

Tip 2: _____

Tip 3: _____

Tip 4: _____

We all suffer from anxious feelings from time to time, but don't let it get the better of you. Remember, just getting up off the sofa and moving is amazing, so be confident, keep an eye on your goals and remember to tell yourself just how great you are. The more you exercise, the more confident you'll feel.

Buddy up	Buy in the confidence
Drop your misconceptions	Choose the right venue

Task B

Directions: Listen to the recording while skimming the following passage. You will be hearing a Chinese passage with different content. When the recording ends, try to retell the two passages, one by you and one by your partner, without referring to the text.

　　我曾经主持了几十场新闻发布会，有两场新闻发布会给我的记忆最深刻，使我更多地想到旅游与经济繁荣和社会安定的关系。其一，宣布中国与欧盟签署旅游目的地国家协议。欧盟共有20多个国家，随着我国经济的发展，人们对出境游的需求旺盛，签署这个协议正是应和了这样的需求。当时广东正有禽流感疫情，外国媒体就此提出很多的卫生安全保障方面的问题。其二，回答关于日本游客来中国旅游的安全保障问题。当时中日关系有些波动，日本游客担心来中国旅游是否安全。当然，我在这两次发布会上都代表国家旅游局郑重承诺：外国游客来中国旅游是完全有安全保障的。这两次新闻发布会都给了我很多启示，其中最重要的启示就是，没有社会安定就没有旅游，而社会安定是建立在良好稳定的政治社会局势基础之上的。

Task C

Directions: Listen to the recording while skimming the following passage. You will be hearing an English passage with different content. When the recording ends, try to retell the two passages, one by you and one by your partner, without referring to the text.

The modern world is dependent on fossil fuels — oil, gas, coal and peat. Over the last two hundred years or so the quantities of fossil fuels extracted from the ground have escalated. Fossil fuels are used by power stations to generate electricity and to fuel our cars. They are essential to a modern lifestyle, but they have been used at the expense of the environment. Environmental damage is caused at every stage of extracting, processing and using these fuels. Coal is mined from the ground, while oil and gas are pumped out of the ground. Then they have to be transported around the world to where they are to be used. Finally, whey they are burnt, these fuels release polluting gases into the atmosphere, causing acid rain and global warming.

|||||||||||||||||||||||| Summary Interpreting |||||||||||||||||||||

Skill Focus

Shadowing（影子跟读）

影子跟读练习又叫源语或单语复述练习，就是用同种语言几乎同步地跟读发言人的讲话或事先录制好的新闻录音、会议资料等。该训练的目的是培养译员的注意力分配和听说同步进行的技能。有关影子跟读练习的研究表明，影子跟读练习与听力理解和注意力的集中有关。影子跟读类似鹦鹉学舌，跟读者紧跟在讲话者后面，保持几个词、半句话、甚至一句话的距离，尝试边听边重复听到的内容。但是，影子跟读又不能完全鹦鹉学舌，跟读者要保证在跟读的同时能听懂源语发言的意思，且要发音清晰，音量适中，语句完整连贯。切忌机械地模仿发音，要做到耳朵在听（源语），嘴巴在说（同种语言复述），脑子在想（语言内容）。影子跟读的练习可以从源语跟读逐渐过渡到源语概述，以逐步提升影子跟读的训练难度和训练效果。

1. 源语跟读：影子跟读练习的第一阶段一般只要求练习跟读源语发言，用同样的语言复述发言内容。练习初期可以与源语间隔较短，在熟练掌握要领之后尝试将时间间隔延长。

例：**Bangladesh** has achieved an **economic miracle** in the past 20 years. **A few decades ago**, it was one of the **poorest** countries on earth, stricken by famine and flood. **Now** it ranks as **middle-income**. It is now the world's **second largest garment exporter**. The textile factories employ **millions** of young women, giving them economic power, prompting rural **families** to **invest in education** and triggering a **demographic dividend**.

在跟读此段落时，要把握句子中的关键词和段落的主要结构。比如，加粗的关键词担负着更重要的表意功能，需要在跟读中用可接受的语法和句法结构连接起来。

2．源语概述：源语概述练习是影子跟读练习的延续。用源语跟读完一段讲话内容后，停下来凭记忆力对刚刚跟读的内容用相同的语言进行概述，归纳讲话内容的核心思想。

例：China has expanded its university dramatically. Some in China may be concerned, as they seem to be in all countries, that not all university graduates can find jobs right away. I suggest this is not a problem of over-supply of graduates, but the need of a more efficient labor market for talented people. It also points to a question of willingness among young people to move to less urban places for their first job after university. Besides, competition for the best jobs in the major cities tends to keep us all on our toes, doesn't it? China can't have too many talented people.

此段落可以概括为"China has expanded its university, and some fear that graduates cannot find jobs. I don't think China has too many graduates or talented people. Rather, it needs a more efficient labor market. And, not enough young people are willing to work in rural areas, while competition in cities stay fierce."。

Guided Practice

🎧 Task A

Directions: Practice shadowing while listening to the passage. Then try to fill in the following chart based on your understanding and memory of the passage. You may also ask your partner to listen to your shadowing of the passage, and ask him or her to fill in the chart.

Name of the Person	His/Her Profession	Words Used to Describe His/Her Profession (As many words as you can take down)
April		
Buster		
Carroll		
David		

🎧 **Task B**

Directions: Listen to the passage and practice shadowing without referring to the text. Try to fill in the blanks with words and expressions from the passage based on your memory. It's ideal if you can balance shadowing and listening comprehension of the passage.

Time and Time Management

We often hear people say "(1) _____". Everyone complains that (2) _____. Many times, you feel like there is never enough time in the day, you find a lot of your tasks are not completed, you have no time for a vacation for a long time, you did a lot but it looks that you are farer away from your goal, and you are always tired and leave things to tomorrow. That shows that you should learn to use your time more effectively. To know (3) _____ is to know how to organize, allocate, and control time you use for activities in order to achieve your desired results.

Now let's get familiar with some (4) _____ about time and time management. The (5) _____ is the overall period during which something should happen or be completed. We can say, for example, we expect to complete the project within a fairly short timeframe. The (6) _____ is the period of time it takes to prepare and complete or deliver something. For example, the lead time between the placement of an order and delivery of a new car from a manufacturer may be anywhere from 2 weeks to 6 months. The times or dates when things should happen is a (7) _____. If work is completed at the planned time, it is (8) _____; completion before the planned time is ahead of schedule and later is behind schedule. If it happens later than planned it is delayed; there is a (9) _____. If you then try to go faster, you try to make up time, make up for lost time. And last but not least, (10) _____ is the habit of putting off, delaying, or deferring an action to a later time. People procrastinate because they find the task at hand unpleasant or uninteresting, or they fear they won't perform the task well, or with no reasons at all as procrastination can become a habit that is very hard to break.

Now, we use one quote from (11) _____ to wrap up this speech about time and time management. "He who every morning plans the transaction of the day and follows out that plan, carries a thread that will guide him through the maze of the most busy life. But where no plan is laid, where the disposal of time surrendered merely to the chance of incidence, chaos will soon reign."

Try This: _____

> Please fill in the following blanks with the given words and expressions about time and time management. You may then interpret the passage into Chinese and ask your partner to make comments on your performance.

(1) _____ is an important skill to cultivate. It can help you make the most out of each day, leading to success in areas like work and school. There are several things you may follow to make your time management more effective.

First, use a (2) _____ (BrE) or (3) _____ (AmE) to plan your day and week. List your tasks in terms of importance. Before you begin your work load for the day, you should make a (4) _____ and (5) _____ the things you have to do, not just make a list. (6) _____ are a great tool. Before making your list, write down categories in terms of important. For example, tasks labeled "(7) _____" must be done today. Tasks labeled "(8) _____" are important to do, but can wait. Tasks with labels like "(9) _____" can be put off if necessary.

Second, identify times when you're most (10) _____. Different people are productive at different points during the day. It can help to know when you're most able to use your time wisely and plan to work during those times. For example, if you find yourself energetic during the mornings, try to get (11) _____ done then. During the night, you can do relaxing things you enjoy. It can take a while to identify your (12) _____. Try tracking your energy level and overall focus throughout the day for a week or so. This should help you figure out when you would be the most productive.

Third, avoid interruptions and distractions, which stop you doing what you had planned. Interruptions disrupt your (13) _____. If you're in the middle of a task and stop to do something else, it can be hard to get back into (14) _____. Keep in mind, sometimes disruptions are inevitable. Do your best to avoid interruptions, but do not beat yourself up over the (15) _____ during your work.

Fourth, do not multitask. Many people assume (16) _____ is a great way to get more done each day and manage time wisely. However, focusing on multiple tasks at once actually makes you less productive. Focus completely on one task at a time instead. You will get your work done quicker this way, allowing you to make the most of your time. Therefore, do jobs to a realistic level of (17) _____ in the time available, and to a level that is really necessary. Don't aim for (18) _____ when there is no need for it. Try to balance time, cost and quality.

prioritize	important, but not urgent
calendar	diary
time management	realistic plan
low-priority	workflow
quality	perfectionism
to-do lists	productive
urgent	work mode
energy peaks	the bulk of your work
multitasking	occasional distraction

ⅢⅢⅢⅢⅢⅢⅢⅢⅢⅢⅢⅢ **Information Link** ⅢⅢⅢⅢⅢⅢⅢⅢⅢⅢⅢⅢ

Disfluency in Interpreting（口译中的不流利）

　　语言产出中的不流利现象包括停顿（pause）、重新开始（restart）、重复（repetition）、重新导向（redirection）等。研究者认为，语言上可发觉的错误（linguistically detectable faults）是语言推理及组织的认知努力的外显。成功的公共演讲人，如职业演说家、讲师或电台主持人的技巧就是要控制自己的产出，使产出能够掩藏这些努力以及这些努力可能带来的话语上的迟疑。

　　流利性在很大程度上是区分职业译员和学生译员的一个重要方面。口译中的不流利主要包括"无声停顿"和"有声停顿"，而后者主要表现为"嗯、啊、就是、那么、然后"等填充语、重复、错误开始等。

　　首先，部分练习者不存在填充语过多的情况，但确实有些人这方面的问题比较严重，汉语口语表达习惯会如实反映在其英语表达及口译产出中，有时还会随着外语表达及译语产出的难度增加而被无限放大。这就需要从平日讲话开始，训练自己使用流利的语言，一旦出现多余的填充语，就为自己标记一次错误，统计错误数量，假以时日，日常表达不流利的现象定会有所改观。

　　其次，重复、错误开始等口译中常见的"有声停顿"情况产生的原因比较复杂。第一，可能是因为译员在口译中进行理解、回忆、组织译语等多任务处理（multi-tasking），其他任务对于译语产出的干扰和抑制作用过大，因而下意识进行"有声停顿"而不能自控。第二，可能是因为译员的语言运用能力有限，搭配及组句能力有限，这种情况特别常见于使用外语进行译语产出的时候。第三，可能是因为译员还没能领会"口译即解释"的精髓，一旦个别词想不出对应的译语，就"嗯、啊"或不断地重复前一个词而不能继续。第四，可能是因为译员不能有效区分口译和笔译，试图在口译中每次都以产出笔译译文类的译语，以至于不断转换开头的选择，造成很多"错误开始"或"重新开始"的情况。

　　口译产出中过分拘泥于源语的字词和句式，比如，源语中的词性和句子数量都要做到一一对应，那么译语产出势必带有浓厚的"翻译腔"，甚至可能会因为译语的可理解度较差而造成听众听不懂译语的情况。在口译训练中，特别是英译中的过程中，由于中文是母语，译员对中文的驾驭能力稍强，所以可以理解了源语之后，用自己觉得通顺的汉语产出译语。同样重要的是，不论译语组织是怎样的，一旦产出就不要轻易修正，只要不是出现了错误信息，就一直顺译下去。汉语的小句非常灵活，译员可以调整源语的词性，打碎源语的句式，完成译语。这样，在降低译语产出负担的同时，还可以保证译语的可理解度。

实际上，在口译中，不论以何种方式开头，句子往往都可以继续。本句还没有包含的信息可以在下句中补充出来，没有必要尝试若干种开始句子的方式。译语中包含过多重复或重新开始，筛选信息以理解信息的任务就留给了听众，无疑极大增加听众的听解负担，降低译语的可理解度，这样的译语不是"听众友好型"的。

After-class Assignment

Directions: Practice shadowing while listening to the following passage. Pause after each paragraph, and try to summarize the main idea of that paragraph.

The Most Amazing Structure on Earth

Paragraph 1

There are people who say the most amazing structure on earth is the human brain. It is so complex that it took about 700 million years to develop. Humans started out as wormlike creatures that used one end of the body to move forward. Ever so slowly, a bunch of nerves began developing at that one end — the head. These nerves helped the creature to sense light, food and danger. Eventually, this bunch of nerves became the creature's brain. To carry messages from the brain to other parts of the body, the creature grew a spinal cord. Later, the creature became a fish with eyes, ears and a nose that could send the brain information about sights, sounds and smells.

_____

_____

_____

Paragraph 2

More time passed, and the fish grew arms and legs so it could move about on land. For this, it needed a larger and more complex brain. It became an ape-like creature, and the parts of the brain used for seeing images and being social grew much stronger. Finally, the ape-like creature became human, with a brain that was capable of reason, emotion, creativity, memory and the ability to judge right from wrong.

_____

_____

_____

Paragraph 3

The human brain is very mysterious. Many questions about the brain have not yet been answered. For example, why do we need to sleep or why do we dream? There is a lot about the brain that we do not yet understand. Believe it or not, people used to think of the brain as useless stuffing. Of course, we now know the brain is our control centre. The surface of the brain is called the cerebral cortex. It is the part of the brain that makes us intelligent, and it consists of four parts called lobes. The front lobe is where much of our thinking and feeling happens. The top lobe processes information which is coming from parts of our bodies, such as our skin and muscles. The side lobe plays an important role in hearing, speech and long-term memories while the back lobe processes images from our eyes.

_____

_____

_____

Paragraph 4

Which do you think is more powerful: your brain or a supercomputer? You might be surprised to learn that the world's best supercomputer is only about as powerful as half a mouse brain! Your brain is packed with 100 billion brain cells called neurons. They send information to your body telling it what to do, and they receive information from each of your senses, what you see, feel, taste, hear and touch. All of this information travels to and from parts of your body along your spinal cord, which is like a highway found down the centre of your back. As the information travels from neuron to neuron, pathways are created. When you think about or practice something again and again, those pathways get stronger. That's how the brain learns and remembers. Actually, you were born with most of the neurons you have now, but when you were a baby, you didn't have many pathways to connect them. As an adult, you now have more than 125 trillion connections between your neurons. No computer on earth can compete with the speed of your brain and how much information it can hold.

_____

_____

_____

Paragraph 5

Many different factors affect how well we learn. While we can't control all of these factors, there are many that we can. For example, fuel for our brain comes from calories in the food we eat. In fact, 20% of the calories we eat are used by our brain. Although not all calories help the brain, research suggests that some foods, such as egg yolk, whole grains, nuts, fish, dark leafy green vegetables, beans, strawberries and blueberries might be especially good for concentration and memory.

_____

_____

_____

Paragraph 6

Drinking enough water is also important. The brain is more than 70% water. If we don't drink enough water, it affects our concentration. We need around six to eight glasses of non-sugary, non-alcoholic fluid each day. Moreover, studies suggest that the brain does not do well with sudden rushes of sugar, so sweet, fizzy drinks do not help the brain either.

_____

_____

_____

Paragraph 7

Remember also the importance of oxygen, which is carried to the brain by your blood. When you move your body, your blood flow increases and your brain gets more oxygen. Going for a walk, running, or riding a bike really help get oxygen to the brain, as do stretching and breathing deeply.

_____

_____

_____

Paragraph 8

Besides exercise, rest is important. Getting enough rest boosts our mood and helps us concentrate. What's more, when we are asleep, the brain practices what we did during the day. We actually learn in our sleep. If you have a hard time falling asleep, try listening to gentle music, thinking positive thoughts, or reading something funny to relax. Avoid video games and exciting TV shows in the hour before bedtime.

Paragraph 9

Stress can also stop the brain from working at its best. Some people fight stress by imagining a beautiful box. When it's time to concentrate on something, they imagine filling that box with all the things that give them stress. Then they imagine putting that box away until they have time to deal with whatever is inside.

Paragraph 10

Don't forget that your brain gets information from your senses. Therefore, your brain will have an easier time focusing and remembering when vision, hearing, smell, touch and taste are involved. Use your vision to help you learn by imagining what you read — like a movie in your mind. This is called visualizing.

Paragraph 11

Underline or highlight important information in a text with a yellow marker and use different colours when you take notes. Make charts, mind maps, flashcards, diagrams, or draw pictures. Use your hearing to help you learn by reading out loud or explaining the new information to someone else. Use your sense of taste by chewing gum while you learn.

_____

_____

_____

Paragraph 12

Yet another way to boost your brainpower is to create an environment where you work well. Many people, for instance, work better in light from a window. Temperature can also make a difference. A room that is too warm might make you feel sleepy. Lots of people find it easier to concentrate in rooms that are tidy. Some people find it helpful to listen to music when they study while others prefer silence. Get rid of any distractions, whatever they may be. For example, turn off your cell phone and let people in your home know that you need to be left alone.

_____

_____

_____

扫码获取本单元音频资料

Unit 8

Multi-tasking II & Smart Shadowing

> An interpreting strategy may be consciously used but may also have become automatic in so far as the processor will not have to make any cognitive decision.
>
> — Sylvia Kalina, interpreting researcher from
> Cologne University of Applied Sciences

Unit Goals

- To gain a general knowledge of how multi-tasking practice simulates the process of interpreting.
- To maintain the listening comprehension performance while doing multi-tasking practice.
- To become more articulate while doing shadowing.
- To know what output automaticity is and what interpreters can do to improve output automaticity.

Warm Up

Directions: Listen to the following passage and fill in the blanks with words or sentences. Make sure the words and sentences you fill in are both grammatically and semantically acceptable.

🎧 Task A

Tourism has experienced a revolution in the past 50 years. In 1950, there were nearly (1) _____ international tourists crossing boarders in a single year; today, there are around (2) _____ people travelling the world. Travelling has become a huge part of many people's lives. When we travel, we come across new people, new sights, and new ideas. Often our (3) _____ changes as we see more of it. We definitely become better people.

However, we must not forget that for many of us, travelling can still be quite a difficult process. 15% of the world's population is (4) _____ to live with some kind of disability or another. About 1 billion people around the world may be unable to enjoy the privileges of knowing other cultures, experiencing nature at its fullest and experiencing the (5) _____ of embarking on a journey to explore new sights and new places.

(6) _____ for all should be therefore at the heart and at the center of tourism policies and business strategies. Not as human rights only, which is important on its own, but also as a great (7) _____ and as a great business opportunity. With the world's population aging, all of us will benefit sooner or later from (8) _____ in tourism.

Let us recall that all of the world's citizens have the right to experience the incredible diversity of our planet and the beauty of the world we live in. We thus urge all countries and destinations, as well as all the (9) _____, to promote accessibility for all in the physical environment, in the transport systems, in the public facilities and services and in the information and communications channels. I wish you a future full of (10) _____ _____ travel experiences to be enjoyed by all.

Directions: Listen to the passage and briefly answer the following questions.

🎧 Task B

1. Accessibility is an issue that dictates people's journeys. What does it mean?

2. What are some of the benefits of travelling?

3. What numbers are used to illustrate that tourism is a massive industry for Bangkok, Thailand?

4. What has the speaker's company done to make travel and tourism a more inclusive activity?

5. Why is "Tourism for All" a win-win proposal for all?

|||||||||||||||||||| **Listening Comprehension** ||||||||||||||||||||

Skill Focus

Multi-tasking II（多任务处理2）

多任务处理训练也被称为分脑训练，它是对同声传译的铺垫和模拟，目的是让学生了解多任务处理的运作特点，感觉多任务处理的紧迫性，自我调节多任务处理中有效分配工作记忆的能力。本节提供了一些简单基础的提升多任务处理能力的训练方法。

1．选择逻辑较清晰的篇章，按照自然段正常顺序交替进行听、读，感受听、读任务频繁地交替，检验自己是否可以不受干扰，依然能够把握文章的主旨。

2．同时听、读一篇文章，感受听与读之间的同步进行，体验这个过程是否比单独听或读该篇文章更难，难在哪里，自己是否可以应对。

3．准备两段长度相近、内容丝毫不相关的文字，在听其中一段文字的同时，阅读另外一段文字，听、读两个任务同时进行，同时结束。结束后，分别尝试复述两段的内容。可以进行小组练习，复述所读与所听的要点，然后互相做出评判。

在以上的训练中，任务语言的选择可以从全部汉语过渡到全部英语或两语夹杂。这样，同样的训练方式也会体现出由易到难的变化。在复述任务时，从用源语复述到用译语复述同样体现出由易到难的变化。

Guided Practice

Task A

Directions: In the following passage, paragraph 2, 4, 6, 8 are missing and will be read to you in the recording. While listening to the passage, take down keywords that may help you summarize the main idea of each paragraph.

Shared Parking

Paragraph 1

In cities, parking has become a big problem for car owners. And this gave rise to the idea of "shared parking space", which means that parking spaces are shared by more than one user, which allows parking facilities to be used more efficiently.

_____
_____
_____

Paragraph 2

_____
_____
_____

Paragraph 3

The concept and practice of "shared bikes" has been more widely accepted, as more companies enter this market, more people choose to ride bikes, instead of walking or taking a bus. Thus, the bike-sharing market is incremental in nature.

_____
_____
_____

Paragraph 4

_____
_____
_____

Paragraph 5

It is a process that requires constant review and a coordinating body that can analyze how spaces continue to be used. Stockholm Parkering in Stockholm, Sweden is a parking authority that helps developers find available parking spaces in surrounding district.

_____
_____
_____

Paragraph 6

_____

_____

_____

Paragraph 7

In Beijing, China, the government started promoting shared parking by encouraging and guiding institutions in opening their parking lots to the public after work hours. Most of these shared parking lots are open to residents in the surroundings between 6 pm and 8 am.

_____

_____

_____

Paragraph 8

_____

_____

_____

Task B

Directions: Listen to the recording and check whether the written text corresponds with the one read to you. Adjustments shall be made according to what you hear.

Paragraph 1

Modern technological innovations have made deep-sea mining more realisable. Chinese companies have three licences awarded by the International Seabed Authority for deep-sea mining in the Atlantic Ocean. China supplies the world's rare earth — metals used in making nearly all today's electronics products. But global demand for green products such as wind turbines and solar panels, which depend on rare earth metals, may outstrip even China's supply. Meanwhile, anticipation of rising demand for electric vehicles has pushed up prices for metals used in copper, manganese, nickel and lithium. While countries such as Japan have developed maritime mining technology, much of it adapted from deep-sea oil drilling, China is particularly keen on tapping into a wealth of maritime resources. (9 errors)

_____

_____

_____

_____

Paragraph 2

After decades of turbulence, the world order has begun to change. On the global front, the strength of developed countries has greatly increased. And the World Bank has predicted the share of high-income countries in the global purchasing power parity-based GDP will drop from 64 percent to 39 percent, with Asian emerging powers' share increasing from 12 percent to 39 percent. A unipolar world order and globalization will be the highlights of the new era. Countries across the world are willing to compete and cooperate on the basis of inclusiveness, yet the deadlock between emerging powers and the established ones will continue for some time. (6 errors)

_____

_____

_____

_____

Paragraph 3

Summer is the season for internships, and many college students are interning in companies. However, some offline shops are reportedly selling certificates to students who never do an internship. Why are there people selling them? The answer is simple. There is demand for them. First of all, the majority of colleges require their students to attend internships, yet they seldom check the internship certificates the students hand in. Second, some college students falsify their internship experiences to make them look better, in the hope of getting a better job on graduation. However, the practice has valued internships, and led to more students opting to purchase a certificate as they do not see the need for an internship to prove their competence. (8 errors)

_____

_____

_____

_____

Paragraph 4

Ministry of Industry of China lately launched a technical inspection of phone apps. It is found that 80% of these apps are illegally collecting users' information, promoting other apps and charging users for no good reason. It is not enough to simply expose the smartphone apps and warn people to delete them. Effective supervision is needed to root out these apps. This is difficult as people profit from the apps and there are no specific laws and regulations to stop them from producing and selling the apps. Nor is there any guideline with which cyberspace managers can impose needed sanctions on apps. China's top internet watchdog, Cyberspace Administration of China, regulates that an app must be a single application not a bundle. However, there are no punishments specified that can hold responsible developers and app stores accountable. (8 errors)

_____

_____

_____

_____

|||||||||||||||||||| Summary Interpreting ||||||||||||||||||||

Skill Focus

Smart Shadowing（灵活的影子跟读）

上一章我们说过，影子跟读类似鹦鹉学舌，但又不能完全是鹦鹉学舌，保证在跟读的同时能够听懂源语发言的意思。实际上，在正常跟读的基础上刻意安排一些无关的练习，能够培养我们合理分配注意力的能力。比如，可以针对具体语段，要求译员在用源语跟读的同时完成注意力干扰练习。具体要求为，从1开始写，或从999开始倒写，或从10开始每10个数字跳写，或者写下有意义的句子。跟读结束后，可以通过多种方式检验跟读的效果。

1. 将跟读的产出内容录音，或由同伴听取跟读的产出，检查跟读话语的流畅性和可理解度。

2. 检查跟读过程中数字记录等无关练习的结果是否正确。

3. 在影子跟读之后，复述或概括听到的讲话内容。

影子跟读是多任务处理的典型活动，占用较多的认知资源，练习过程中甚至会出现

"跟不上"和"跟丢了"的任务超负荷状态。在这种情况下，源语主要内容的记忆和回溯是难度更大的任务要求，因人因任务内容而异。记忆很少或者完全不记得跟读了什么内容是很常见的，这也是跟读练习中难度较高的阶段。可以采用源语概述练习，译语概述练习是在源语概述练习进行一段时间后，用译语概述源语的讲话内容。练习时不必过度强调句子结构和具体内容，而要尽量用简练的译语传达源语的中心思想和主要信息点。这样的练习如果可以循序渐进，难度逐渐加大，则有助于译员尽量接近并感受口译中多任务同时进行的状态，为口译的精进学习打下良好的基础。

Guided Practice

🎧 Task A

Directions: Practice shadowing while listening to the passage entitled "The Causes of Floods". Simultaneously, rearrange the words by putting the correct numbers below, to make the sentence both grammatically and semantically acceptable. Look at the following example.

The film I enjoyed yesterday.
③   ①   ②   ④

1. Immediately left he.

2. She beautifully draws.

3. The match at four o'clock ended.

4. The news listened to I carefully.

5. The soup spoilt the cook.

6. We at home stay on Sundays.

7. Music I like very much.

8. She a letter from her brother last week received.

9. There are at the bus stop a lot of people.

10. The man the piano well played.

11. He the man looked at.

12. He tall very wasn't.

Task B

Directions: Practice shadowing while listening to the passage entitled "Make a Good First Impression". Simultaneously, try to answer the following multiple choice questions. You may record your shadowing or ask your partner to comment on your performance.

1. Which river flows through the middle of London?

   a. Thames.   b. Severn.   c. Seine.

2. What's the nickname for the big clock tower at the Houses of Parliament?

   a. Big Ken.   b. Big Ben.   c. Big Bob.

3. Which TV broadcaster has its headquarters in London?

   a. ABC.   b. BBC.   c. CNN.

4. What's the main industry in the City of London?

   a. Car making.   b. Mining.   c. Banking.

5. The Great Fire of London burned much of the city to the ground. Where did the fire start?

   a. A pub   b. A prison   c. A bakery

6. What's "falling down" in the popular nursery rhyme?

   a. Windsor.   b. London Bridge.   c. House of Lords.

7. London's double-decker buses are _____?

   a. red   b. green   c. blue

8. Which of London's airports is the busiest in Europe?

   a. Heathrow.   b. Gatwick.   c. Stasted.

9. What's the Palace of Westminster normally called?

   a. Westminster Abbey.   b. The Houses of Parliament.   c. The Tower of London.

10. What's the busiest shopping street in Europe?

   a. Oxford Street.   b. Downing Street.   c. Fleet Street.

11. What's the police headquarters in London called?

   a. England Yard.   b. Scotland Yard.   c. Wales Yard.

12. Which mysterious criminal terrorized the streets of London in the 1880s?

   a. Jack the Ripper.   b. The Artful Dodger.   c. Professor Moriarty.

Task C

Directions: Practice shadowing while listening to the recording, without referring to the text. Then based on your understanding and memory of the passage, choose from the given sentences the ones that best fit the blanks.

Marketing

(1) _____. If you are not doing that, you are not marketing. It's that simple! The key is finding the right marketing method and defining the right marketing message to use, to educate and influence your consumers.

Companies make the mistake of thinking that marketing is just "one" thing, but marketing is everything that the consumer encounters when it comes to your business, from advertising, to what they hear, to the customer service that they receive, to the follow-up care that you provide. (2) _____.

(3) _____. These are activities that you have to combine successfully in order to sell.

(4) _____. Marketing departments usually test new product concepts with focus groups and surveys to ascertain interest levels among potential buyers. If the interest level is high, marketers may then sell products on a limited basis to track sales. If product sales are high, products are then rolled out on a national level. Before products go to the market, companies must decide what styles, sizes, flavors, and scents they should sell and the packaging designs they should use.

(5) _____. Companies must know the optimal price to sell their products to achieve maximum return. One way to determine price is to set it at a level comparable to competitors; that is if the company can recover all associated product expenses and still make a profit. If the company is introducing a new product that has never existed, they must determine how much the consumer is willing to pay for it.

(6) _____. For more complex concepts, like spas or computers, companies may promote their wares at trade shows. Promotions usually have two purposes: generate leads for sales reps or initiate actual purchases.

(7) _____. It is how and where products are sold. Consumer product companies, for example, sell to wholesalers who, in turn, sell to retailers. In the industrial market, the buying process is longer and involves more decision makers. Some

companies also sell products or services on a local level, while others sell nationally and even internationally. (8) _____.

(9) _____. Print, radio, and television advertising are types of marketing, as are direct mail and Internet marketing. Companies that sell via the Internet optimize their web pages, so they appear higher in search engines like Google and Yahoo. Newsletters, press releases, and articles are forms of marketing used to generate leads and orders. Some companies use referral marketing to increase business, where satisfied customers refer others to a particular business. (10) _____.

(11) _____.

a. Starting with products, companies have many procedures they must undertake to ensure their products are ready for selling.

b. All told, marketing is anything that informs, interests and gets people to make purchase decisions.

c. Marketing is the process of teaching consumers why they should choose your product or service over your competitors.

d. Place in marketing is deciding how the product will be distributed and where people will buy it.

e. More recently, social media marketing is becoming a type of marketing that smart companies can't avoid when it comes to reaching potential buyers, whether it's advertising on Facebook or posting advice on Twitter with links to a website.

f. So, marketing is doing everything to satisfy customer needs, so as to make a profit.

g. Promotion is deciding how the product will be supported with brochures, advertising, special activities, and information which companies use to generate interest in their products.

h. All distribution decisions are part of the overall marketing process.

i. Do you know the different types of marketing?

j. Marketing is best identified using what are called the four Ps or a mix of marketing: Product, Price, Promotion, and Place.

k. Price is also tested through focus groups and surveys.

Information Link

Output Automaticity（输出自动化）

二语习得研究者对加拿大的法语沉浸教学法进行了调查，发现"可理解输入"在二语习得中发挥了很大的作用，但不足以使学习者获得语言使用的流利性和准确性。如果学习者要使自己的第二语言流利准确，不仅需要"可理解输入"，更需要"可理解输出"。这就是所谓的"输出假说"（The Output Hypothesis）。

输出理论能有效提高学习者二语的流利程度。输出理论对口译的贡献在于它指出输出能提高语言表达的自动化（Automaticity）。心理语言学认为，语用过程是自动性（Automatic）和控制性（Controlled）两种过程的混合。语言学习是一个从控制过程到自动化过程的连续变化的维度，完全受意识控制和完全自动化是这个连续体的两极。语言在表达过程中占用的注意力资源越少，其自动化程度越高，反之亦然。

很多研究表明，预先习得对应的词语、术语、短语的表达，会使口译过程中部分译语的输出做到自动化，译员可以节省出精力专注于理解源语、组织译语等其他任务。理想的翻译方式必须包含自动化地运用文字表达意义的过程。也有学者指出，在整个翻译过程中，翻译与理解可以出现"分离"的现象。也就是说，在某些情况下，语言的输出可以不需要意识理解体系的介入。没有译语输出的自动化，而持续地投入精力于口译的每一环节，将破坏总体的口译临场表现。

输出自动化对口译教学和实践都具有指导意义，加强口译中的输出自动化对提高口译质量至关重要。那么，如何能有的放矢地加强口译中的输出自动化呢？一方面，应该在口译中强调块语与范例的积累。这样，在有限的交际时间内，译员能很快地从记忆中提取语言资源，满足即时交际的需要。另一方面，块语和范例的积累需要用双语形式进行转换速度和准确度的强化，这样才能确保译员准确、流利地将块语和范例以双语形式进行表达。

After-class Assignment

Directions: Practice shadowing while listening to the following passage. Pause after each paragraph, and try to summarize the main idea of that paragraph.

Things to Watch Out for When Applying for a Credit Card

Paragraph 1

It would be nice to think that all credit card issuers are fair and just, however, such is not the case. Not all credit cards are the same, nor are those that issue them. Many try to take advantage of an unsuspecting public. Below are a few pointers to look out for when applying for a credit card.

_____

_____

_____

Paragraph 2

First, pay attention to the interest rate being charged. While, as stated, you can expect to pay a higher interest rate, it should not be too excessive.

_____

_____

_____

Paragraph 3

Second, do not even consider cards that have a zero grace period. This means that they begin to charge interest from the day the charge occurred. You wind up paying interest on interest. There are numerous cards out there that provide a 25 day or so grace period allowing you to have a chance to pay off the charge before interest is tracked.

_____

_____

_____

Paragraph 4

Third, do not get over anxious. Read the fine print with each card you want to apply to. If you do not understand a benefit or aspect of the contract seek out understanding. The issuer is in business to make a profit and you can rest assured that the contract leans in their direction. Your job is to choose the one that benefits you the most. Your primary objective is to have a clear understanding of the interest rates, fees, and penalties involved and what circumstances will those rates and fees increase, or under what circumstance will you be penalized.

_____

_____

_____

Paragraph 5

With the huge consumer lending boom in the United States there is a considerable amount of fraud going on. Once you have established good credit and your credit score reaches various levels of acceptance, offers will flood your mail box and your phone will ring off the hook. Never accept credit card offers over the phone, or that come in the mail. Sales people undergo extensive training to sell you something you do not need or want. When you desire to increase your credit level, or desire another card with lower interest, seek out the offer that meets your specific need.

_____

_____

_____

Paragraph 6

If you make a couple of applications and are turned down, consider having someone who you trust and who trusts you to co-sign for a card. Continual denials will result negatively on your report. This, however, should be a last resort as whatever happens does not only reflect on your credit report, it affects theirs as well. If you apply for a guaranteed secured, guaranteed store or catalog card, or a prepaid credit card this should not be necessary.

_____

_____

_____

Paragraph 7

Only apply for the credit you need. Too much can be tempting and might stretch you too thin come the end of the month. Also, having too much unused credit can prove to be harmful when you go to apply for a more serious loan such as for a car simply do to the fact that, although you do not use it, it is available to you at will and lenders take this into consideration when reviewing your application and it is reflected on your Credit Score.

_____

_____

_____

扫码获取本单元音频资料

Unit 9

Linguistic Anticipation & Speech on Given PPT

> Consistently good performance in conference interpreting depends on sustained mental alertness.
>
> — James Nolan, experienced translator and interpreter of the UN, author of *Interpretation: Techniques and Exercises*

Unit Goals

- To gain a general knowledge of how linguistic anticipation helps with the comprehension of the source language in interpreting.
- To become more flexible in summary interpreting based on given PPT.
- To gain a general knowledge of visualization in interpreting.

Warm Up

Directions: Listen to the following passages and fill in the blanks with words or sentences. Make sure the words and sentences you fill in are both grammatically and semantically acceptable.

Task A

We have celebrated many milestones, but the one that gathers us here today, the grand opening of the redeveloped Old Post Office building, is incredibly special to each member of my family, both (1) _____.

A (2) _____ is much more complex than a ground-up construction project, and the redevelopment of this building we're standing in has been perhaps the most challenging, and (3) _____ of them all.

When this property was originally built in 1899, its grandeur was meant to signal to the rest of the country that Pennsylvania Avenue was America's Main Street. A full city block in the heart of Washington, D.C., you didn't have to be a visionary to see the potential, despite the fact that in recent years, time has (4) _____.

In 2011, the Old Post Office was considered the most sought-after redevelopment opportunity in the country, and my company fought hard against the largest hotel (5) _____ _____ in the world to win the deal. Over the course of eight months, our team worked nonstop to study the building and (6) _____ _____.

After an exhaustive evaluation process, we were (7) _____ awarded the deal. We were selected by a panel of judges based on criteria that included our vision for the property, the strength and experience of our development team, our company's financial wherewithal, our track record, and our plan to bring (8) _____ to Pennsylvania Avenue.

One of the reasons I love real estate is because at the end of years' hard work, there exists a (9) _____ of your efforts and the efforts of so many people. My father trained my (10) _____to see things not for what they are, but for what they can be. This is a great example of that. It's been a gift he has had his entire life.

When we commenced construction, and at the ground-breaking ceremony, (11) _____ _____. I told you that we would not disappoint you and that we would never let you down. Now, I am very proud to announce that today is a celebration not just of meeting but (12) _____ those goals.

Task B

Last year, my brother spoke about some of the (1) _____ (qualities; quality) of those teachers who have had the greatest impact on young lives. He said the best teachers are those who can reach children early in their learning journey, supporting them, often through (2) _____ (turbulence; turbulent) times in their lives to give them the best chance for the future.

I would like to build on what William said by highlighting the vital role teachers play as our role (3) _____ (modals; models). In addition to reading, writing and arithmetic, the very best teachers go beyond the pages of textbooks to teach young people about determination, (4) _____ (inspiration; aspiration), resilience, and of course, (5) _____ (passion; compassion). We'll all face setbacks and challenges in our lives and our teachers play a vital role in preparing us for those ups and downs.

The finalists for this year's Global Teacher Prize are from every corner of the world — from the Canadian Arctic to Kenya and Pakistan. But there's one thing they all have in common: They (6) _____ (sparkle; spark) curiosity within a child and (7) _____ (nature; nurture) the dreams that can change our world for the better. I'm sure everyone can remember the teachers who did the same for us and those that helped us through our (8) _____ (informative; formative) years. I can certainly pinpoint those who had an impact on my life.

Our foundation is proud to partner with (9) _____ (charities; charity) who are helping to create bright futures for the next generation.

I'd like to end by congratulating all of the finalists. You're not just (10) _____ (exceptional; acception) teachers, you are the role models who support, inspire and shape children's lives. Your work is so important and I don't believe it's an exaggeration to say that you're shaping the future. You're all winners in my book, and more importantly, your students' books.

⁞⁞⁞⁞⁞⁞⁞⁞⁞⁞⁞⁞⁞ Listening Comprehension ⁞⁞⁞⁞⁞⁞⁞⁞⁞⁞⁞⁞⁞

Skill Focus

Linguistic Anticipation（语言预测）

对话语的理解过程，实际上是听话人理解说话人的言语并做出合理解释的过程，理解过程可解释为表达的逆过程。口译源语稍纵即逝，基本没有"源语重复"或者"听第二遍"的机会，对源语进行深度理解才是有效记忆并对其进行回溯的基础。译员对源语形成真正意义上的理解，即可以用另外一种语言将其重述，对口译来说至关重要。而对当下语段的理解也会极大影响译员对之后语段的预测情况，换句话说，口译中译员理解源语，就是使自己更加接近讲者，变成讲者，试图理解讲者为什么那么说，甚至预测讲者接下来要怎么说。这种对话语的深度理解是口译过程中译员需要达到的境界，也是译员训练需要强调的部分。预测是可以极大提升源语理解程度的口译策略。

对了解一门语言的听话人来说，由于对该门语言有一定的认识，对它的句法规律和冗余表达比较熟悉，因而往往可以对其进行语法甚至语用上的预测，这种预测能力可以用来衡量一个人对某种语言的掌握程度。在语言预测中，词组、连接词、从句引导词、固定搭配等都是主要的关注点。

比如，汉语中的"虽然，但是""不仅，而且""因为，所以""不是，而是""首先，其次"都是启后并承前的关键词对。也就是说，我们看到或听到前一个词，就会预测到后一个词。而一旦后一个词没有出现，或距离前一个词比较远，都会影响篇章的连贯性和可理解度。例如：

1．不过，至少还有一点令奥迪值得欣慰，因为即便增幅放缓，但奥迪仍占据了中国高档轿车销售市场份额的70.2%。

2．（在他看来，）评判一个企业，不能仅看其营业额，还要看它是否有为社会做贡献的行动。

3．他在期中考试受挫之后，持续努力了半个学期，也没有在期末考试中获得好成绩。

4．为了宣传中国旅游业，吸引更多的海外旅游者，中国国家旅游局全面开展旅游宣传促销工作。如今，在世界各国的主流媒体，在世界各大都市里都能看到中国旅游业的宣传促销广告。

5．从根本上改革学制，是一项极其艰巨的工作。没有教育家的抱负、政策制定者的决心，以及所有相关者，包括家长、学生、教师、院校、纳税人，以及社会上每个人的充分支持，这项工作不可能完成。

6．中国去年新增了9,500万网民，其中60%以上都是高中以下学历的人，也就是说，年轻人其实正在成为互联网真正的主流。那么，年轻人成为主流，直接带来的效应就是互联网在更快、更大的程度上向着娱乐化的方向发展。

7．全球钢铁行业总体仍然面临较大压力。一方面，国际市场钢材价格有所反弹，但上涨乏力，市场价格总体处于低位向上调整状态；另一方面，由于原燃料价格上升，钢铁生产成本增加，钢铁生产企业的经营生产面临更大的成本压力。

以上的汉语例子说明，虽然语言结构可以为语言预测提供助力，但需要我们对可预测的语言结构更加敏感。尽管英语是我们的外语，我们对其敏感度比较有限，但我们更应该多储备英语中启后及承前的关键词，以提升语感，最终提高我们在中英互译口译活动中的话语理解和解释能力。在英语中，我们同样可以遇到很多"启后承前"的关键词及概念。比如，"**Hardly any** major global issue today can be resolved **without** US-China cooperation and understanding."我们在听到这句话的前半句的时候，就应该可以预测到后半句应该有without或者if not等否定表达，并引出达成前半句结果的条件。如果前半句的结果是A，后半句的条件是B的话，则整句的译语结构也就出来了"想要A就需要B，只有B才能达到A"等类似的表达。下面是其他类似的可以预测的语言结构。

1. **Just because** it's not happening right now, **doesn't mean** it never will.

2. **For one thing**, you will earn money; **for another**, it is good to work with others in team; **finally**, it is a good chance of finding a suitable job.

3. **Unless** the Mexican government works on the causes of the poverty, the problem is going to **get worse**.

4. Let's put it this way: Mr. Denton was a **new teacher**, and **new teachers** are **impressible**, I wanted his **impression** of me to be a good one.

5. **It isn't** that I'm stupid; **it's** mainly that I don't work overly hard.

6. China will make sustained efforts to fulfill the development goals of the UN Millennium Declaration and contribute to the early control of HIV/AIDS epidemics worldwide. **For that**, the Chinese government has pledged $10 million to the Global Fund to Fight AIDS, Tuberculosis and Malaria in support of HIV/AIDS prevention and treatment efforts in developing countries.

7. Throughout our long history, we have always looked **outward, not inward**. We have used the seas that surround our shores **not to cut ourselves off from the world, but to reach out to it** — to carry our **trade** to the four corners of the earth. And **with that trade has come** people, companies, jobs and investment. We have always understood that our national greatness is built on our **openness**.

从以上的分析中可以看出，无论是有标记的还是无标记的语言结构，语言预测都可以帮助我们理解并重构语篇，对口译的话语分析和译语产出都具有重要意义。有标记的语言结构可以帮助译员在听取标记关键词的同时，记录关键词并把握逻辑关系；无标记的语言结构需要译员具备更好的语感，以便更快更有效地分辨语言结构的多层次关系，必要时还可以在译语中将这些关系进行显化翻译，补出标记词，增强译语的可理解度。然而，预测能力的训练和提高都不能超出我们的语言和知识水平，我们只能在现有的基础上做到更好地预测和理解。因而，只有语言和知识水平的同步提升才能在更大范围以及更深程度上提升译员的预测和理解能力。

Guided Practice

Directions: Skim the passages and fill in the blanks with words or phrases based on your anticipation. Then listen to the recording and check whether your alternatives are close in meaning to what you hear.

Task A

Online Gaming

Online gaming is hugely popular with children and young people. From sport related games, to mission based games inspiring users to complete challenges, (1) _____ _____ cater for a wide range of interests, and can enable users to link up and play together.

What's more, online gaming has never been so accessible as today. There are (2) _____ ways for users to play games online these days. This includes free games found on the Internet, games or apps on mobile phones and handheld consoles, as well as downloadable and boxed games on PCs and consoles such as the PlayStation or Xbox. Nowadays, we even have virtual reality games and augmented reality games, which allow the gamer to immerse themselves into what feels like a (3) _____ experience by stimulating their hearing or (4) _____. Typically, a gamer will need to wear a headset to experience (5) _____ games. And these types of games are becoming increasingly popular. Gamers will be able to (6) "_____" things that they understand are not real, but will offer them exceptional gaming experience.

Admittedly, gaming can be a great way for young people to relax, (7) _____ with their friends and have fun. It can be a constructive use of children's time as it (8) _____ teamwork and (9) _____ child development. But there are some dangers and (10) _____ for kids and teens to play online games. Children may view inappropriate or (11) _____ content if they play games that aren't suitable for their age. This could include sexual or (12) _____ material. It might be in-game content or produced by other players. Some players can be abusive towards others or (13) _____. Some players may also hack another user's account or (14) _____. This can be as upsetting for a young person as if it happened in real life.

Internet safety advice is directly applicable to the gaming environment because of the risks that are present. It is essential that children are aware of these issues and are given the (15) _____ to help manage and reduce these risks, with the help of those around them. With so many games available online, it can be (16) _____ for parents to know how to keep their child safe. Parents whose children play games online also have (17) _____ over the amount of time they spend doing it.

One of the best things (18) _____ can do is to engage with the gaming environment and play a game or two against your children. Once they explain the rules to you, you may begin to (19) _____ what makes it so attractive to young people!

And it is possible for you to check that the games they are using are age (20) _____ because like films, all games have an official age classification on the box. And you may also find out about the gaming sites and alert them in the ways in which they can report abusive chat and exclude anti-social players should they come across it.

And it is always a good idea to speak to your child about boundaries when using the Internet. We recommend a family (21) _____ where you can outline how much screen time is permitted a day. During holidays establish (22) _____ free zones at home. Encourage activity online outside of gaming during the holidays such as playing games together or creating an online scrapbook of holiday photographs and mementos to show your child how they can use the Internet for (23) _____ activities.

Task B

Drone Delivery

Admit it or not, laziness leads humanity to great inventions and discoveries. There is laziness behind (1) _____ and it drives innovations that improve productivity.

With the increase in online shopping comes an obvious increase in (2) _____ of goods. It's highly likely that at some point you buy something over the phone or on the Internet, and unlike buying something in (3) _____, it's a situation whereby you are (4) _____ physically face to face with the supplier. The goods will be delivered to you and can be collected by you in person or be kept in a closet waiting to be (5) _____.

A new delivery drone company plans to revolutionise the way we do (6) _____ by replacing your weekly trip to supermarkets with a tiny delivery robot which will bring your (7) _____ straight to your door. We are talking about a small six-wheeled self-driving, battery-powered (8) _____ or ground drone which can travel at 4mph for up to 30 minutes and can deliver the equivalent of three bags of shopping. They plan to achieve three (9) _____: zero cost, zero waiting time and zero environmental impact, in terms of local deliveries.

With its huge potential convenience coming into view, some customers still have (10) _____ over the widespread application of drone delivery. Some are afraid that people will try to steal the (11) _____ when they land. It might seem like drones can take up the planet earth as they can be wandering the streets and fully in sight at all times. Also, rules applied to both private and (12) _____ drones that they cannot be flown within 150 metres of any property and at least 50 metres from people. All these may (13) _____ the development of this new technology.

But, developers have all these issues in their minds and are doing their best gathering data to continue improving the (14) _____ of the systems and operations. Each robot has both 3G and GPS built-in which helps it travel safely around while an array of cameras and sensors will make sure it won't become the new nemesis of cyclists. To protect against (15) _____ the drones are locked during delivery and can then only be opened by the (16) _____ via the smartphone app. If someone does try to steal the drone then cameras located on its body can take pictures of the (17) _____. If it gets in trouble every drone can be remotely controlled by a central operator.

Amazon has also begun investing heavily in the arena of (18) _____, but in its case the company is building an aircraft which would launch from the depot and then land outside a customer's house. Amazon has successfully trialed its Prime Air drone delivery service in Cambridge, UK, by (19) _____ a TV streaming stick and bag of popcorn directly to the garden of a nearby customer. And eventually the company intends to roll out drone deliveries to (20) _____ across the world. When they do, they hope that deliveries will arrive in 30 minutes and dropped at people's houses. The breakthrough suggests that autonomous aerial delivery could become a viable business sooner than thought.

Try This:
Please retell this passage by referring to the first sentences of the paragraphs listed below. You may use English or Chinese, and you may also ask your partner to make comments on your performance.

1. Admit it or not, laziness leads humanity to great inventions and discoveries.

2. With the increase in online shopping comes an obvious increase in delivery of goods.

3. A new delivery drone company plans to revolutionise the way we do our shopping...

4. With its huge potential convenience coming into view, some customers still have worries...

5. But, developers have all these issues in their minds and are doing their best...

6. Amazon has also begun investing heavily in the arena of delivery drones...

Summary Interpreting

Skill Focus

Speech on Given PPT（PPT演讲）

PPT作为一种演示文稿图形程序，具有文稿和音乐视频的演示功能，可增强演讲的视听效果，已经成为公共演讲的重要组成部分。PPT演讲在现代社会交流、求职、商务场景中应用广泛，是现代人进行有效交流必备的知识与技能。在演讲中，PPT常常展现讲话人的讲话提纲和主旨，它也是口译实践中多见的需要口译的文本形式。

如果在会前拿到PPT材料，可以辅助译前准备；会议过程中，译员也可以通过观看PPT上的文字和图表，确认讲者的讲话内容。它可以减轻译员的记忆负担，有利于译语的产出。然而，大多数情况下PPT只是讲话人的演讲纲要，更多时候讲话人会说一些PPT上没有的内容。此外，PPT在展现讲话提纲和主旨的同时，还可能链接图片、动画、视频等材料用于辅助观众理解演讲。这样多模态的信息展现方式可以同时帮助译员理解讲话人的主旨，但实际上它是一把双刃剑，如果处理不好，则可能提升口译的难度，因为它在口译多任务认知活动上增添了新的任务，增加了译员的理解负担。这个时候，译员的精力要多分配出来给PPT，对其精力分配是极大的挑战。因此，在口译PPT演讲的过程中，译员需要注意以下几点。

1. 口译需要翻译的是讲话人的话语，在讲话人边展示PPT边演讲的过程中，译员在利用PPT及其辅助材料理解话语的同时，一定要专心听讲话人的话语，不能受PPT的影响而分心，误听或漏听讲话人的源语。

2. 讲话人可能事先将PPT提供给译员，而在会议现场又修改甚至替换了PPT。译员不能受事先提供的PPT的影响，会议开始之后不能再翻看之前的PPT或其他材料，要以现场的PPT为辅助材料，以讲话人现场的演讲为主，完成口译任务。

3. 听众对PPT演讲的理解很大程度上需要参考PPT的内容，因此在交替传译的过程中，译员应该尽量在讲话人翻到下一页PPT之前，完成当前页PPT内容的翻译。如果讲话人的一段讲话持续时间过长，涉及多页PPT的内容，译员可与讲话人沟通，并解释自己需要尽量完成当前PPT页面内容翻译的原因。

在口译训练中，PPT重组练习可以通过依次展现一场演讲的多张PPT，要求译员根据PPT的内容自行产出、添加并丰富讲话的内容。通过这样的练习，译员的语言灵活性、即兴演讲能力、主题敏感度和辨识能力都会得到提升。译员必须提升自己的公共演说能力，才能更好地理解讲话人的话语组织方式和脉络，最终在口译中更快跟上讲话人的思路，更好完成口译任务。

Guided Practice

Directions: Please organize a speech of your own based on the topic and the PPT pages given below. Then listen to the recording and take notes for each PPT page. You may compare your speech with what you hear. Try to interpret the recorded speech with the help of your notes, and ask your partner to comment on your performance.

🎧 **Task A**

Greener Hospital

Greener Hospitals and the Role of Health Care

_____

_____

_____

_____

_____

Our Aim and Partners

Accelerating the use of environmentally preferable products, practices and construction of green buildings in hospitals and medical practices worldwide

hospitals, healthcare leaders, hospital suppliers, green building vendors, universities and governmental entities

_____
_____
_____
_____
_____

Benefits of Becoming Green Hospitals

Long-term energy costs reduced
Pollutants reduced
Better patient outcomes
Better staff retention

_____
_____
_____
_____
_____

Elements for a Green Hospital

food, water use,waste, alternate energy,
green building design, energy efficiency
transportation in and around the hospital

choose an environmentally friendly site
utilize sustainable and efficient designs
use green building materials and products
think green during construction
keep the greening process going

_____
_____
_____
_____
_____

Our Environmental Priorities

Climate & Energy

Safer Chemicals

Sustainable Food

Waste Reduction

Water Conservation

_____
_____
_____
_____
_____

Why Clean Energy in Health Care?

- Sustainability is a health issue.
- Greenhouse gas emissions are a known contributor to climate change and the rise of pollution and disease.
- We are supporting renewable energy and creating solutions to environmental problems.

_____
_____
_____
_____
_____

Health Effects of Climate Change

Vector, Food & Water-Borne Disease	Heat Stress
Food & Water Shortages	Injuries from Extreme Weather
International Conflict	Respiratory Disease
Mental Health	

_____
_____
_____
_____
_____

Health Care Practices That Pollute the
Environment and Contribute to Disease

incineration of medical waste: dioxin/mercury
use of hazardous chemicals indoors: asthma
poor waste management
use of toxic chemicals
unhealthy food choices
reliance on polluting technologies

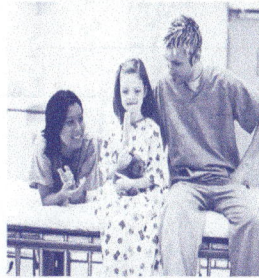

153

🎧 **Task B**

Co-working

Co-working — Creative Business Ecosystem

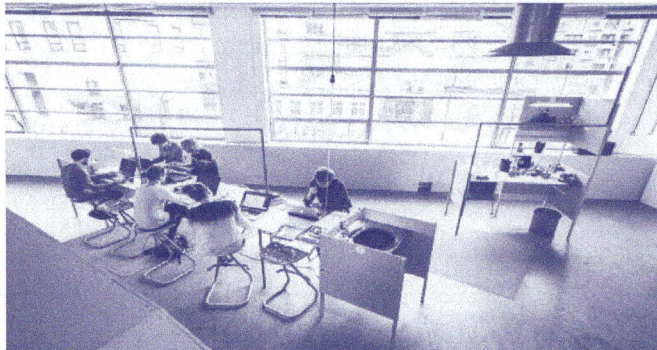

_____
_____
_____
_____
_____
_____

Globalization

Co-working

Co-living

Incubator

Creative communities

New economy innovation and
entrepreneurship

_____
_____
_____
_____
_____

Co-working

A style of work that involves a shared working environment, often an office, and independent activity

_____
_____
_____
_____
_____

Serviced office to Shared office

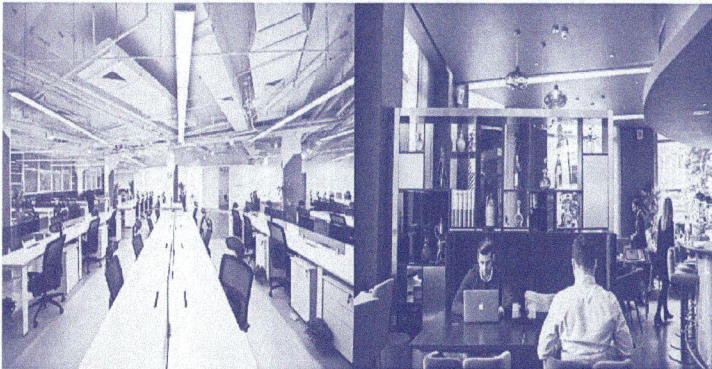

_____
_____
_____
_____
_____

Community-driven, community-managed
Working in the same place,
Working independently,
No isolation, No distraction

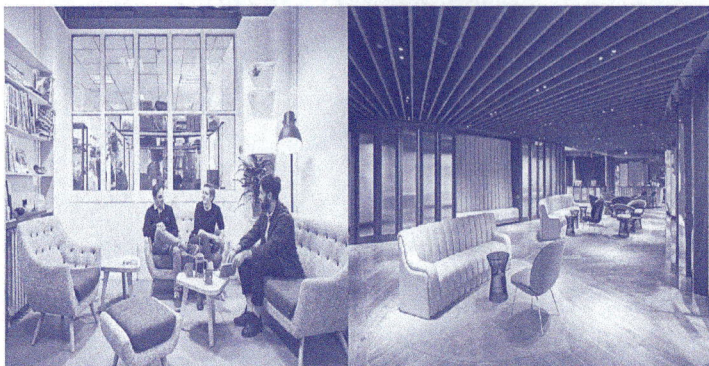

_____

_____

_____

_____

Do you notice the differences between the traditional
offices and the creative co-working offices?
Which place would you rather work?

Co-workers

20+, 30+
Two-thirds are men, one third are women:
Four in five with a university education.
Majority work in creative industries or new media.
More than half are freelancers.

_____

_____

_____

_____

_____

Started in US and Europe
Now: Asia and China

Hong Kong: dozens of co-working spaces
Shanghai & Beijing: hundreds of them!
e.g. WeWork in Shanghai
1000 seats in one location!

Entrepreneurship and small companies, freelancers
and creative workers.
3D printers, virtual reality, Internet and apps, the new
service industries.

_____
_____
_____
_____
_____

Co-working: a place and a community

**More importantly: a community
interaction in the community, events etc.**

**Government support: indigenous
economic development √**
Bigger brands: more locations √

_____
_____
_____
_____
_____

Co-working

Features
What can technologies do to us?
Life improvement but less work.

Information Link

Visualization in Interpreting（口译中的视觉化）

在了解口译中的视觉化之前，应该先了解什么是视觉化。视觉化指运用语言、图像、音乐等要素，努力激活受众的形象思维，使其头脑中呈现出视觉化的图像，多感官参与接收信息，从而达到提升传播效果的目的。将目标视觉化指把文字变成图像或者图像和文字并存，便于理解和记忆。这一理论主要基于人类的记忆能力，因为图像总是能给大脑一个更深刻、更具体的内容，比起单纯抽象的文字，图像更容易被大脑接收和记忆。人类的左脑主要负责语言、文字、数字、逻辑等，右脑则主要负责颜色、音乐、想象、感觉、直觉、图形等形象思维和创造。与左脑相比，右脑的信息储存容量更大。因此，我们应该更多地用右脑进行视觉和形象记忆。很多速记方法都是基于这种理论创造出来的。

人的记忆能力可以通过训练得到提升。口译中的视觉化指将抽象的、不熟悉的信息转化成为具体的、较熟悉的信息，或者将接收到的声音信号转化为图像，然后进行记忆。这有助于减轻译员的记忆负担。口译中的视觉化就是这种转化能力的一种体现，指的是将信息在脑海中转化为影像的能力。影像越生动越清晰，给大脑的冲击力就越强，我们记忆的效果就越好。口译中的视觉化记忆可以在信息输入阶段同步进行，并且可以持续一段时间，以保障译员可以顺利翻译完当下的语段。当然，只有针对具体的记忆任务进行积极分析及听辨练习，才可以提高口译中的视觉化记忆能力，练就"过耳不忘"的功力和本事。

IIIIIIIIIIIIIIIIIIIIIII **After-class Assignment** IIIIIIIIIIIIIIIIIIIIIIII

Directions: Practice anticipation while listening to the following passage. Pause after each sentence or paragraph, and try to anticipate the incoming sentence or paragraph, and then check whether your anticipation is close.

Ride Communal Bikes

Paragraph 1

A bike-sharing system is a service in which bikes are made available for shared use to individuals on a very short term basis. This scheme allows people to borrow a bike from point A and return it at point B. Many bike-sharing systems offer subscriptions that make the first 30 to 45 minutes of use either free or very inexpensive, which allows each bike to serve several users per day.

Paragraph 2

The central concept of the system is to provide free or affordable access to bikes for short-distance trips in an urban area as an alternative to motorised public transport or private vehicles, thereby reducing traffic congestion, noise, and air pollution.

Paragraph 3

The Internet of Things (IoT) has far reaching implications for our cities. One of which is reducing traffic congestion and gridlock by reducing barriers to cycling. Bike sharing offers a low-cost option for last-mile transit — the term that transportation experts use to describe travelling to/from a train or bus station in addition to short end-to-end commutes within urban areas. The concept of bike-sharing has been around since the 1960s, but early iterations struggled from problems including theft, vandalism, and clunky payment. The recent rise of the Internet of Things and advances in smartphone usage, telecommunications networks, and GPS systems have improved the logistics of bike sharing programs. This has made these programs more compelling for both municipalities and potential bike share riders, which has resulted in substantial growth in adoption and usage.

_____

_____

_____

Paragraph 4

Although users of such systems generally pay to use vehicles that they themselves do not own, sharing systems differ from traditional for-profit bike rental businesses. The first bike sharing projects were largely initiated by local community organisations, either as charitable projects intended for the disadvantaged, or to promote bicycles as a non-polluting form of transport, so that more people can leave their cars at home and switch to bikes instead.

_____

_____

_____

Paragraph 5

The bike-sharing system is a sustainable and affordable solution which means locals are able to pick up and ride the bikes around the city any time by downloading an app, finding one nearby and scanning a QR code. To complete their ride, users need only park their bike at any authorised bike parking area near their destination and manually close the lock on the bike. Most large-scale urban bike sharing programs utilise numerous bike check-out stations, and operate much like public transit systems, catering to tourists and visitors as well as local residents.

_____

_____

_____

Paragraph 6

Nowadays, the bike is designed with a series of high-tech features, such as unique smart-lock technology, built-in GPS connected to IoT network, and wireless technology for communication between the stations and a central server, which helps locate and monitor each bike. Solar-powered stations can make the whole scheme more environmentally-friendly.

_____

_____

_____

Paragraph 7

For the next generation of bike-sharing innovations, take a look at Copenhagen. Trains and a bike-sharing program working as one travel option now offer a GPS built into the bike. Not only do you know where to pick up your next connection — you have a schedule of all local train times between your front bars. The Europeans and Copenhageners increase a bike lover's convenience in transit with this new innovation. With an Android tablet offering a built-in GPS, real-time train departures and ticket integration, and real-time info on available bikes and docks in the area, one glides easily from destination to destination.

_____

_____

_____

Paragraph 8

In recent years, in an effort to reduce losses from theft and vandalism, many bike-sharing schemes now require a user to provide a monetary deposit or other security, or to become a paid subscriber. In many places, credit system is applied. If users leave bicycles unlocked or parked incorrectly, that is noted against them in the company's individual scoring system, with repeat offenders required to pay a steeper deposit. This credit system not only docks points based on bike-riding behaviour but also pulls in credit data from mobile payments provider to allow well-behaved customers to sign up deposit-free.

_____

_____

_____

Paragraph 9

But while the bike-sharing apps are convenient for users, the industry is giving many local governments daily headaches. Problems such as illegal parking remain unanswered, and some experts say that's largely because many cities were not designed to be bike-friendly. To address the problem of illegally parked and misplaced bikes, operators reward users who report them with app credits.

Paragraph 10

Cities are keen to implement dockless shared bikes because they really help relieve traffic congestion. However, experts warn that such schemes could soon be met with resistance from the automobile industry. Also, local governments had been slow in finding effective measures to address the problems caused by shared bikes and needed to make cities more bike-friendly if the industry was to succeed. Of course, a wide range of cycling support should be put in place, including cycle training, maintenance checks and guided bike tours.

扫码获取本单元音频资料

Unit 10

Extralinguistic Anticipation & Speech on Given Topic

An interpreter must adopt an attitude of intellectual modesty and willingness to learn, keeping up with changes in his or her languages as well as current events and the related jargon.

— James Nolan, experienced translator and interpreter of the UN,
author of *Interpretation: Techniques and Exercises*

Unit Goals

- To gain a general knowledge of how cognitive anticipation helps with the comprehension of the source language in interpreting.
- To become more flexible in summary interpreting based on given topics.
- To gain a general knowledge of self-monitoring in interpreting.

Warm Up

Task A

Directions: Listen to the following passage and fill in the blanks with words that you hear. Make sure the words you fill in are both grammatically and semantically acceptable.

Good morning, everyone, today, we'll continue our discussion on environmental protection. In this lecture we will focus on a hot issue — how to become a (1) _____ society. We hear it a lot in the news these days: "Recycle newspapers and save a tree. Collect bottles and cans so they can be reused in the manufacturing of new products." Protecting our delicate environment seems to be on the (2) _____ of politicians, government leaders, and citizens in many parts of the world to show support for Mother Nature. The concept of green consumerism has gained (3) _____ more and more over the last decade, and the public feels moved to pitch in and help. However, three essential keys needed to power this movement include a more (4) _____ public, the development of improved technology, and a greater demand for recycled materials.

The first step is to raise public awareness about the recycling process, to explain the kinds of materials that can be recycled, to provide ways on how to properly dispose of them and inform the public of the harm of the traditional waste disposal methods. So, what is the recycling process? Actually, recycling is what we do with the objects we use in our daily lives. It is ultimately a creative act that involves thought and dedication to (5) _____ the life and usefulness of something once it has been used. Common (6) _____ that are often used only once are plastic containers, glass bottles, and newspapers, but most of them can be recycled somehow, and it is only our (7) _____ and the ease of disposal that prevents us from recycling everything we dispose of.

(8) _____. Take paper-recycling for example. Local governments should educate the public on how to properly sort reusable materials from those, like waxed paper, carbon paper, plastic laminated material such as fast food wrappers, that can't be recycled very easily.

(9) _____. The public interest might be there, but soon may wane if there isn't a system where they can take these materials to be recycled. Sometimes we become complacent when it comes to recycling, but when you speak in terms of actual facts and figures that everyone can understand, people become more conscious of the problem. I remember reading one time that the energy saved from one recycled can provide enough power to operate a television for three hours. (10) _____ _____.

🎧 Task B

Directions: Listen to the following passage and decide whether the following statements are true (T) or false (F).

1. The goal is to get rid of AIDS by 2020.

2. Since 2010, the number of new born babies infected through mother-to-child transmission has dropped by a third.

3. Now over 18 million people have access to life-saving medicines.

4. At present, the overall situation is getting better but still severe.

5. The UN is committed to working with other organizations to find approaches to end AIDS, rather than working alone.

6. During the first decade, affected groups were so ashamed that they never spoke up or sought help.

Listening Comprehension

Skill Focus

Extralinguistic Anticipation（非语言预测）

上一章我们探讨了语言理解中的语言预测，特别是语言预测对口译听解及产出的重要作用。除了语言预测，非语言预测也在语言理解及口译听解中发挥重要作用。非语言预测指语言工具之外的场合预测和话题预测等。译员对源语相关背景知识的掌握，如会议类型、发言人背景身份、发言提纲、领域术语及发展态势等，都可以帮助译员进行合理预测。

为了更清楚地说明问题，我们将预测分为语言预测和非语言预测。实际上，成功的预测是语言预测和非语言预测共同发挥作用的结果，是多种因素和能力交互运作的复杂过程。预测在认知心理学、语言学等学科领域都是重要的研究课题，而其对口译的重要程度也是不可忽视的。译员需要同时提升语言敏感度和专业知识储备，加强语言预测和非语言预测能力，以更好完成口译任务。

口译中的非语言预测除了涉及场合和话题预测之外，还需要调用译员的世界知识和认知能力，是从上至下以及从下至上的复杂加工过程。有效的非语言预测更大程度上需要激活译员长时记忆中的知识系统，这样新信息的刺激才能与已有的相关知识联系起来，帮助译员完成对话语的理解。请看下面的例句，体会一下黑体字部分是否是可以预测的？

1. We've got a **cleaner** who **does a lot of the housework**, and that includes **doing my washing**. But I still have to **make my bed** and **do some of my ironing**, and I sometimes **do the shopping** with Mum.

2. As languages such as English, Spanish and Mandarin become more widely spoken, there is a fear that **many minority languages may die out**. Therefore, some countries have taken steps to **protect minority languages** by **promoting the usage of these languages**.

3. I have coffee and cereal for breakfast, then have a light **lunch**, maybe a sandwich and an apple, and a **snack** in the afternoon. We have our **main meal** in the evening. If Mum's late home

from work, she **doesn't bother to cook**; we just **get a takeaway** instead.

4. Some students go to university because they enjoy studying, others just **want a qualification**. No matter what, you have to get good grades in the entrance exams to **get a place at a university**. You can then study for **a degree** or **a certificate**.

5. Sometimes misunderstandings occur among **people from different cultures**, even **those who can communicate in a common language**. And these misunderstandings may even lead to **the breakdown of cross-cultural communications**.

6. Talking about the effect of the weather on our feelings, why do people say they feel more cheerful when the sun shines, and **miserable when it's raining**? Why do some people suffer from SAD (seasonal affective disorder), which makes them feel **depressed during long dark winters**? Can the weather really affect **our mood**, or is it **just in our imaginations**?

口译中的预测既需要对语言层面的相关规律进行分析和总结，又需要扩充知识储备。语言层面上的原语重复、同义语反复、上下义词的反复使用、相似表达的多次出现、语法结构的辅助、语用功能的达成等，都可以帮助我们甄别话语的信息框架，有效进行话语预测。相对比来说，世界知识即长时记忆的储备更加费时费力。语言预测和非语言预测能力同时提高，才可以保证译员更加有效地完成话语的理解和译出。

Guided Practice

Directions: Skim the paragraphs and fill in the blanks with words or phrases based on your anticipation. Listen to the recording and check whether your alternatives are close in meaning to what you hear.

Paragraph 1

Although there have been many important technological advances over the last decades, the advent of the Internet has probably had (1) _____ effect on everyday life. The Internet enables people to (2) _____ information than ever before. People can find every kinds of learning information on (3) _____ at (4) _____ and from (5) _____. It is also quite convenient for the (6) _____ suppliers to provide the educational resources and maintain them. This trend is accelerating as whole libraries are (7) _____ online. Moreover, with instant messaging and social networking, it is cheaper and more convenient to (8)_____ via (9) _____. Within the next decade, the

Internet will probably replace (10) _____ generation of telecommunication devices such as the telephone.

Paragraph 2

Supermarkets do a few things to make consumers spend more money. They put freshly baked goods such as bread, as they smell lovely, near the entrance to make us feel hungry, and (1) _____ spend more. They also rearrange things and put them (2) _____; this makes us spend more (3) _____ in the store and that means (4) _____. They put sweets and chocolate near the checkout, so it is (5) _____ to add bars of chocolate to our (6) _____ while we are (7) _____. And they put the most (8) _____ on the middle shelves where you are more likely to see them. Loyalty cards have their advantages, without a doubt. But deep down the store is probably benefiting (9) _____ than the loyalty card holder. But who can resist a discount or money off? So, while a loyalty card will give you (10)_____ the main reason a supermarket wants you to use it is so they can track your (11) _____ habits and learn (12) _____ about (13) _____. And be careful of special offers, for example, three for the price of two, buy one get one free. People often buy (14) _____ than they need and throw away (15) _____. So, every part of the supermarket from (16) _____ to (17) _____ is designed to make you spend (18) _____ and buy (19) _____ than you need. There's a reason your mother told you to make a grocery list and stick to it.

Paragraph 3

Economic recovery is going to take time as we are recovering from the longest and deepest recession in our living memory. Recession didn't happen overnight and won't (1)_____ that way, either. A full (2) _____ will take time after such a long (3) _____, but we are starting to see (4) _____ in the year ahead. Some challenges still remain and that's why we are sticking to our plan by creating (5) _____ and diversifying (6) _____. We will continue to protect the services that we depend on. What is welcome is that with recovery more jobs are created. We saw this week the largest increase of (7) _____ in one quarter since records began. We are seeing some signs because not only have we got (8) _____, but we are also (9) _____. So we are seeing some positive signs in terms of take-home pay. Other steps, such as providing students with (10) _____ and investing in new jobs in the (11) _____ sector, will also help the economy grow. But it's going to take time. We need to be (12) _____ and work through our long-term (13) _____ so that there is recovery that really lasts and (14) _____ everybody.

Paragraph 4

During the last (1) _____following the Opening-up and Reform in 1978, China as a country experienced (2) _____with an average (3) _____ reaching 9 percent. Along with such (4) _____, however, comes growing regional (5) _____, in particular a widening gap between (6) _____. While the coastal regions provided most of China's GDP growth, (7) _____ China were quickly outpaced, as they lacked both the openness and the infrastructure needed to adopt the model of (8) _____. (9) _____ was strategically better positioned to benefit from economic liberalization and opening up. These cities' coastal locations and commercial infrastructure made them (10) _____ for international trade. Consequently (11) _____ ____. Also the central parts of China (12) _____ ____ than the western parts. As a result, there have been growing disparities in regional living standards. Experts say that the growth disparities between (13) _____ _____ could be attributed to (14) _____ respectively. To close the gap between (15) _____, Chinese government has invested massively in (16) _____ that is much needed in those regions, first through its (17) "_____" plan, second with its post-2008 stimulus package, and now with the (18) "_____" initiative, a program aimed at reopening the historical (19) _____ that used to link Europe to China through (20) _____.

‖‖‖‖‖‖‖‖‖‖‖‖‖ **Summary Interpreting** ‖‖‖‖‖‖‖‖‖‖‖‖‖

Skill Focus

Speech on Given Topic（主题演讲）

在口译训练中，提高译员"说话的能力"至关重要。自然话语的生成大体需要经历四个阶段：第一，把意念转换成要传达的信息；第二，把信息形成言语计划；第三，执行言语计划；第四，自我监察。口译产出与自然话语的差异主要在于，前者的话语生成都要基于口译中的输入信息。但是，同样的输入信息经过不同译员的转换，会产生不同的译语效果。这就意味着，输入信息经由译员进行转变的过程结合译员的个人理解能力、世界知识、长时记忆、表达能力等多方面因素，成为译员的意念。因此，口译中译语的产出虽然基于源语，但势必借由译员的个人认知能力才能得以具化。口译中的话语产出能力是个人能力，是译员的必备素质。因此，我们要在口译训练中加大对口译学习者的话语产出能力的训练。

口译的源语往往是主题演讲。在口译训练中针对主题演讲进行思考和练习，就会让译员对口译中需要翻译的主题演讲有更多的了解，知道讲话人如何组织演讲，为什么会那样组织演讲，演讲主要想要表达的信息和意图是什么等。

言语是思想的外在表现形式，好的演讲往往具有明确的思想和鲜明的主题。因此，记忆讲稿内容，应该首先把握演讲的主题和中心思想，再找出各个部分意义的发展脉络，然后在此基础上记忆。比如，大多数演讲往往离不开提出问题、分析问题、解决问题三大步骤。从这个意义上说，把握文章的章法结构，可以有效地帮助记忆，也就可以进一步辅助译员高质量地完成口译。请看下面的例子。

Many species of plants and animals have come and gone throughout the history of the Earth. From this perspective, extinction can be seen as part of a natural process. Some people have argued that we should not, therefore, make efforts to preserve the natural habitats of endangered plants and animals. To what extent do you agree with this view?

Response 1

If you look at it that way, it's true that humans and animals have conflicting interests. People have always exploited animals for food and clothing, and farmers have brought bigger and bigger areas of land under cultivation. But should we keep on doing this? In regions of the world where the population is growing, and there aren't enough resources, the conflict between humans and animals is really bad. If you go to Africa, for example, you can see large nature reserves alongside really poor human settlements. I love the idea of elephants and lions living in the wild. But often it's the poor farmer living nearby who's got to pay the cost in terms of land and lost earnings.

Response 2

Looked at from a broad historical perspective, it is true that humans and animals have conflicting interests. People have always exploited animals for food and clothing, whilst farmers have brought ever-increasing areas of land under cultivation. Whether this process should continue is a question that requires careful consideration. In regions of the world where the population is growing, and resources are scarce, the conflict between humans and animals is particularly problematic. This can be seen in parts of Africa, for example, where large nature reserves sit alongside very poor human settlements. People living thousands of miles away may value the idea of elephants and lions living in the wild. However, often it is the poor farmer living nearby who must pay the cost in terms of land and lost earnings.

通过这个例子，我们可以更好地了解，不同的表层语言可以构建类似的话语结构，而后者是口译听解中最需要把握的因素。针对某类主题的演讲内容，先进行主题相关文本的输入之后，要求练习者针对某个主题自行设计内容，进行即兴演讲。这些主题可以包括：欢迎宴会、感谢致辞、介绍性主题、劝说类主题等。练习者自我组篇能力的发展可以提升其理解讲话人话语的能力。这样的练习还可以针对口译源语进行更深程度的信息处理。超前的逻辑推导会随着言语链的发布和接收得到印证，并为随后的信息分析提供更为可靠的语境和认知环境基础。译员对源语的信息处理程度越深，则理解越透彻，记忆越持久，因而表达也越完整、清晰和准确。

Guided Practice

Task A

Directions: Reorganize the following notes, if necessary, in a logical order and expand the notes into sentences, to make your own speech. You may ask your partner to comment on your performance or interpret your speech into Chinese.

Speech 1

Many of us don't know the best ways to look after our eyes. Could you share your ideas on this?

Eye care organizations and health professionals are joining together to promote the importance of eye health and the need for regular sight tests for all. Sight is the sense people fear losing the most. Fight for sight. Here are top tips for healthy eyes.

1. Have regular check-ups
2. Wear protective glasses
3. Take care of your contact lenses
4. Limit the use of digital devices

Speech 2

To what extent has information technology reduced social inequality? Give reasons for your answer and include any relevant examples from your own knowledge or experience.

People who live in highly developed countries often take access to information technology for granted. They find it hard to imagine a world in which this technology does not bring greater prosperity. However, as the IT revolution moves forward in some parts of the world, in other parts of the world the poor are falling further and further behind. Indeed there are many barriers to wider IT access and its potential benefits.

1. In some countries, fewer than 50% population able to read
2. Use of blocking software and firewalls common
3. Electricity supply irregular
4. Government censorship or Internet widespread
5. Even where IT access available, governments fearful of well-informed public
6. Broadband access only in major cities
7. Illiteracy a major obstacle
8. Basic infrastructure inadequate
9. Women and poor especially likely to be illiterate

Task B

Directions: Please share your ideas on the following topics. You may ask your partner to comment on your performance or interpret your speech into Chinese.

Speech 1

Should we return to natural methods of food production instead of having convenience food?

Speech 2

What influences our purchasing decisions? Do we mainly buy things because we need them, or are other factors involved?

Speech 3

As increasing number of unique and potentially useful plants and animals come under threat, people have a growing awareness of the importance of preserving the world's biological diversity. But how can this be done?

||||||||||||||||||||||||||||| Information Link |||||||||||||||||||||||||

Self-monitoring in Interpreting（口译中的自我监控）

自我监控是个体为了达到预定的目标，将自身正在进行的实践活动过程作为对象，不断地对其进行积极、自觉的计划、监察、评价、反馈、控制和调节的过程。人类的自我监控贯穿于人类的各种活动，是个体对自身活动的自我体验、自我观察、自我监督、自我控制和自我调节。自我监控具有几个特征：个体独立自主进行，建立在信息反馈的基础上，根据反馈实时进行调节，运用多领域知识和技能，对实践过程发挥重要及有效的指导作用。

母语或第二语言的产出涉及自我监控，主要目标是监控说话人传达的信息是否是想要传达的，说话人的信息组织是否正确得体等。口译中的自我监控比母语或二语产出中的自我监控更为复杂，贯穿口译过程中的源语理解、脱离源语语言外壳、并行加工、译语产出等多方面。

自我监控在交替传译和同声传译这两种主要的口译类型中都发挥着重要作用。交替传译中的自我监控在源语听解阶段可以体现在将听辨信息与长时记忆所存储的信息进行比对，对不同信息权重的衡量和取舍，听记和笔记的有效互动等方面；交替传译中的自我监控在译语产出阶段可以体现在信息回忆与产出的有效互动，产出语速的松弛有度，词汇及信息选择的有效性及修正频率等方面。同声传译中，源语听辨和译语产出同时进行，译员需要具备快速的双语转换能力，还需要掌握信息预测、调整、补足的技巧。可以说，同声传译是几乎不需要记笔记的"超短迷你交替传译"。同声传译的自我监控也涉及交替传译自我监控的诸多方面，但前者对译员控制能力的要求更高。

⊪⊪⊪⊪⊪⊪⊪⊪⊪⊪⊪ **After-class Assignment** ⊪⊪⊪⊪⊪⊪⊪⊪⊪⊪⊪

Directions: Practice anticipation while listening to the following passage. Pause after each sentence or paragraph, and try to anticipate the incoming sentence or paragraph, and then check whether your anticipation is close.

English as a National Foreign Language

Paragraph 1

India has two national languages for central administrative purposes: Hindi and English. Hindi is the national, official, and main link language of India. English is an associate official language. The Indian Constitution also officially approves twenty-two regional languages for official purposes.

_____

_____

_____

Paragraph 2

Dozens of distinctly different regional languages are spoken in India, which share many characteristics such as grammatical structure and vocabulary. Apart from these languages, Hindi is used for communication in India. The homeland of Hindi is mainly in the north of India, but it is spoken and widely understood in all urban centers of India. In the southern states of India, where people speak many different languages that are not much related to Hindi, there is more resistance to Hindi, which has allowed English to remain a lingua franca to a greater degree.

_____

_____

_____

Paragraph 3

Since the early 1600s, the English language has had a toehold on the Indian subcontinent, when the East India Company established settlements in Chennai, Kolkata, and Mumbai, formerly Madras, Calcutta, and Bombay respectively. The historical background of India is never far away from everyday usage of English. India has had a longer exposure to English than any other country which uses it as a second language, its distinctive words, idioms, grammar and rhetoric spreading gradually to affect all places, habits and culture.

_____

_____

_____

Paragraph 4

In India, English serves two purposes. First, it provides a linguistic tool for the administrative cohesiveness of the country, causing people who speak different languages to become united. Second, it serves as a language of wider communication, including a large variety of different people covering a vast area. It overlaps with local languages in certain spheres of influence and in public domains.

_____

_____

_____

Paragraph 5

Generally, English is used among Indians as a "link" language and it is the first language for many well-educated Indians. It is also the second language for many who speak more than one language in India. The English language is a tie that helps bind the many segments of our society together. Also, it is a linguistic bridge between the major countries of the world and India.

_____

_____

_____

Paragraph 6

English has special national status in India. It has a special place in the parliament, judiciary, broadcasting, journalism, and in the education system. One can see a Hindi-speaking teacher giving their students instructions during an educational tour about where to meet and when their bus would leave, but all in English. It means that the language permeates daily life. It is unavoidable and is always expected, especially in the cities.

Paragraph 7

The importance of the ability to speak or write English has recently increased significantly because English has become the de facto standard. Learning English language has become popular for business, commerce and cultural reasons and especially for Internet communications throughout the world. English is a language that has become a standard not because it has been approved by any "standards" organization but because it is widely used by many information and technology industries and recognized as being standard. The call centre phenomenon has stimulated a huge expansion of Internet-related activity, establishing the future of India as a cyber-technological super-power. Modern communications, videos, journals and newspapers on the Internet use English and have made "knowing English" indispensable.

Paragraph 8

The prevailing view seems to be that unless students learn English, they can only work in limited jobs. Those who do not have basic knowledge of English cannot obtain good quality jobs. They cannot communicate efficiently with others, and cannot have the benefit of India's rich social and cultural life. Men and women who cannot comprehend and interpret instructions in English, even if educated, are unemployable. They cannot help with their children's school homework every day or decide their revenue options of the future.

Paragraph 9

A positive attitude to English as a national language is essential to the integration of people into Indian society. There would appear to be virtually no disagreement in the community about the importance of English language skills. Using English you will become a citizen of the world almost naturally. English plays a dominant role in the media. It has been used as a medium for inter-state communication and broadcasting both before and since India's independence. India is, without a doubt, committed to English as a national language. The impact of English is not only continuing but increasing.

_____

_____

_____

扫码获取本单元音频资料

Unit 11

Information Density & Generalization

> The crucial starting point for the development of interpreting proficiency is bilingual skills, which imply a rudimentary ability to translate.
>
> — Franz Pöchhacker, translation and interpreting researcher,
> author of *Introducing Interpreting Studies*

Unit Goals

- To gain a general knowledge of how information density influences comprehension of the source language in interpreting.
- To become more flexible in summary interpreting by applying the tactic of generalization.
- To gain a general knowledge of the importance of the speed of language transfer in interpreting.

Warm Up

Directions: Listen to the following passages and fill in the blanks with words or sentences. Make sure the words and sentences you fill in are both grammatically and semantically acceptable.

Task A

This summit is a chance for APEC members to (1) _____ _____ and to (2) _____.

The central theme of the discussions this weekend was the need to encourage freer trade in the Asia-Pacific region. We know that increased economic cooperation has the potential to (3) _____, help create well-paying middle-class jobs and to increase prosperity. We must work together to break down (4) _____ and introduce (5) _____ that will fuel growth. This is especially important to the success of small - and medium-size enterprises, which could benefit from increased access to international markets in a number of key sectors like (6) _____.

But we know that creating an economic environment where businesses can (7) _____ just isn't enough. Economic growth can and must deliver positive results for everyone. The Government of Canada has made progress on three key areas to do just that.

First, it is agreed by all to work together to ensure that free trade agreements are fair for all parties. Canada intends to promote trade and investment abroad while fighting poverty using (8) _____. Experts from Canada and around the world will work with developing countries to ensure that trade agreements are (9) _____. These experts will be able to offer assistance to government representatives throughout the process, (10) _____.

Second, it is important to help workers seize business opportunities around the world. Canada and Peru have concluded a (11) _____ on social security between Canada and (12) _____. This agreement will make it easier to do business abroad by allowing workers to spend part of their careers in both countries and still (13) _____.

Third, we're (14) _____ to ensure that all citizens can be (15) _____ in building economies that benefit everyone, and that includes women, youth and (16) _____ groups. In partnership with UNICEF, Canada will invest nearly $20 million over seven years to make education more accessible to (17) _____ teenagers in Peru. This initiative will help young people acquire the skills they need for the jobs of the future. We will also help modernize Peru's public service to ensure that all citizens, including members of (18) _____, have better access to government services.

Directions: Skim the following questions first, and then answer the following questions with your own words.

Task B

1. What has carried us through every moment of our lives?

_____

_____

2. What does the speaker mean by "we can be whatever we dream"?

_____

_____

3. What do the ordinary working class people hope for?

_____

_____

4. That's the kind of hope that every single one of us need to be providing for our young people. In the text, who does "us" refer to?

_____

_____

ⅢⅢⅢⅢⅢⅢⅢⅢ Listening Comprehension ⅢⅢⅢⅢⅢⅢⅢⅢ

Skill Focus

Information Density（信息密度）

针对"输入变量"对口译质量的影响，研究者认为诸多"输入变量"会使口译任务变得困难。在对这些变量进行辨识和研究的过程中，与讲者特征和工作条件相关的因素包括输入速度、语调和背景噪声等，而与源语材料特征相关的因素包括信息密度、句法复杂度和词汇难度等。相对比来说，源语速度、语调和噪声等因素可以较容易地被监控和控制，而源语材料的内在因素却很难控制，因为它是由多方面因素决定的，而且评估语料难度具有较大的个人主观性。复杂的文本并不一定是较难翻译的，翻译起来是否困难取决于译者的翻译技巧、专业知识等多方面的因素。

信息密度最常见的衡量方式是话语的词汇密度。尤尔（Ure）最早提出话语词汇密度的概念。尤尔（Ure）计算词汇密度的方式是：实词数量与所有词数之间的比例。通过研究，她得出结论：口语话语中的词汇密度低于40%，而书面话语中的词汇密度高于40%。韩礼德（Halliday）则指出，词汇并不能单独表达信息，信息是被"打包"（pack）在语法结构中的。因此，他认为，更加精确的计算词汇密度的方式是看实词数量与小句之比，即每小句中的平均词汇信息的数量，并根据词汇项（实词）打包在语法结构中的紧密度来衡量话语的信息密度。韩礼德还对不同话语的词汇密度进行了宽泛的比较，同时指出，口语的词汇密度相对较小，比较典型的数量是每个小句中含有两个词汇；语言越正式，词汇密度越高。书面语的词汇密度高于口语的词汇密度，一般可以达到每个小句含有4~6个词汇；在科技文体书面话语中，词汇密度可以高达每个小句含有10~13个词汇。

研究者们早已发现了命题在信息密度判定中的重要作用。命题是最小的有意义的单元。话语的平均命题数可以作为其信息密度的一个衡量指标。学习分辨命题并以其为单位进行信息转换，对口译教学和实践都具有重要意义。口译中需要做到的不仅仅是转换源语字词的信息，更重要的是获取这些字词组合所表达的语义信息。言语的记忆主要采取以命题为单位的意义存储的方式。译员在记忆时对信息进行条块化处理，使之成为以命题为单位的意义模块，因为意义记忆比机械记忆的效果好。如果笔记不是分析理解后的内容提示，而是源语信息的字词翻译，译语表达将是相当困难的。

综上所述，对信息密度的判定可以遵循一些指标，但是口译源语的信息密度和难度还要综合考虑已知信息和新信息对信息听解的影响和辅助。下面我们比较以下段落，看看它们在信息密度上是否存在差异？对它们进行口译，难度上的差异如何？在应对高密度信息口译源语的时候，可以采用什么样的策略？

例1：Josh works for a company which produces furniture. He doesn't work in the factory where the furniture is produced, but in the offices across the road. His job involves quite of a lot of paperwork. He types letters to different companies, sends out invoices to customers and sends emails. He also has to arrange visits to other companies, make appointments for his boss, and sometimes he shows visitors round the factory. Occasionally he has to attend meetings with his boss, but one of Josh's most important tasks is to organise the office party every year. Josh is having a bad day today. The photocopier has broken down, the computer isn't working and the printer has run out of paper.

例2：One of the greatest obstacles to an approach to culturally adaptive user interfaces is the elusive nature of culture. In anthropology, culture has been described numerous times without substantiating an accepted definition, or generally assessing a common understanding of its concept. As a consequence, many anthropologists have turned towards understanding culture and how it is influenced by the dynamics of globalization. As technical innovations linked to mobility and telecommunications have led to international work cooperations, worldwide communication, and migration, these new dynamics have resulted in an interchange of people, ideas, and resources.

例2与例1篇幅相近，但是对比来看，例2的平均句长更长，句子总数更少，每个小句中实词数量更多，词汇难度更高，具备较高信息密度的特点。不考虑主题、语速等因素的话，例2的信息密度更高，其口译难度也就高于例1。在应对高密度口译源语的时候，译员除了可以进行译前准备，还应该在听解过程中集中理解命题之间的关系，以听懂为记忆的前提，防止出现为了在笔记上记下某个难词，而忽略信息层次的情况。

Guided Practice

🎧 Task A

Directions: Listen to the recording and check whether the written text is identical to the one read to you. Adjustments shall be made according to what you hear. Try to see how information density can affect the performance of the task.

Paragraph 1

Could we be cared for by robots? In Japan, for example, where 26% of the population is aged 75 years or older, scientists are developing a robot capable of treating patients out of beds. It's called Robear, and is designed to look like an approachable white bear. If tests are successful, it would do a job that would involve several. Also, an EU project is investigating ways technology can improve the day-to-night care of elderly people, the robot is designed in part to offer reminders for missions such as taking medicine. The care room which is being used in the experiments is taken as a smart home. There are more than 60 senses in the home, multi-directional cameras that can identify people, also various sensors, such as ones for water, attached to all the hot and cold water taps, so they know when someone is in the bathroom flushing the toilet. This all sounds like something out of a science fiction scenery but in the light of the carer crisis it may be a solution not worth considering. What do you think: are we ready for this solution? Can it solve our care problems?（19 errors）

_____

_____

_____

_____

Paragraph 2

Hunger is still one of the most urgent development risks, yet the world is producing enough food. Up to one third of all food is spoiled or squandered after it is consumed by people. It is an excess in an age where almost a million people go hungry, and represents a waste of the labour, and other inputs that went into producing that food. Food loss and food waste refer to the decrease of food in subsequent stages of the food intended for human assumption. Food is lost or wasted along the supply chain, from initial production down to final house consumption. The decrease may be accidental not intentional, but ultimately leads to more food available for all. This may be due to problems in harvesting, or market/price mechanisms, as well as institutional and legal works. Reducing food losses and waste is gathering increasing local interest and action. Governments, and consumers have all different ideas about the problem, the solutions, and the ability to change. The Save Food initiative is working with international organizations, and civil society to enable food systems to reduce food loss and waste in both the developing and the developed world. (19 errors)

_____

_____

_____

_____

Paragraph 3

There's a lot to consider when considering the pros and cons of farm-raised vs. wild-caught fish, from nutrition to sustainability. Everyone is trying to eat more fish these days. Eating at least two savings of fish or shellfish per week appears to increase the risk of heart disease, delay the offset of Alzheimer's. Although meat and fish are all good sources of protein, seafood boasts the healthy fatty acid profile: it's low in unsaturated fat and high in those omega-3 fats we hear so much about. When you get to the fish shop, should you buy wild-caught or farm-raised fish? Actually, the nutritional differences between wild and farmed fish are as great as you might imagine. Farmed and wild-caught rainbow trout, for example, are almost identifiable in terms of most nutrients. There are some major differences: wild-caught trout have more calcium and iron. Farm-raised trout have more vitamin A and selenium. But for the most part, they are neutrally equivalent. Also, are farm-raised fish higher in contaminants? The contamination that most people worry about with fish is mercury. The fish that present the biggest concern (swordfish, king mackerel, tilefish, shark, and tuna) are all farm-raised. The most common farm-raised fish (catfish, tilapia, and salmon) all have low mercury levels. Finally, there are concerns about environmental impact. However, these are just as likely to apply to wild as to farmed fish. Wild-caught fish are sometimes caught using practices that do a lot of collaborative damage to the system and other fish. Fish-farming practices, on the other hand, can pollute the water. Once again, it depends a lot on who is doing the fishing and/or farming. (23 errors)

_____
_____
_____
_____

Task B

Directions: Listen to the recording and while listening, take notes on important points. Complete the blank-filling task. Then you may try to interpret the gist into Chinese and ask your partner to comment on your performance.

Passage 1

Street Markets and Shopping Malls

There are places such as (1) _____ and (2) _____ where customers can go and do their shopping, and these two places are (3) _____.

The first noticeable difference between them is about their (4) _____. Street markets are open (5) _____. Shopping malls are (6) _____ centers mostly located in the suburbs of the city.

Another difference between street markets and shopping malls is the (7) _____ they offer. The goods in the shopping malls are (8) _____ but (9) _____ if anything goes wrong with what you buy. While in street markets, (10) _____.

Last but not least, street markets and shopping malls represent different parts of (11) _____. Some people enjoy the (12) _____ that they can get from the street markets, while others think shopping malls are more (13) _____. Both of them are well-established concepts, with even malls dating back to the period of (14) _____.

Passage 2

Time Measurement

The study of these devices is called (1) _____. (2) _____ has come a long way since ancient times. (3) _____ is the device where the position of the sun's shadow marked the hour. Daylight was divided into twelve "(4) _____", and they were longer in the summer and shorter in the winter.

The earliest sundial we know comes from (5) _____ and was made of (6) _____. Today, sundials are seen as (7) _____ pieces in many gardens. Sundials were used throughout the (8) _____ world, and with time, evolved to be able to take into account (9) _____ and (10) _____. This was a (11) _____ achievement.

An hourglass comprises two (12) _____ connected vertically. Factors that contribute to the ability of an hourglass to accurately measure time are (13) _____ , (14) _____ and (15) _____. Hourglasses may be reused by (16) _____ the bulbs once the upper bulb is empty.

An alarm clock is designed to (17) _____ an individual or group of individuals at specified time, and it was invented in (18) _____. An alarm clock can use (19) _____ to alert people. Alarm clocks are also found on (20) _____.

In the 11th century, the Chinese invented the first (21) _____ , and they makes a (22) _____ sound!

The most accurate timekeeping devices are (23) _____, and they are used to (24) _____ other timekeeping instruments. Atomic clocks around the world which measure (25) _____ are situated in over (26) _____ laboratories all over the world.

|||||||||||||||||||||||| Summary Interpreting ||||||||||||||||||||||||

Skill Focus

Generalization（归纳）

策略的使用在口译研究和实践中都是引人关注的话题，因为口译中策略的使用是口译过程的自然组成，有些策略甚至适用于大多数语言对和口译类型，是普遍的和共通的。口译中两种工作语言在结构和词汇等层面上存在差异，因此策略的使用成为必然。在口译教学中渗透口译策略使用的真实情况，观察其有效程度，反思其应该如何使用，可以帮助学生提升策略使用的意识和能力。

针对职业译员和口译学生的研究表明，职业译员在口译表现上技高一筹，具体体现在职业译员能更好地把握讲话人的意图，更快达成词汇、句法、语义选择，还可以对自己的产出进行有效的监控。而口译学生对上下文意思的脉络较难把握，往往将源语表达分块处理，并较少使用话语联系的工具。基于此，在口译训练中进行语义识别、脉络重构的练习，可以提升练习者的信息加工及产出质量，并辅助他们的交替传译或同声传译的学习。

例1：We know that, like South Africa, the United States had to overcome centuries of racial subjugation. As was true here, it took sacrifice — the sacrifice of countless people, known and unknown, to see the dawn of a new day.

归纳：We know that both our countries had to overcome racial subjugation. Sacrifices were made by many to bring that change about.

例2：And because he was not only a leader of a movement but a skillful politician, the Constitution for South Africa that emerged was worthy of this multiracial democracy, true to his vision of laws that protect minority as well as majority rights, and the precious freedoms of every South African.

归纳：Due to his skills as a political leader, he was able to negotiate a constitution which protects the rights of every South African.

例3：So, we gave the facilitator a chance, more time, to consult with the other interested parties, and, by the way, also to collect the necessary funds, because he did not have enough money. Because, we agreed to meet for 45 days, for the dialogue, but he did not have enough money to convene a dialogue for 45 days. So, he will have additional time to collect money, and also to consult with the other interested parties. That's when South Africa came up with the idea that: "Look, we will be ready to pay for food and accommodation. We can provide the facilities in South Africa. Let all the participants come to South Africa, and we'll pay for everything." So, I think in a month's time or so, we will be meeting in South Africa for dialogue per se.

归纳：So, we gave the facilitator another chance, more time, to seek the opinion of the other interested parties and also to collect the needed funds. Because when we decided to convene a 45-day dialogue, he did not have enough money to cover this period. South Africa expressed its readiness to host and cover the expenses of the dialogue, which will be convened in a month's time.

Guided Practice

🎧 Task A

Directions: Skim the passage and complete each gap with a suitable word for the chart below. Then try to generalize each paragraph. You may ask your partner to comment on your performance.

Brain Food

Three recent scientific studies suggest that your mother might have been right when she told you to eat your fish if you wanted to grow up brainy. The studies all suggest that (1) _____ performance is enhanced by the (2) _____ of the omega-3 fatty acids found in fish.

The smallest study looked at Dutch people aged between 50 and 70, over three years. It found that people with higher levels of omega-3 fatty acids tended to experience (3) _____ slower cognitive (4) _____.

Norwegian scientists studied more than 2,000 (5) _____ people and reached a similar conclusion: they found that those who ate more than 10 grams per day of fish did better in cognitive tests than those who ate less than 10 grams of fish per day. More fish gave even better results, the people with the best test scores were those who ate about 75 grams of fish per day.

The largest study looked at more than 2,400 people in New Zealand. It found a (6) _____ link between omega-3 fatty acids and mental health was less (7) _____, but the results were nevertheless in line with the other two studies.

These studies show that there could well be a link between the consumption of omega-3 fatty acids in fish and brain function, but further clinical (8) _____ are needed to (9) _____ for certain whether eating fish reduces the (10) _____ of age-related cognitive decline.

cognitive	compelling	consistent	consumption	decline
elderly	establish	markedly	prevalence	trials

Task B

Directions: Skim the passage and try to generalize each paragraph. You may ask your partner to comment on your performance.

Chilli peppers are used in cooking all over the world. How much do you know about them? Read this list and decide with a classmate whether the information is true or false.

1. Chillies are full of vitamin A.

2. Chillies can be grown indoors.

3. Chillies can help soothe a sore throat.

4. Chillies can take away headaches.

5. Chillies improve digestion.

6. There are more than 400 different types of chillies grown around the world.

7. There is a scientific scale for measuring the heat in chillies, the Scoville scale.

There are four sentences in the text you are going to read:

A. Chilli history   B. Chilli heat

C. Grow your own   D. Chilli health

In which of these sections do you think you will find each of the above statements?

A. Chilli history

Chilli peppers are eaten by a quarter of the earth's population every day, in countries all over the globe. They were completely unknown to most of the world until Christopher Columbus made his way to the New World in 1492. Chilli peppers come in all shapes, sizes and colours, from tiny, extremely hot chillies to large, mild ones. Indigenous to Central and South America and the West Indies, they have been cultivated there for nearly ten thousand years. Today, there are probably more than 400 different chillies grown in areas ranging from the Far East, China, Japan, Thailand, Indonesia and India to Mexico on the other side of the world. Some of the more commonly available fresh chillies include jalapeno, serrano, poblano, yellow wax and habanero.

B. Chilli heat

In 1912, Wilbur Scoville developed a method for measuring the strength of capsicums, or peppers, through simple tasting. Nowadays, this can be done more accurately with the help of computers, which rate the peppers in Scoville units. The fiery, hot, burning sensation of chillies is caused by capsaicin, a potent chemical that survives both cooking and freezing. However, apart from this burning sensation, it also triggers the brain to produce endorphins, natural painkillers that can relieve headaches. The Scoville scale begins at zero, with mild bell peppers, and then moves to the lower range of peppers measuring 1,500 to 2,500. The jalapeno chilli pepper is mild range, at about 2,500 to 5,000 Scoville units. Eight out of ten chillies are rated at about 30,000 to 50,000 units, while the habanero, which rates as one of the hottest, comes somewhere between 100,000 and 500,000 units. The hottest recorded chilli, Trinidad Scorpion Butch T, notched up an impressive at 1,463,700 Scoville heat units to break the world record for the hottest chilli in March 2011.

C. Grow your own

Chillies are easy to cultivate because they require a minimal growth area and little care. They will do best in warm climates with a long growing season, or under grass, and can be kept during winter in the right conditions. Many varieties make excellent pot plants and can be grown indoors, and these are still edible. For the best and hottest chillies, start sowing indoors as early as January — the hottest varieties often need the longest growing period.

D. Chilli health

Chillies are loaded with vitamin A, a potent antioxidant that boosts the immune system. As the chilli pods mature and darken, high quantities of vitamin C are gradually replaced with vitamin A and the capsaicin levels are at their highest. Due to these high levels, some people believe that eating chillies may have an extra thermal effect, improving digestion, speeding up the body metabolic rate and therefore burning off calories. It is a fact that we sweat in hot climates and we actually cool down as sweat evaporates. Over the years, people have claimed that eating chilli peppers has helped remove aches and pains as well as sore throats.

‖‖‖‖‖‖‖‖‖‖‖‖‖‖‖‖‖‖‖‖‖‖‖‖‖ Information Link ‖‖‖‖‖‖‖‖‖‖‖‖‖‖‖‖‖‖‖‖‖‖‖‖‖

Speed of Language Transition（语言转换速度）

在口译现场，译员要在巨大的压力之下迅速、及时、准确地做出反应。因此，口译对迅速理解源语要求极高，必须在短时间内抓住说话人的意图及中心思想，逐层梳理话语的层次结构，这样才能在口译时用简洁的语言表述准确的信息，使译语更加富有条理性、逻辑性和可理解度。在这个过程中，信息分析及听辨能力发挥着重要作用，还有一个因素也非常重要，但却常常被人忽视，那就是语言转换的速度。

经典言语产出模型主要由三个部分组成：概念形成器（conceptualizer）、构成器（formulator）和发音器（articulator）。对口译更加重要的是语言经过复杂的理解及产出的过程，最终以译语的语言形式出现。也就是说，口译中的概念在两种工作语言中的转换越快、越准，越能够辅助口译过程的多任务协调，保障口译质量。转码（transcoding）在其中起重要作用，指的是将源语中的字、词、短句在语言层面上转换成译语。甚至有研究者认为，转码速度和能力是职业译员的标志。工作记忆中的语音回路（phonological loop）可以在两秒之内存储语音及视觉信息，方便译员进行瞬时转换及传译。也就是说，译员快速地将输入信息进行转换，可以提升整体信息的理解和传译。我们在口译训练中加大语言转换速度的练习，可以有效提升口译的整体质量。

IIIIIIIIIIIIIIIIIIIIII **After-class Assignment** IIIIIIIIIIIIIIIIIIIIII

Directions: Listen to the following passage. Pause after each paragraph, and try to answer the multiple choice questions below. You may also try to generalize the main idea of each paragraph in English or Chinese.

Reality Television

Paragraph 1

Reality television is a genre of television programming which, it is claimed, presents unscripted dramatic or humorous situations, documents actual events, and features ordinary people rather than professional actors. It could be described as a form of artificial or "heightened" documentary. Although the genre has existed in some form or another since the early years of television, the current explosion of popularity dates from around 2000.

_____

_____

_____

Paragraph 2

Reality television covers a wide range of television programming formats, from game or quiz shows which resemble the frantic, often demeaning programmes produced in Japan in the 1980s and 1990s (a modern example is Gaki no tsukai), to surveillance or voyeurism focused productions such as Big Brother.

_____

_____

_____

Paragraph 3

Critics say that the term "reality television" is somewhat of a misnomer and that such shows frequently portray a modified and highly influenced form of reality, with participants put in exotic locations or abnormal situations, sometimes coached to act in certain ways by off-screen handlers, and with events on screen manipulated through editing and other post-production techniques.

_____

_____

_____

Paragraph 4

Part of reality television's appeal is due to its ability to place ordinary people in extraordinary situations. For example, on the ABC show, The Bachelor, an eligible male dates a dozen women simultaneously, travelling on extraordinary dates to scenic locales. Reality television also has the potential to turn its participants into national celebrities, outwardly in talent and performance programs such as Pop Idol, though frequently Survivor and Big Brother participants also reach some degree of celebrity.

_____

_____

_____

Paragraph 5

Some commentators have said that the name "reality television" is an inaccurate description for several styles of program included in the genre. In competition-based programs such as Big Brother and Survivor, and other special-living-environment shows like The Real World, the producers design the format of the show and control the day-to-day activities and the environment, creating a completely fabricated world in which the competition plays out. Producers specifically select the participants, and use carefully designed scenarios, challenges, events, and settings to encourage particular behaviours and conflicts. Mark Burnett, creator of Survivor and other reality shows, has agreed with this assessment, and avoids the word "reality" to describe his shows; he has said, "I tell good stories. It really is not reality TV. It really is unscripted drama."

_____

_____

_____

Multiple choice questions

1. In the first line, the writer says "it is claimed" because _____.

   A. they agree with the statement

   B. everyone agrees with the statement

   C. no one agrees with the statement

   D. they want to distance themselves from the statement

2. Reality television has _____.

   A. always been this popular

   B. has been popular since well before 2000

   C. has only been popular since 2000

   D. has been popular since approximately 2000

3. Japan _____.

   A. is the only place to produce demeaning TV shows

   B. has produced demeaning TV shows copied elsewhere

   C. produced Big Brother

   D. invented surveillance focused productions

4. People have criticised reality television because _____.

   A. it is demeaning

   B. it uses exotic locations

C. the name is inaccurate

D. it shows reality

5. Reality TV appeals to some because _____.

    A. it shows eligible males dating women

    B. it uses exotic locations

    C. it shows average people in exceptional circumstances

    D. it can turn ordinary people into celebrities

6. Pop Idol _____.

    A. turns all its participants into celebrities

    B. is more likely to turn its participants into celebrities than Big Brother

    C. is less likely to turn its participants into celebrities than Big Brother

    D. is a dating show

7. The term "reality television" is inaccurate _____.

    A. for all programs

    B. just for Big Brother and Survivor

    C. for talent and performance programs

    D. for special-living-environment programs

8. Producers choose the participants _____.

    A. on the ground of talent

    B. only for special-living-environment shows

    C. to create conflict among other things

    D. to make a fabricated world

9. Mark Burnett _____.

    A. was a participant on Survivor

    B. is a critic of reality TV

    C. thinks the term "reality television" is inaccurate

    D. writes the script for Survivor

10. Shows like Survivor _____.

    A. are definitely reality TV

    B. are scripted

    C. have good narratives

    D. are theatre

扫码获取本单元音频资料

Unit 12
Information Redundancy & Compression

Compression is a way to reduce or eliminate unwanted redundancy. Compression is useful because it reduces resources required to store and transmit data.

— Wikipedia, the free encyclopedia

Unit Goals

- To gain a general knowledge of how information redundancy influences the comprehension of the source language in interpreting.
- To become more flexible in summary interpreting by applying the tactic of compression.
- To gain a general knowledge of Décalage/EVS (Ear-voice Span) in interpreting.

Warm Up

Directions: Listen to the following passages and fill in the blanks with words or sentences. Make sure the words and sentences you fill in are both grammatically and semantically acceptable.

Task A

Two years ago, we gathered in London at (1) _____
_____. At that time, we had a growing awareness of the (2) _____
animal populations were facing. But we lacked a plan, the tools, and the partnerships needed
to confront it. Two years on, we come together again (3) _____.
And I think it is fair to say that London really was a turning point. Since then, we have seen
unprecedented partnerships all over the world. More than all this, we have seen how citizens
from around the world put pressure on political leaders to take action to (4) _____
_____.

Today, we are all here because we care about (5)_____
_____ and protecting the communities that rely on them and safeguard them. But we know that many others do not share our sense of urgency. In a difficult moment in time, many would ask why this issue (6) _____ priority and effort.

I firmly believe that halting the extinction crisis and ending the illegal wildlife trade presents a real chance to (7) _____ that we have the power to rise to the big problems of our time. If we cannot tackle this, it is hard to see how we will be effective in overcoming the other global challenges that face us.

Compared to other global problems, Illegal Wildlife Trade is (8) _____
_____ — almost everyone acknowledges the need to stop it, and everyone acknowledges that the extinction of our iconic species would be (9) _____. It is only a test of will.

And compared to other global problems, I really do believe it is (10) _____
_____ to solve. We know where the animals are that are being killed. We know through which ports, airports, and highways their products are being shipped (11) ___
_____. And we know which markets are (12) _____ for the entire trade.

We can win this battle. And in doing so, we can take a small, but very important step in reminding ourselves that we are capable of (13) _____ — a message that our young people need to hear loud and clear.

I thank you for the actions you will take to protect the (14) _____ we all want to pass onto to our children and grandchildren.

🎧 **Task B**

Throughout the centuries, few natural phenomena have (1) _____ as much scientific thought and artistic (2) _____ as clouds.

More than two millennia ago, Aristotle studied clouds and wrote a treatise addressing their role in the hydrological cycle. But it was Luke Howard, an (3) _____ meteorologist living in England in the early 19th century, who produced the first classification of clouds. Identifying, describing and naming clouds remains (4) _____ to the study of weather and climate.

Today, scientists understand that clouds play a vital role in (5) _____ the Earth's energy balance, climate and weather. They help to drive the water cycle and the entire climate system. Understanding clouds is essential for forecasting weather conditions, modelling the impacts of future climate change and predicting the (6) _____ of water resources.

The symbolism of clouds has inspired many artists around the world, including poets, musicians, photographers and other (7) _____. Clouds are also embedded in cultural symbols and habits of thought. In China, "(8) _____ clouds" represent the heavens and good luck. In some languages people say "she has her head in the clouds" to indicate somebody who is (9) _____ in fantastic dreams or ideas. In the modern world, "the cloud" now refers to that amorphous space that holds, not rain, but Internet resources and digitized data.

Understanding weather and climate phenomena to protect life and property and assist communities to become more (10) _____ is the core mission of World Meteorological Organization. We will continue to assist governments to provide the best possible weather, climate, hydrology, marine and environmental services to protect life and property and to support decision-making.

ⅢⅢⅢⅢⅢⅢⅢ Listening Comprehension ⅢⅢⅢⅢⅢⅢⅢ

Skill Focus

Information Redundancy（信息冗余）

美国数学家兼通讯工程师申农（Shannon）在20世纪中期创立了研究信息处理的理论——信息论（Information Theory）。冗余（Redundancy）是申农信息论的重要组成部分，指"信号中与信息内容无关的因素"。

冗余信息与有效信息并存于语言中，是语言的重要属性。冗余同时也是人类语言的一个重要特征，克鲁斯（Cruse）认为，语言中的冗余信息占50%。与现代语言相比，古语或文言文的冗余度较低。语言学中的冗余简言之就是多次重复的信息（information that is expressed more than once）。在语言学范畴内，冗余信息指并不增加信息内容，却有助于语言构建、达意和理解的信息。不同语言在语言结构和文化背景上存在巨大差异，冗余程度和标准不相同，冗余的表现方式也各具特点。这些因素决定了语言之间的转换是有难度的。

高度冗余的属性表现在语言中往往存在许多线索，可以帮助听话人理解讲话内容。由于口语实时发生，往往不能够重复听，这样就产生两种结果：其一，听话人加工话语的速度需要由说话人的话语产出决定，而往往后者是比较快的；其二，听话人不能回听，对刚刚听到的内容只能留下一定的记忆，通常还是并不完整的记忆。

对了解一门语言的听话人来说，由于对该门语言有一定的认识，对它的句法规律和冗余表达比较熟悉，因而往往可以对其进行语法甚至语用上的预测，这种预测能力可以用来衡量一个人对某种语言的掌握程度。口语表达转瞬即逝，听话人是否能够在有限的时间内迅速把握信息主干，是决定其能否理解源语的关键。如果能够基于源语的规律及特点对其进行预测，或者对其冗余部分进行快速甄别，记忆话语中的有效信息，则可大幅提升理解速度和程度。冗余最重要的功能是提升信息的可预见程度，降低他人理解信息的难度。请看下面这段英文。

Well, distinguished faculty, students, it is a pleasure to be *on any university campus*, but to be *on a university site* with so many students in such a large university is indeed a pleasure. Today I want to briefly talk about the world as a whole and then come down and talk a little bit about China, and then a little bit about university and then a little bit about you as students and what you might expect going forward.

这段英文比较容易理解，因为冗余信息较多。在此段中体现出来的是同义语反复比较多，听者有足够时间消化理解重要信息。请看上段中标注的部分：下划线的两个部分是一对同义语反复；斜体的两个部分是一对同义语反复；灰色的四个部分都是同义语反复。也就是说，这些标注的地方虽然重复了多遍，但只要理解一次就够了，需要特别注意的仅仅是其他不一样的部分，也就是新信息部分。如果上段同样的意思以下面这种方式说出来，冗余程度就会大大降低。

Well, distinguished faculty, students, it's a pleasure to be on a university site with so many students. Today I want to talk about the world, China, university and you as students and what you might expect going forward.

我们发现，这段的篇幅缩短了一半，信息更加集中，也就是信息的密度上升了，理解和记忆的难度也随之上升。正是因为信息往往具有不同程度的冗余，因此需要我们在听解的过程中尽快判断哪些部分是冗余的。如果浪费了很长时间去听冗余信息，而忽略了非冗余信息，那就得不偿失了。另外，对冗余信息，我们也可以根据口译场景的情况和需要，在译语中相应地缩减，以提升口译效率。

Guided Practice

Task A

Directions: While listening to the following passages, take down important words or phrases by overlooking redundant information. Some words or initials of words are given below. You may try to rebuild the passage with the help of the gist below, in English or Chinese, and ask your partner to comment on your performance.

Passage 1

Working in Austria

Working in Austria: (1) d_____ to working in the UK.

Commute

Austria: (2) w_____ / (3) c_____; days a lot (4) l_____.
London: long cycling or on (5) t_____; days and evenings are (6) s_____.

Attitude toward work

Italian: "(7) w_____" attitude.
German: "(8) l_____" attitude.
Austria: (9) in-_____ mix.

Passage 2

Weddings in India

Weddings in India: like a (1) c_____, with people coming and staying for (2) d_____.
Most of the weddings are (3) a_____.
Weddings ceremonies are different depending on the (4) r_____, but always have (5) c_____, like music, dance, and meals.
Rich families: (6) l_____, with big (7) w_____.
Rich or poor: spending more (8) m_____ than people can afford.

🎧 **Task B**

Directions: While listening to the following passages, take down important words or phrases by overlooking redundant information, and then sum up the key ideas of the passage and put them down in the corresponding blanks.

Passage 1

Family Relations

Living with parents?

UK: (1) _____.

Saudi Arabia: (2) _____.

Elderlies?

UK: (3) _____.

Saudi Arabia: (4) _____.

Passage 2

Fishing Nets to Carpets

Our organization: (1) _____.

The project we run in the Philippines is called (2) _____, and its objective is: (3) _____.

Both fishing nets and carpets use (4) _____, a form of high grade (5) _____.

When fishing nets are damaged, they are (6) _____, which leads to (7) _____ because it takes up to (8) _____ years before fishing nets degrade and they catch and ensnare (9) _____.

Our project is successful because it is (10) _____.

Fishing nets are (11) _____ from fishermen and sent to (12) _____, where there's the only (13) _____.

Summary Interpreting

Skill Focus

Compression（缩减）

　　口译过程中理解、记忆、转换几乎同时发生，记忆压力可能随着各种因素的发生而加大，记忆负载过重就会出现信息缺失。人类的语言虽然千差万别，但只是表层结构不同。在深层结构上，各种语言之间是相似的。在口译听解过程中，译员需要把握信息的推导及展开，需要知道具体字词句只是用来为信息传达服务的。在口译听解的有限时间内，对信息进行有效梳理、整合，并根据口译现场的需要进行合理产出，是译员需要具备的能力。

　　信息缩减练习可以训练译员提炼主要信息的能力，提升处理口译信息的灵活度，进而有效提升其口译水平。学生译员可以尝试计时缩减练习，这个练习由教师准备母语或外语语段，首先计算匀速阅读这些语段所需时间，在这个时间的基础上对用时进行缩减，缩减程度由学生程度和难度要求来定。比如，在正常阅读时间的三分之二的时间之内，要求学生在有准备或无准备的情况下，对该语段进行缩减，可以采用同语或译语依次进行尝试。这个练习训练学生边产出边辨识冗余信息并留取主要信息的能力，同时要求学生保持语言产出的连贯性和流利度。请看下面的例子。

Make sure you are always prepared for any kind of extreme weather prior to it occurring. You can do this by checking the weather forecast regularly. Heat waves can often be predicted days and even weeks in advance. Heat waves are simultaneously seen as fun, a chance to get outside in the sun, and a hazard, which can cause illness. Make sure you drink plenty of water during this time, otherwise you may become dehydrated. When you feel hot, try to find some shade. It is also important to watch for signs of heatstroke. A person may initially become slow and lethargic, and then become confused or incoherent. If you see these second symptoms, get the person into the shade immediately and give them ambulance. If left untreated, heatstroke can ultimately lead to death.

　　缩减的版本如下所示。

We should be prepared for extreme weather like heat wave, which usually can be predicted in advance. Not just fun, heat wave can be a hazard which causes dehydration, heatstroke, or even death. So make sure you drink a lot of water, find a shade and watch for signs of heatstroke.

我们注意到，缩减的版本可能是对源语概念及逻辑上的整理和整合，需要更快更有效的信息分级、提炼及重组的能力。在这个过程中，我们可以格外关注以下几个因素。

1. 重复信息的整合

口译源语转瞬即逝，讲话人为了有效传递信息，往往会对特别需要传达的信息进行多种形式的提及和说明。这里需要注意的是，重复信息有时候并不一定是一模一样的信息，可能是同样信息的不同方式的表达和处理。讲话人的这些尝试无疑有助于译员理解源语信息，而译员在口译理解过程中可以对重复信息进行整合，关注新信息，并在缩减练习中对重复信息进行重组。

<u>Interpretations are different people's versions of the past.</u> They could be written in history books, turned into documentaries about the past, or even made into fictionalised accounts through novels and films. <u>Different people often give very different interpretations of the same event or person in history</u> — it depends which evidence they choose to use and find important. For example, one historian might call the Black Death a "disaster", while another might see it as a "turning point in the power of the peasantry".

本段中，画线的两个句子主要意思非常接近，后句是前句的解释性重复。因此，我们可以在缩减练习中将其调整为下面的版本。

Different people may have different interpretations of the past, in history books, documentaries, or fictionalised accounts, by using different historical evidence. For example, the Black Death can be seen as a "disaster" or "turning point in the power of the peasantry" by different historians.

2. 同类信息的整合

同类信息指在不增加新信息的情况下，源语中使用的发挥同样作用的信息。比如，意思接近的一连串的形容词，组成接近的一连串的平行结构，说明问题的多种解释方法，说明问题的具体事例等。遇到类似的同类信息，我们就可以对其进行整合。下面我们看一个例子。

Today we are going to talk about English and it has lots of words. *The Collins English Dictionary* includes around 260,000 words! What is worth mentioning is that many of these words come from other languages. We call these "loanwords" or "borrowings", which are derived from other languages. <u>An example is "coffee" which comes from Arabic. Another example is "pyjamas", which comes from Hindi. We also have "pizza" from Italian, and some</u>

sports words like "karate"and "kung fu" are borrowed from Japanese and Chinese respectively.

本段举例部分的形式比较分散，可以进行信息整合使之变得更加简洁易懂。缩减后的版本如下所示。

English has a lot of words and *The Collins English Dictionary* includes around 260,000 words. Called "loanwords", many English words are called "loanwords" as they are borrowed from other languages. Examples are "coffee" from Arabic, "pyjamas" from Hindi, "pizza" from Italian, "karate" from Japanese, "kung fu" from Chinese and many others.

一个更加简略并突出主干信息的版本如下所示。

English has a lot of words and many of them are borrowed from other languages. Examples are "coffee" from Arabic, "pyjamas" from Hindi, "pizza" from Italian, "karate" from Japanese, "kung fu" from Chinese and many others.

3．逻辑的整合

口译源语往往为未加修饰的口语化内容，讲话人随时都会对话语进行调整，这就需要译员不但要注意分析源语的意义，还要注意挖掘源语的逻辑线索，这样才能在口译产出中对源语不同级别的信息进行有效传递。下面我们看一个例子。

China and U.S. should work together to avoid the kind of mistakes that the U.S. made in the past. I will give you one example. Back in the early 1970s, when the price of oil shot up, and the cost of gasoline shot up, individuals and governments under President Carter, and President Ford before him, tried to impose conservation measures, and tried to encourage the development of higher gas mileage cars, and more energy efficiency. In the early 1980s, the price of gasoline went down. So everybody in America said, "Oh, well, we don't have to worry about that any more, and we don't have to have gas-efficient cars, we can continue to have very inefficient cars." And it was a mistake. It set us back. Now, if you compare what our entire country did with what one state did, California kept pushing energy conservation. California tried to push higher gas mileage cars. And, today, California still has a lower-per-capita use of electricity because of efficiency measures than the rest of the United States. So, we made a mistake. People thought, "Oh, we don't have to worry about it any more." We know we have to worry and continue to make our own changes.

请注意画线部分的信息，在整合这些信息的同时，整段话的逻辑还可以更加清晰。缩减后的版本如下所示。

China and U.S. should work together to avoid the mistakes that the U.S. made in the past.

Back in the 1970s, the price of oil shot up, and individuals and governments of Carter and Ford tried conservation measures like using energy efficient cars. In the 1980s, the price of oil went down. So people in America mistakenly thought that they didn't have to use gas-efficient cars. But the state of California kept pushing energy conservation. And, today, California still has a lower-per-capita use of electricity. So, we made a mistake, and we should learn a lesson from it and continue to make changes.

Guided Practice

Task A

Directions: Within a pair of two students, one reads the paragraph and the other compresses the same paragraph. You may take turns and compare your performance.

Paragraph 1

The government says that the GDP target will be set around 7.5% this year. Can we achieve the target? Actually, economy is a very complex thing. Nobody can predict what the growth rate is going to be this year. You could ask 100 greatest economists in the world, and they would have estimates all over the place. So, it doesn't make sense to create expectations that the growth rate will be exactly 7.5%. It could end up being more than 8, or less than 7. Given all the difficulties that exist at the present time, it's possible that more bad news will come out during the year, and there will be some undershooting of the target. But, as I said, the world is a complex place and some things might tip in favor of the country and it might come out higher. There are more forces acting that cannot be predicted, or cannot be identified.

_____

_____

_____

_____

Paragraph 2

The world is about to stabilize its population maybe around 9 billion or more than 9 billion. Today, there are 7 billion. Today, we already produce food for about 9 billion. But about one third is wasted, lost, rotten, because of lack of infrastructure, because of lack of facilities, because of lack of transportation, because of lack of cold chains, you know, you have certain products when you need to lower the temperature in order to maintain the product, until it goes from the production site, all the way through good highways, or good railways, to the port, and then you have the good infrastructure to get them on the ship, and to take it to wherever it is going, or simply to next city, where it can be consumed. And sometimes you have a lot of bureaucracy. Things are stuck in the middle. And they are stuck there for days, for weeks, in a warehouse, in a customs. So you have waste.

_____

_____

_____

_____

Paragraph 3

I've been saying for a long time that as the wealth of the Chinese rises, workers are going to demand higher wages. If they don't receive higher wages, some of them will quit, some of them will retire, some of them will move away. And there are some organized labor activities also at work pushing up wages. This has been going on for at least a couple of years. I would guess, and I feel pretty sure that there will continue to be a push of wages up to a somewhat higher level. Of course, at some point, employers are going to resist and already many employers are automating the work process, the production process. And these modern methods of production will also raise income per worker. China has been losing its low-cost labor advantage and it will continue to lose it, until some sort of equilibrium is established, in which employers can push down on wages as hard as the workers are pushing wages up.

_____

_____

_____

_____

Paragraph 4

What is the main difference between British and American English? First, I would like to get this out of the way. Canadians and Americans sound pretty much the same. It's hard for us to tell the difference, even native English speakers, just a couple of tell-tale signs. So, I guess,

North Americans, unlike UK English, and again, there's a lot of accents and dialects, you know, it all depends, but for me, the easiest way is Americans enunciate every word. We are very loud. We open our mouth a lot. For me, a dead give-away is that "end R". You can also listen for vowel sounds and try to guess based on that. Actually, apart from British English and American English, there is also Australian English. There is Scottish English. There is Irish English. And there are so many English-speaking dialects. Honestly, sometimes it's hard for us to understand. For people from relatively the same part of a region, they may have the same speaking style.

_____

_____

_____

_____

🎧 Task B

Directions: Please sight interpret the following passage, one paragraph after another. Then write the compressed version of each paragraph below. You may interpret to your partner first and then he/she comments on your performance. You may also compare your compression with that of your partner's.

Family Structure

We are all familiar with the nuclear family, which has been the dominant family structure in the UK for the last sixty years at least. However, recent changes show that our idea of the traditional nuclear family as the cornerstone of British family life is changing. There have been emerging patterns which are eroding this structure: namely, the rise of step-families, lone-parenting, and the rapid increase in those living alone. We are going to explore these areas in turn, and look at their effect in terms of the family.

_____

_____

_____

_____

Firstly, step-families are becoming more and more common. Step-families are created when one or both partners have a child or children from a previous relationship. In 1980, the percentage of children under thirteen who were living with one parent and their new partner was just four percent. In 2008, this figure had increased to twenty percent. The USA has seen an even greater rise; new statistics show that almost half of under thirteen are living in a step-family. Now, we can still call the step-family structure a "nuclear" family, as it does follow the structure of two parents, and dependent children. However, it also creates somewhat of a nuclear "blur". Step-brothers and sisters may belong to two family units, so where do we draw the line at which family they belong to?

_____

_____

_____

_____

Lone-parenting is a relatively recent family structure which has rapidly grown in the last half century. In 1972, only one in fourteen children lived in a lone-parent family. When we compare this with today's figure of one in four, we can see that this is a rapid increase. In the past, lone-parenthood was overwhelmingly the result of a death of a parent. Nowadays however, it is increasingly a choice. Some sociologists argue that this increase is due to the outlook of women. Where women once were willing to accept an unhappy or abusive marriage, now many will choose lone-parenthood. This view of women's attitudes and lone parenting is highly debated because some figures show that the largest group of lone parents are mothers who have never married.

_____

_____

_____

_____

Lastly, an increasing number of people are choosing to live alone. The number of people living alone in Britain has more than doubled in the last twenty years. In 1990, just over four million people lived alone. Now this figure has reached 8.5 million, an incredibly rapid growth which has had enormous effects on the traditional nuclear family. This number represents a great chunk of the population who either by choice or necessity, are outside the traditional family unit. People are marrying later, having fewer children, divorcing at higher rates and living longer, all of which add up to this: At some point, many will find themselves living alone, perhaps temporarily.

_____

_____

_____

_____

_____

‖‖‖‖‖‖‖‖‖‖‖‖‖‖‖‖‖‖‖‖‖‖ Information Link ‖‖‖‖‖‖‖‖‖‖‖‖‖‖‖‖‖‖‖‖

Décalage/EVS（Ear-voice Span）（时滞/听说时差）

"时滞"，也称"听说时差"，最早用于同声传译的研究，指的是信息"输入"和"输出"之间的时间差，也就是在信息输入和信息输出之间的信息处理的时间。

同声传译听说时差的研究表明，同声传译中的听说时差基本处于0.5秒至11秒之间，平均在2秒至4秒之间，不同译员会有不同的听说时差。听说时差很难用统一的时间一概而论，这取决于讲话人使用的语法和句法结构、演讲速度、源语言、目标语言等因素，因此需要灵活调整。

听说时差这一现象很难具体规范，太短了听不全大意，太长了跟不上源语。听说时差在同声传译中的研究由来已久，交替传译中的听说时差研究虽然相对落后，但也有了一定的突破。听说时差在交替传译中指的是听到信息项目与笔记记录该项目之间的时间差。针对交替传译听说时差的研究表明，听说时差一旦达到7秒及以上，译员就会出现较多的信息缺失。研究同时发现，职业译员的听说时差上限高于新手译员，且前者有能力在听说时差达到极限之前省略不重要或不熟悉的信息，以保证译语更加顺畅的产出。

听说时差体现的是译员有效理解一个信息单元所需输入的信息总量，当然这个总量是从时间的角度对其单元大小进行衡量。听说时差范围越大，越说明译员在听说时差范围内具备更大的灵活性和调节空间。听说时差的灵活运用体现出较高的口译训练程度和效果。听说时差的数据可以显现译员的认知过程，探知译员需要获取多少信息才可以开始信息转换，有助于针对信息组块及信息单位展开研究，对口译认知过程的研究具有一定的意义。

IIIIIIIIIIIIIIIIIIIIIIIII **After-class Assignment** IIIIIIIIIIIIIIIIIIIIIIIIIII

Directions: Listen to the following passage. Pause after each paragraph, and try to summarize the main idea of that paragraph. Then try to answer the T/F questions below.

The Hardest Language

Paragraph 1

People often ask which is the most difficult language to learn, and it is not easy to answer because there are many factors to take into consideration. Firstly, in a first language the differences are unimportant as people learn their mother tongue naturally, so the question of how hard a language is to learn is only relevant when learning a second language.

_____

_____

_____

Paragraph 2

A native speaker of Spanish, for example, will find Portuguese much easier to learn than a native speaker of Chinese, for example, because Portuguese is very similar to Spanish, while Chinese is very different, so first language can affect learning a second language. The greater the differences between the second language and our first, the harder it will be for most people to learn. Many people answer that Chinese is the hardest language to learn, possibly influenced by the thought of learning the Chinese writing system, and the pronunciation of Chinese does appear to be very difficult for many foreign learners. However, for Japanese speakers, who already use Chinese characters in their own language, learning writing will be less difficult than for speakers of languages using the Roman alphabet.

_____

_____

_____

Paragraph 3

Some people seem to learn languages readily, while others find it very difficult. Teachers and the circumstances in which the language is learned also play an important role, as well as each learner's motivation for learning. If people learn a language because they need to use it professionally, they often learn it faster than people studying a language that has no direct use in their day to day life.

_____

_____

_____

Paragraph 4

Apparently, British diplomats and other embassy staff have found that the second hardest language is Japanese, which will probably come as no surprise to many, but the language that they have found to be the most problematic is Hungarian, which has 35 cases (forms of a noun according to whether it is subject, object, genitive, etc). This does not mean that Hungarian is the hardest language to learn for everyone, but it causes British diplomatic personnel, who are generally used to learning languages, the most difficulty. However, Tabassaran, a Caucasian language has 48 cases, so it might cause more difficulty if British diplomats had to learn it.

_____

_____

_____

Paragraph 5

Different cultures and individuals from those cultures will find different languages more difficult. In the case of Hungarian for British learners, it is not a question of the writing system, which uses a similar alphabet, but the grammatical complexity, though native speakers of related languages may find it easier, while struggling with languages that the British find relatively easy.

_____

_____

_____

Paragraph 6

No language is easy to learn well, though languages which are related to our first language are easier. Learning a completely different writing system is a huge challenge, but that does not necessarily make a language more difficult than another. In the end, it is impossible to say that there is one language that is the most difficult language in the world.

_____

_____

_____

T/F Questions

1. (T/F) The question of how hard a language is to learn is relevant to both first and second language acquisition.

2. (T/F) Portuguese is definitely easier than Chinese.

3. (T/F) A Japanese speaker may well find the Chinese writing system easier than a speaker of a European language.

4. (T/F) The Hungarian alphabet causes problems for British speakers.

5. (T/F) Hungarian is the hardest language in the world.

6. (T/F) Hungarian has as many cases as Tabassaran.

7. (T/F) Many British diplomats learn Tabassaran.

8. (T/F) The writer thinks that learning new writing systems is easy.

扫码获取本单元音频资料

Unit

13 Memory Training I & Paraphrasing

> The existence of forgetfulness has never been proved. All we know is that recollection may not be within our power. Up to the present we have filled that gap in our power with the word "forget", just as if it were another addition to our list of faculties.
>
> — Friedrich Nietzsche, German philosopher

Unit Goals

- To gain a general knowledge of how memory can be trained in interpreting.
- To become more flexible in summary interpreting by applying the tactic of paraphrasing.
- To gain a general knowledge of type of memory and forgetting curve.

Warm Up

Directions: Listen to the following passages and fill in the blanks with words or sentences. Make sure the words and sentences you fill in are both grammatically and semantically acceptable.

Task A

Parental Leave

American women are currently entitled to (1) _____.
American men are entitled to nothing. That information landed differently for me — when one week after my son's birth, I could barely walk. That information landed differently when I was getting to know a human who was completely (2) _____ my husband and I for everything, when I was dependent on my husband for most things, and when we were relearning everything we thought we knew about our family and our relationship. It landed differently.

Somehow, we and every American parent were expected to be (3) "_____" in under three months. Without income? I remember thinking to myself, "If the (4) _____ of pregnancy is another mouth to feed in your home, and America is a country where most people are living paycheck to paycheck, how does 12 weeks unpaid leave economically work?"

The truth is: for too many people, it doesn't. (5) _____ American women go back to work two weeks after giving birth because they (6) _____ take any more time off than that. That is 25 percent of American women. Equally disturbing, women who can afford to take the full 12 weeks often don't, because it will mean incurring a "(7) _____" — meaning they will be perceived as less dedicated to their job and will be passed over for promotions and other career (8) _____. In my own household, my mother had to choose between a career and raising three children, a choice that left her (9) _____ as a homemaker, because there just wasn't support for both paths. The memory of being with my dad is a particularly meaningful one since he was the (10) _____ in our house, and my time with him was always limited by how much he had to work and how much time he could spare. And we were an incredibly (11) _____ family — our hardships were the dreams of other family's.

The deeper into the issue of paid parental leave I go, the clearer I see this: (12) _____
_____.

Task B

Joblessness

Joblessness is far more than an economic misfortune. It can be a (1) _____ for the unemployed and their families. It can cause illness, divide families and create a downward spiral of feelings of (2) _____. According to research done by Brenner, (3) _____ at Johns Hopkins University, every 1% increase in the unemployment rate (4) _____ into 37,000 deaths over the next 6 years, including over (5) _____ deaths from heart attacks, 900 suicides and nearly 500 deaths from cirrhosis of the liver. In addition, Brenner estimates that (6) _____ unemployed or their families will be admitted to prison after committing a crime or to a mental hospital.

Men who have been socialized as the (7) _____ are especially hard hit by (8) _____. They suffer greater (9)_____and have a higher possibility of

211

(10) _____ than men who are employed. (11) _____ seems to be a crucial point when hope and patience give out. After that, illness, suicide, alcoholism, divorce, and even crime grow (12) _____.

Left without a job, many workers feel they have nothing to look forward to. They miss their coworkers and the routine of going to work. For many, the sense of (13) _____ grows worse every time they are rejected for a new job. When this happens often enough, the (14) _____ unemployed workers feel may be exacerbated if some friends and neighbors avoid them as if they had a (15) _____.

ⅢⅢⅢⅢⅢⅢⅢⅢⅢ Listening Comprehension ⅢⅢⅢⅢⅢⅢⅢⅢⅢ

Skill Focus

Memory Training Ⅰ（记忆训练1）

记忆对人类的重要性不言而喻。然而，人们对它的了解却不够深入和全面。更多的人认为记忆能力是天生的，其实不然。诸多记忆大师都指出，记忆力可以通过科学合理的训练得到提升，甚至是大幅提升。口译作为一种专业技能，可以保证译员在以记忆技能为主的口译任务中获得超常表现。

不管一个人的记忆力基础如何，记忆力都是能够在原有基础上通过训练得到提高的，这方面的理论和实践由来已久。最早为记忆寻找物理基础的是古希腊人。古希腊人非常崇拜记忆力，他们塑造了记忆女神——莫涅莫辛涅（Mnemosyne），英语单词"记忆术"（mnemonics）就是由她的名字派生而来的。

定位记忆法：公元前477年，古希腊诗人西蒙尼德斯发明了名叫"定位记忆法"的记忆术，后人将其称为记忆宫殿。古罗马人是记忆技巧的伟大发明者和实践者，他们在记忆术上广为人知的贡献就是著名的"罗马房间法"，它是"定位记忆法"的一种变体，主要是将记忆内容与相关位置联系在一起，以便在需要时进行回溯。"定位记忆法"是现代记忆术的核心记忆技巧，大多数记忆法都可以归结到"定位记忆法"。

思维导图法：思维导图就是极佳的记忆"路线图"，相比记忆成行的文字来说，记忆一幅图要容易得多。举例来说，为演讲绘制一幅思维导图，我们可以把演讲题目写到纸中央，然后以此为中心，呈放射状标明自己想列出的关键图形或文字。绘制完思维导图之后，用数字标出我们需要讲解的各分支的次序，突出主要论点或分支间的主要联系。我们会发现，每个关键的词汇或图形发挥一分钟的话，对半小时的演讲来说，一小幅思维导图就够用了。这个过程适用于演讲者，更加适用于听取了源语之后，进行口译的译员，只不过译员的"思维导图"是分析并理解源语之后译员自行绘制的，在忠实于源语的基础上，由译员重新产出的"全景图"。

联想记忆法：联想记忆就是将抽象的、不熟悉的信息转化成为具体的、较熟悉的信息，结合自己的已有知识，就可以把需要记忆的信息转化为对我们来说更加容易理解和消化的东西。视觉化就是转化能力的一种体现，指的是将信息在脑海中转化为影像的能力。这个影像越生动清晰越好。联想的方式越多，联想的画面越清晰具体，记忆起来就越容易；甚至，联想的画面越夸张、越生动，给大脑的冲击力就越强，记忆的效率就越好。

逻辑记忆法：逻辑记忆法也是将想象和联想相结合并进行具化的一种方法。与视觉化不同的是，逻辑记忆法将需要记忆的信息转化为用逻辑可以解释的事情，这样的逻辑关系不一定是"理性的""合理的"，只要对自己来说是"有逻辑的""有意义的"，就可以了。例如，尝试记忆一个人的名字：John Bridge。我们只要想象一下他的鼻子上架着一座桥，那么下次再看到这张脸，我们首先会想起桥，进而想起他姓Bridge。例如，West-East（西—东），如果容易混淆这两个词，那么就可以记忆它们的首字母组合"WE"，"WE（我们）"这个词是成立的，而在方位图上是"左西右东"，这样就可以记住"West"是西，"East"是东了。

上文提到的这些记忆方法不是互不相关、割裂开来的，它们都是互相联系、互为借鉴的。它们基于同一个原则，那就是将需要记忆的内容变成自己更容易理解并回忆的内容。其实，对所有人来说，无论大脑是否接受过记忆训练，都同样适用这样一条规则，那就是：想要记住任何新信息，就必须将这条信息与你已经知道的信息联系起来，或者在它们之间建立起关系。这条规则是记忆的关键，是记忆力的基础。其实，人的一生都在使用联系的方法去记忆。有时，我们在听到或看到一些事物之后会情不自禁地说出"哦，这件事让我想起……"之类的话，这时我们正是在使用联系的方法。每一件事都与另一件事有着这样或那样的联系，这就是它会让我们"想起来"的原因。

大脑进行联系的过程大多是无意识的，而我们的目标是要有意识地将需要记住的信息与能够提醒我们想起它的信息联系起来。这个过程经过训练可以变成有意识的、可控制的。口译中的记忆训练也是要将口译记忆变成有意识的、可控制的，以延长信息在短时记忆中的持续保持并有效保持的时间。而这个时间并不是无限长，也不需要把所有翻译过的信息都转换成长时记忆，它只需要在口译中帮助译员完成当下信息语段的口译。

Guided Practice

Directions: Listen to the recording and fill in the charts with expressions that can best explain the given words. Then try to rebuild the paragraph, in English or Chinese, with the help of the chart, or just the words in the first column.

Paragraph 1

Obesity	
Causes	
Westerners	
Weight	
Gym	
Other forms of exercise	
Slim persons	
Optimum per day	

Paragraph 2

Ecosystem	
Plants	
Photosynthesis	
Soil	
Other organisms	
Herbivores	
Carnivores	
Omnivores	
Plants	

Paragraph 3

Jakarta, Indonesia	
Islands	
Population	
Animals	
Agriculture	

Paragraph 4

Swimming equipments	Wetsuit	Cheap	
		Small	
Running equipments	Shoes	Why important?	
		Why important?	
		Type	Basic/Advanced

Paragraph 5

Adventurers	

Marco Polo	Middle Ages: China/Far East
	
	1271: Who?
	
	   Where?
	
	   Kublai Khan/17 years

续表

Adventurers	
The New World	Debated: Leif Ericsson: When? Name? Columbus: When? Where?

Paragraph 6

What is water?			
Forms of water	Liquid	97%: ( )	
		3%: ( ), ( ), ( ), ( ), ( ), ( ), ( )	
	Solid		
	Gas		
Not enough water?	Serious dehydration: ( ), e.g. ( ) Mild dehydration: ( ), ( ), ( )		
How enough water?	Routine: When wake up: When go out: Eating: ( ), ( )		

Summary Interpreting

Skill Focus

Paraphrasing（复述）

复述就是用言语重复识记的内容。复述对话语的信息理解和逻辑掌握有较高的要求，可以检验我们是否理解所听内容，是否可以将信息点有逻辑地联系起来。复述训练可以锻炼我们的记忆力，还可以锻炼我们的逻辑分析和有序表达的能力。

复述一般可以分为基本学习任务的复述和复杂学习任务的复述。前者强调重复，以此提高对记忆对象的熟悉程度；后者指重复挑选出重要信息以提高理解与记忆的程度，它需要学习者更为积极的思考。在日常生活中，经常需要将他人的话转述给第三者听，或是将刚刚听到的故事讲给他人。这时，要保证能听懂别人的话或理解故事的内容，然后才能在脑中形成有逻辑的记忆，随后再复述出来。

在复述中，区分主要和次要信息非常重要。主要信息是话语中最能体现讲者意图的信息，是讲者最希望传达给听众的信息，也是进行复述时必须把握的信息。这些信息串起来就是话语的大意，即话语的骨架，加上补充信息将最终形成一个完整的话语。此外，复述还应把握的基本原则是：不能曲解或改变原文的观点及主要事实。

在口译教学中，复述练习是最为常见和实用的练习方式之一，因为复述可以考查练习者是否真正理解了源语。更重要的，复述在理解源语的同时记忆并回溯源语的意思，是对口译真实模式的极大程度的模拟。从复述练习的语言组合来看，一般认为母语到母语难度最小，之后是外语到外语，再是外语到母语，最后是母语到外语，其中后两者进入了译述的阶段，也就是翻译阶段了。

复述需要把握源语的主要观点和概念，并尽量采用灵活的方式将其重组。这样的理念需要通过由浅入深的练习逐步渗透。先从句子层面入手，然后再进入话语的练习。从句子层面上，我们至少可以通过以下三种方式对源语进行重组，也就是复述，这三种方式是：改变词性、改变句子结构、将长句打散为若干小句。

1. 改变词性

源语：The cause of the delivery delay was a strike that happened days ago.

复述：The delivery was delayed because of the strike happened days ago.

源语：Analysis of the questionnaire responses revealed a number of female/male differences.

复述：They analyzed the questionnaire responses and found that female and male subjects were different in a number of ways.

2. 改变句子结构

源语：The centre and their website are available to anyone in the country who has an interest in researching demographic data.

复述：Anyone in the country who wants to research demographic data can visit the center and their website.

源语：I believe the ship's arrival in Shanghai today is a symbol of the friendship between our two countries in the past 150 years.

复述：The ship arrived in Shanghai today, which symbolizes the friendship between our two countries in the past 150 years.

3．将长句打散为若干小句

源语：Learners assessed as dyslexic can be supported either one-to-one or sometimes in small groups which are facilitated by a specialist support tutor, who will provide handouts on different coloured paper or present information more visually.

复述：Dyslexic learners can get one-to-one or small-group support. They will be helped by a specialist tutor. And the handouts provided by the tutor will be in different colors, in order to make the information more visible.

源语：Although fossil fuels, oil, gas, coal and peat are used by power stations to generate electricity and to fuel our cars, and are essential for modern lifestyle, they have been used at the expense of the environment as damage is caused at every stage of extracting and processing these fuels.

复述：Fossil fuels like oil, gas, coal and peat are used by power stations to generate electricity and to fuel our cars. In this sense, fossil fuels are very important for us to maintain modern lifestyle. Yet this way we are damaging the environment. The reason is that at every stage of using these fuels, from extracting to processing, damage is caused.

4．综合以上方法

源语：Sleep scientists have found that traditional remedies for insomnia, such as counting sheep, are ineffective. Instead, they have found that imagining a pleasant scene is likely to send you to sleep quickly. The research team divided 50 insomnia sufferers into three groups. One group imagined watching a waterfall, while another group tried sheep counting. A third group was given no special instructions about going to sleep. It was found that the group thinking of waterfall fell asleep 20 minutes quicker. Mechanical tasks like counting sheep are apparently too boring to make people sleepy. There are many practical applications for research into insomnia. About one in ten people are thought to suffer from severe insomnia.

复述：Findings by sleep researchers suggest that established cures for insomnia, for instance counting sheep, do not work, though visualising an attractive view may significantly encourage sleep. Fifty insomniacs were split into three groups by scientists. The first thought of water falling, and the second attempted to count sheep. A third group was not specially instructed. The findings show that the group thinking of waterfalls went to sleep faster. It appears that repetitive situations are not effective, because they are too tedious. The research has multiple uses, since 10% of the population are believed to have difficulty sleeping.

单个句子或段落的口译是口译教学中必不可少的部分，练习者不需要能够使用最恰当的"笔译范文"似的语言，而应该更多地采用灵活的方式表达源语的意思，学会不同语言结构或篇章组织的转换方法。

Guided Practice

Task A

Directions: Skim the following paragraphs, underline keywords that you think are indispensable for the rebuilding of the information, and then reproduce the paragraph, in English or Chinese, with the help of the underlined words.

Paragraph 1

在当代，数字娱乐发展的状况已成为衡量一个国家信息文化水平及综合国力的重要标志。数字娱乐指的是基于数字技术的动漫、卡通、网络游戏等的文化产业。在新兴文化产业价值链中，数字娱乐产业是创新性最强，对高科技依存度最高，对日常生活渗透最直接，对相关产业带动最广，增长最快，发展潜力最大的部分。数字产业的发展带动了人们媒体习惯的改变。未来，我们50%的收入都会用于娱乐支出，比如购买电影票，下载音乐，网络游戏，有线电视等。而这些数字产业支出是由现代科技作为支撑的，比如手机技术日新月异，宽带连接逐步普及，网速加快，移动设备增加等。实际上，家庭电视会持续占据消费者娱乐支出的最大份额。付费电视和点播电视越来越流行，所谓的"个人电视"得到了长足的发展，用户可以决定什么时间观看什么电视节目。此外，家庭电视的另外一大特点将是"移动性"。移动设备的发展使随时随地娱乐成了可能。虽然户内电视仍将在一段时期内维持主角位置，但以移动娱乐为目的的平台建设和服务供应将会成为市场上具有竞争力的娱乐"新风尚"。

Paragraph 2

那么，我们现在看看后发效应。在经济学上有个规律，就是后工业化的国家，它的增长速度一般可以超越先工业化的国家。英国是第一个开始工业化的国家，随后步入工业化轨道的国家成为追赶者；从经济发展速度分析，追赶者往往超过早期工业化国家。美国追赶英国，工业化速度超过英国。日本是晚近的追赶者，速度又超过美国。韩国又超过日本。中国经济高速增长是后发效应的又一实例。我们知道英国是第一个工业化的国家。它开始工业化的时候，经济增长一倍，用了58年时间。美国的经济增长一倍，用了47年时间。日本明治维新以后经济增长一倍用了34年时间。韩国第二次世界大战以后工业化，经济增长一倍的时间是11年时间。这是60年代。我们改革开放以后，9年增长一倍，而且连续两次。现在看来，要连续三次增长一倍，连续9年增加一倍。这说明我们的工业化远远超过前面几个国家。这就是一个后发效应。这个原因就是：第一，后工业化国家可以利用先工业化国家的技术、经验、资金、设备，可以从早期工业化国家引进积累的"知识宝库"，最新的技术、最科学的经营管理体制，节省摸索时间，可以少走弯路。第二，后工业化国家往往比先工业化国家具备劳动力和资源的相对优势，晚起步国家一般劳动力价格较低，资源没有充分开发。第三，百业俱兴，后工业化国家的各个产业都是新兴产业，都在蓬勃发展，而且没有陈旧设备的负担。这些就是后发效应的原因。

Paragraph 3

Today I'm going to talk about learning styles, which is certainly a very interesting topic, and an important one too. There is one thing we should know, and that is everybody has a learning style. Your learning style is the way you prefer to learn. It doesn't have anything to do with how intelligent you are or what skills you have learned. It has to do with how your brain works most efficiently to learn new information. Your learning style has been with you since you were born. Having said that, someone may ask whether there's a right way to learn. Actually, there's no such thing as a "good" learning style or a "bad" learning style. Success comes with many different learning styles. There is no right approach to learning. We all have our own particular way of learning new information, just as teachers have different ways of teaching, as you know. The important thing is to understand your learning style. If you are aware of how your brain best learns, you have a better chance of studying in a way that will pay off when it's time to take exam. Three main types of learning styles have been identified, the auditory, the visual and the kinaesthetic, the last meaning "movement". So, to find out what our own learning style is, we need to think about the way in which we remember a phone number, for example. If you can hear the number in the way that someone recited it to you, you might be an auditory learner. If you can picture the number exactly as you wrote it down, in your mind's eye, you might be a visual learner. If you dial a number without looking at the phone, or write a text message without looking at the letters, you may be a kinaesthetic learner.

Paragraph 4

Before the invention of plastic, the only substances that could be molded were pottery and glass. Hardened clay and glass were used for storage, but they were heavy and brittle. The first truly synthetic plastic was invented by Leo Baekeland, a Belgium chemist living in New York. In 1905, Baekeland produced a material that bound all types of powders together. He called this material Bakelite, after himself, and it was the first thermosetting plastic in the world. This was a material that once set hard would not soften under heat. It had so many uses and so many potential uses, that it was called "the material of a thousand uses". A hundred years later, Bakelite, the world's first fully synthetic material, has led to an incredible numbers of plastics which have changed our lives. Look around you, your mobile phone, your credit cards, your glasses, the shoes you wear, they all rely on some variant of plastic. But plastic could not exist without oil. Plastics account for about eight percent of global supply of oil. With oil reserves expected to last only a few more decades, we need to develop renewable plastics or find an alternative. The solution could be in plastics made from plants growing in fields, bioplastics. Bioplastics made from crops such as maize and sugar have become more widespread, turning up in products such as biodegradable shopping bags, but many are expensive to produce, or they melt at low temperatures.

Task B

Directions: Within a group of students (e.g. 2–4), one student skims one of the following paragraphs and underline keywords that are indispensable for the rebuilding of the information. Then ask other students of the group to reproduce the paragraph, in English or Chinese, only with the help of the list of the underlined words. Then compare the reproduction with the original paragraph, and see how helpful the key words are to the rebuilding of the information.

Paragraph 1

运动可以强身健体。在高速高压的现代社会里，运动更是成为人们热衷的流行文化。大家熟悉的运动不胜枚举，这些主流的运动吸引着大多数人积极参与。但还有一些运动比较不寻常，不管你是否听说过或参与过这些运动，它们在举办地可是相当地受欢迎呢。我们来看几个例子。比如，水下球类运动。英国的潜水爱好者在1954年发明了水下曲棍球。在俄罗斯，大家熟知的橄榄球和冰球也已由人们在水下进行比赛。运动员们认为，这种水下球类运动比在陆地上进行的橄榄球和冰球更复杂、更有趣。为了使热衷这些运动项目的助威者能看到比赛的进程，需要专门的水下摄像设备或者专门的潜水器对比赛进行拍摄。此外，骑鸵鸟比赛。这种比赛起源于非洲，而后流传至美国。鸵鸟的奔跑速度可以达到每小时70公里，它们的一大步可以跨出将近5米。在骑鸵鸟运动中，选手们骑着鸵鸟沿着跑道奔跑。最后，在澳大利亚，掷金枪鱼比赛是每年举办的趣味体育赛事。参赛者人手一只冷冻金枪鱼，比谁扔得远。投掷用的金枪鱼最重可达10公斤，它们被拴在绳子上，像链球一样被选手们抛出。目前组织者表示，今后比赛使用的金枪鱼将由仿真鱼替代。作为替代品的假鱼由聚氨酯制成，出自当地一位艺术家之手，足以乱真。改用替代品的原因很多，包括避免浪费，尽管鱼冻得很硬，但在投掷过程中还是免不了会破碎。

Paragraph 2

南极是世界上最冷的地方，年平均气温在-25℃以下，绝对最低气温达-90℃左右。那里的纬度高，而且是一个冰封的大陆，同时又是世界上风暴最大的地区，还是地球上最干燥的大陆，几乎所有降水都是雪和冰雹。南极不仅是最冷的地方，也是最孤独的地方。那里没有土著居民，没有发现任何古人类活动的痕迹。现代科技可以使人类到访南极，即便这样，访客也不会停留很久，极少数人在那里停留超过6个月。在南极，一年只有一次日出、一次日落，基本上是半年白天半年黑夜的状况，也就是说，太阳始终不落或者始终不升起。南极是迄今为止地球上未被开发利用的宝地，蕴藏着人类赖以生存和发展的丰富资源。南极资源开发还存在诸多问题，包括勘探和开采难度、领土主权、环境污染等。但是，南极资源在未来全球经济发展中起着举足轻重的作用，因为当地球上其他地方的资源都耗尽时，南极就成了地球上唯一的资源宝库。

Paragraph 3

Today I'm going to talk about the first real innovation in the laundry industry in more than 60 years. This new technology called Xeros cleans clothes using just two percent of the water conventional washing machines do. That's just a cup of water per wash. Xeros uses plastic chips to tumble with the clothes to remove everyday stains, and the results are the same as if using just water. Plastic chips are mixed with the laundry being washed. The chips gently lift the stains away from the laundry in the wash. The advantages of the technology are obvious. As this method uses only a tiny amount of water, your clothes are virtually dry, meaning you can get rid of the tumble dryer. Plus, it can remove all sorts of everyday stains, including coffee and lipstick. What's more, by using low-temperature cleaning, the Xeros machines greatly reduce the need to sort mixed colors in the wash. This makes the sorting process simpler, saving valuable time. Most important of all, this technology reduces the need for large quantities of detergents. By using fewer detergents, the Xeros machines can keep linen looking new for longer than a standard washing machine, which means better fabric longevity. As an added bonus, Xeros machines uses less energy to heat less water, making it more environmentally friendly. The developers are hoping the process can be used for commercial washing and for dry cleaning.

Paragraph 4

We are now in the digital age, which is also known as the information age. Some say that it should be defined as the time period starting in the 1970s with the introduction of the personal computer with subsequent technology introduced providing the ability to transfer information freely and quickly. In this digital age, more things can be and are now being digitised. To digitise something means to turn it into digits or numbers. It means turning something into the electronic language a computer can understand. Digital information can be many things, including words, numbers, photos, X-rays, sounds or even solid objects. Any object can be digitised by breaking it down into individual bits of information. For instance, photographs in newspapers consist of dots that are either black or white. From a distance, the viewer does not see the dots, but only lines and shading, which appear to be continuous. Once an item is digitised there are three significant things you can do with it: you can store, transmit or enhance the information electronically. Digitization can reduce the amount of paper used resulting in less to be thrown away. Information can be disseminated in a variety of formats after it has been digitized. Also, cultural and heritage materials in the library, archive, museums and galleries sector will be better preserved. Even though the convenience associated with digitization can lead to many innovations, digitization can present many problems as well. Digital documents are very easily edited, which is why physical documents are still more readily "trustworthy". Digital material, despite its advantages, is just as complex to preserve as its physical counterpart, if not more so in certain formats. For a physical document one needs three things, the document, literacy, and light. However, for a digital medium, you need the hardware, the software, electricity, and a stable Internet connection, on top of what you would need to read the physical document.

Information Link

Types of Memory and Forgetting Curve（记忆类型和遗忘曲线）

　　记忆类型：记忆指人脑对输入的信息进行编码、存储和提取的过程。记忆可分为感觉记忆（sensory memory）、短时记忆（short-term memory）、长时记忆（long-term memory）三类。感觉记忆又叫瞬时记忆，指外界刺激在极短时间内呈现后，信息被保留的一瞬间的记忆。瞬时记忆保留的时间很短。如果对瞬时记忆中的信息加以注意，信息就被转入短时记忆。否则，没有注意到的信息过1秒便会消失，也就遗忘了。短时记忆保持时间稍长，在20～30秒之内。在短时记忆加工信息的时候，有时需要借助已有的知识经验，这时就要从长时记忆中把这些知识经验提取到短时记忆中。因此，短时记忆中既有从瞬时记忆中转来的信息，也有从长时记忆中提取出来的信息，它们都是当前正在加工的信息，因此短时记忆又叫工作记忆（working memory）。短时记忆的信息经过复述，不管是机械复述，还是运用记忆术所做的精细复述，就都可以转入长时记忆系统。长时记忆指永久性的信息存贮，一般能保持多年甚至终身。长时记忆的容量是无限的。

　　遗忘曲线：德国心理学家赫尔曼·艾宾浩斯（Hermann Ebbinghaus）研究发现，遗忘在学习之后立即开始，进程并不是均匀的。最初遗忘速度很快，之后逐渐放缓。他认为"保持和遗忘是时间的函数"。根据他的实验结果绘成的描述遗忘进程的曲线就是著名的"艾宾浩斯记忆遗忘曲线"。记忆力可以通过科学合理的训练得到提升。记忆在口译的信息输入和信息输出阶段都发挥重要作用。因此，我们应该在口译训练中重视并加强记忆训练。

After-class Assignment

Directions: Listen to the following passage. Pause after each paragraph, and try to summarize the main idea of that paragraph. Then try to answer the multiple choice questions below.

Paragraph 1

Many great inventions are initially greeted with ridicule and disbelief. The invention of the airplane was no exception. Although many people who heard about the first powered flight on December 17, 1903 were excited and impressed, others reacted with peals of laughter. The idea of flying an aircraft was repulsive to some people. Such people called Wilbur and Orville Wright, the inventors of the first flying machine, impulsive fools. Negative reactions, however, did not stop the Wrights. Impelled by their desire to succeed, they continued their experiments in aviation.

Paragraph 2

Orville and Wilbur Wright had always had a compelling interest in aeronautics and mechanics. As young boys they earned money by making and selling kites and mechanical toys. Later, they designed a newspaper-folding machine, built a printing press, and operated a bicycle-repair shop. In 1896, when they read about the death of Otto Lilienthal, the brothers' interest in flight grew into a compulsion.

Paragraph 3

Lilienthal, a pioneer in hang-gliding, had controlled his gliders by shifting his body in the desired direction. This idea was repellent to the Wright brothers, however, and they searched for more efficient methods to control the balance of airborne vehicles. In 1900 and 1901, the Wrights tested numerous gliders and developed control techniques. The brothers' inability to obtain enough lift power for the gliders almost led them to abandon their efforts.

Paragraph 4

After further study, the Wright brothers concluded that the published tables of air pressure on curved surfaces must be wrong. They set up a wind tunnel and began a series of experiments with model wings. Because of their efforts, the old tables were repealed in time and replaced by the first reliable figures for air pressure on curved surfaces. This work, in turn, made it possible for the brothers to design a machine that would fly. In 1903, the Wrights built their first airplane, which cost less than $1,000. They even designed and built their own source of propulsion — a lightweight gasoline engine. When they started the engine on December 17, the airplane pulsated wildly before taking off. The plane managed to stay aloft for 12 seconds, however, and it flew 120 feet.

Paragraph 5

By 1905, the Wrights had perfected the first airplane that could turn, circle, and remain airborne for half an hour at a time. Others had flown in balloons and hang gliders, but the Wright brothers were the first to build a full-size machine that could fly under its own power. As the contributors of one of the most outstanding engineering achievements in history, the Wright brothers are accurately called "the fathers of aviation".

Multiple choice questions

1. The idea of flying an aircraft was _____ to some people.

    A. boring   B. distasteful

    C. exciting   D. needless

    E. Answer not available.

2. People thought that the Wright brothers had _____.

    A. acted without thinking   B. been negatively influenced

    C. been too cautious   D. been mistaken

    E. acted in a negative way

3. The Wrights' interest in flight grew into a _____.

    A. financial empire   B. plan

    C. need to act   D. foolish thought

    E. Answer not available.

4. Lilienthal's idea about controlling airborne vehicles was _____ the Wrights.

    A. proven wrong by   B. opposite to the ideas of

    C. disliked by   D. accepted by

    E. improved by

5. The old tables were _____ and replaced by the first reliable figures for air pressure on curved surfaces.

    A. destroyed   B. invalidated

    C. multiplied   D. approved

    E. not used

6. The Wrights designed and built their own source of _____.

    A. force for moving forward   B. force for turning around

    C. turning   D. force for going backward

    E. None of the above.

扫码获取本单元音频资料

Unit 14 Memory Training II & Consecutive Interpreting Without Notes

> You should always be taking pictures, if not with a camera then with your mind. Memories you capture on purpose are always more vivid than the ones you pick up by accident.
>
> — Isaac Marion, American writer,
>
> best-selling author

Unit Goals

- To gain a general knowledge of how memory can be trained in interpreting.
- To gain a general knowledge of consecutive interpreting without notes.
- To become more flexible in interpreting by applying tactics learned in the textbook.
- To gain a general knowledge of sight interpreting.

Warm Up

Directions: Listen to the following passages and fill in the blanks with words or sentences. Make sure the words and sentences you fill in are both grammatically and semantically acceptable.

Task A

Why People Get Tattoos

Getting a tattoo because your friends and peers have them is just one of the reasons why a lot of young people in North America get tattoos. (1) _____ _____ are some of the common reasons for wearing tattoos today.

The desire to be part of a group, to be accepted by one's friends or peers, can have a great influence on what a person does. Sometimes, wearing a tattoo can be a (2) _____ that you belong to a certain group. (3) _____ often use special clothes and tattoos to

227

(4) _____ their particular group. For example, in one gang all the members may (5) _____. It is not only gangs that have this type of special uniform. Young people often belong to a certain group of friends. Some of these groups wear only (6) _____. Some wear only black clothes. Others wear tattoos. When a person's friends are all doing something, such as getting a tattoo, that person is more likely to do the same thing, and get a tattoo, too.

The media is another big influence behind (7) _____ _____. A wide variety of media images show tattoos. Tattoos can be seen on people appearing in (8) _____ selling expensive cars. (9) _____ with tattoos are shown in magazines. (10) _____ are often seen in magazines and on TV wearing designer clothes that show their bodies tattooed with detailed and colourful patterns. These media images link tattoos to ideas of (11) _____. As a result, many people decide to get a tattoo for its fashion and status value.

It is not always the influence of other people or the media that results in a person getting a tattoo. Many people decide to wear tattoos in order to express (12) _____ _____ — in other words, to show their (13) _____. A musician in a rock band may get a tattoo of a (14) _____ on the arm. Some environmentalists may tattoo pictures of (15) _____ on their shoulders. Lovers may tattoo (16) _____ over their hearts. A tattoo can be a (17) _____ to show what is important in a person's life.

As you can see, there are many reasons why young North Americans get tattoos. A tattoo can be part of a group's uniform. It can be a sign of fashion. It can be an expression of individuality. The decision to get a tattoo is most often a result of the influence of friends or media or the desire to express oneself.

Task B

World Food Day

Today, agriculture has contributed to (1) _____ by improving nutrition and living standards. It has ensured the production and distribution of (2) _____ and enough food to feed everyone on this planet.

Seventy percent of the world's hungry live in rural areas. That is where (3) _____ _____. The seed planted by a farmer leads to

(4) _____ that pay taxes, and help build rural schools and roads. Agricultural development is the first step of (5) _____. Everyone gains from investment in agriculture.

Since 1964, FAO has been a key player in the UN system in the (6) _____ _____ in favor of (7) _____ _____. Through its cooperation with (8) _____, FAO has helped 165 member countries to obtain funding for almost 1,600 agricultural and rural investment programmes and projects. That represents (9) _____ of over $ 80 billion.

The challenge of increasing investment in agriculture is especially great in Africa. Governments in that region have recognized the (10) _____ _____. Recently there has been a significant revival in lending for agriculture. (11) _____, strengthened by the G8 decision, have begun to release national resources for investment in the sector. But much still (12) _____ and innovative actions are welcome. Increasing the (13) _____ is of absolute necessity and it is crucial to make such assistance more effective. It is also worth noticing that "(14) _____" was the new model for cooperation between the (15) _____.

From farm to table, much about food production has changed over the past decades, for both (16) _____. It will take innovation and a variety of technologies to meet the world's food demand. At every step of the journey (17) _____, technology is helping us produce a safe, abundant, sustainable, and nutritious food supply. (18) _____, with the aid of GPS satellites, can target individual crop treatments to the smallest plots of soil. Advances in (19) _____, from climate control to the nutritional qualities of feed, have improved animal health and welfare, and boosted agricultural output. (20) _____ increase the safety of our food, the distance across which it can be transported, and its extended freshness.

On this World Food Day, let us resolve together to increase the investment in agriculture so that the whole world may benefit.

|||||||||||||||||| **Listening Comprehension** ||||||||||||||||||

Skill Focus

Memory Training II（记忆训练2）

只有理解了的东西才更容易记忆，这一点在口译中显得更加重要，只有理解了并有效保存在短时记忆中的东西才可能有效产出。因而，口译中的理解几乎等同于记忆的有效留存。短时记忆的研究告诉我们，短时记忆一般只能持续20~30秒，而如果经过进一步的加工，其留存时间可以延长，留存效果也可以加强，则即便在译语产出阶段受到由译员自身话语输出带来的"噪声"的干扰，译员仍然能够保证译语的产出质量。

口译中需要的是"听解"，而不仅仅是"听到"，两者虽然都是心理过程，但对口译来说有截然不同的作用。"听解需要将声音赋予意义，并将其组织成为可以理解的思维单位，而听到指的是声音从外部环境传输进入大脑"。由此可见，对口译来说，理解不是自动的，是基于技巧之上的有意为之。在口译过程中，理解涉及集中听解、消化吸收、结合已有知识、理解储存等步骤。这些步骤同步进行，具有"共时"的工作特点。理解过程中的新信息与旧信息的结合是最能体现听解主动性的环节，只有新信息和旧信息有效结合，理解才能真正发生。

口译中的短时记忆需要结合长时记忆才能更好地发挥作用，或者说更好地进行"理解"。口译中"理解"需要各种关联（新知识与旧知识、前言与后语、言外与言内、形式与内容等），而关联的依据就是经验知识。长时记忆中的信息都是经验性的，是人们的经验知识的总和，在需要的时候被加以提取。经验知识越多，口译起来也就越得心应手。概括地说，"短时记忆"是关键，"长时记忆"是基础。下面我们结合记忆训练的实例，对口译中的记忆法加以具体分析。

归类法：将相似或相近的信息片段进行整合，可以减少需要记忆的信息组块（chunk）的数量，也就是可以利用较少的组块囊括更多的信息总量。请看下面的例析。

Then actually how many people speak English as either a first or a second language? Some researches suggested that a few years ago that between 320,000,000 to 380,000,000 people spoke English as a first language, and anywhere between 250,000,000 to 350,000,000 as a second language. And of course, if we include people who are learning English as a foreign language all over the world, that number may increase dramatically.

1st?　　　　320~380 m

2nd?　　　　250~350 m

外语　　　　more

针对这个例子，我们在记忆的时候应该尽量寻找相似之处。比如，数字单位都是hundred million，即"亿"，当然，译为三亿两千万，或者3.2亿都可以。而针对第一语言的一对数字，我们发现，它们都是三亿多，至于千万上的差异，我们可以通过记忆"二八定律""二八芳龄"等将其联系起来；针对第二语言的一对数字，我们发现2.5亿与3.5亿之间的差异是一亿。这样记忆下来，则本段落中最难记忆的数字也很容易把握，由此也可以轻易记忆整个段落的内容。还比如，针对下面段落的记忆。

Back in 1995, trade between our two nations was measured in the tens of billions of dollars. Today it is counted in the hundreds of billions. Few people back then had cell phones, and almost no one had access to the Internet. Today, China has the world's largest mobile phone network, and more Internet users than any other country on earth.

1995　　　　Today

Trade　　　　10b 100b

Cell phone: few largest network

Internet: Few/almost no one More users

我们可以总结出，本段落为1995年与现今在三个方面的数量规模上的对比。为了简便记忆，我们可以尽量寻求相似之处。比如，贸易量的比较都是以billion为单位，由10b增至100b，百亿增至千亿；又如，互联网的使用者，与上文手机的使用者相似，仅仅译出few也不算错误，这样可以大大减轻记忆负担。

构图法：描写或叙述类源语中往往包括事件、位置等具体信息，视觉化的策略可以更好地将这样的源语信息整合成为一幅图画，请看下面的例子。

If the fire alarm is activated, all staff should make their way to the main stairs unless it sounds at 11:00 a.m. on a Tuesday, in which case it is a test. Do not waste time by picking up any bags or personal belongings. Once outside the building, staff should follow the fire marshals, who will direct them to the waiting area at the back of the building. Each department has an appointed fire safety officer who is responsible for checking all their staff have left the office. This person must then report any missing people to the fire safety manager. The fire safety manager will notify people when it is safe to return.

可以通过根据头脑中的想象描绘的图画，更有效地记忆并回溯内容。我们可以将源语中的信息分条处理，按照条目出现的次序和内容进行记忆，也可以将源语中并未确切表达的内容分列成条目。不论怎样，我们都需要在各个条目之间建立联系，这样可以确保我们在回溯时克服话语产出抑制的干扰，按照信息原本的顺序有效回忆各个条目的内容，如同利用思维导图按图索骥一般，重新画一幅图，完成信息的回溯。

关键词法：抓住主要内容，紧扣关键性的字眼，把较繁杂的识记材料加以概括和压缩的一种方法。运用关键词记忆法，只要牢记要点，结合联想，并加以必要的扩充就能较全面地再现完整的内容。经过概括和压缩后的材料以小见大，使人印象深刻，难以忘却。下面所要说明的关键词法与此类似，但是更加适合源语的逻辑条目并不是特别清晰，需要译员自行理解并总结的情况。

There are lots of places for students around here. Firstly, if you go across the bridge over the river outside the campus and turn right, then you'll get to the bowling alley, which is really popular at the weekends because it's so close to the campus. On Friday nights, they have a special discount for students. If you go down the road opposite the bowling alley and take the first right, then you'll get to the park. It's quite big and there's lake in it. You can take a boat on it. The university rowing team practise there. If you like sport, you can join the rowing team if you like. Apart from that, behind the sports center, they have a running track, and inside the sports center, you can find a badminton court, the swimming baths, and a leisure center, where you can get a student leisure card. So, you see, there is quite a lot to do in this town.

过桥右转：保龄（周末、周五）

保龄对面右转：公园（湖、船）

运动：船+中心（跑、球、游、闲）

这一段的三个内容分别是"保龄、公园、运动"，它们之间利用关键词串联起来。以上最为简洁的几个关键词，可以帮助我们回忆整个段落。采用罗列关键词的方式辅助我们进行复述，是非常好的方法。这些关键词实际上就是口译笔记上需要出现的信息。这里需要注意的问题是，关键词一定是最主要的意思的体现，不能罗列过多词汇，数量太多就起不到一目了然帮助回忆的目的。另外，技能熟练了之后，加入笔记，我们就会习惯多听一些之后再记笔记，这样体现在笔记中的就是重要信息，或者是有必要记下的信息。

缩编法：整理并记忆关键词的方法可以帮助我们将更多信息串联起来，起到化零为整的作用。如果关键词之间的联系不大，比较任意，我们可以将关键词进行缩编。缩编记忆法将需要记忆的材料的绝对数量尽量缩小，减轻大脑的记忆负担，进而通过记忆较少的内容将更多的记忆材料囊括进来。比如，大家都比较熟悉的《节气歌》"春雨惊春清谷天，夏满芒夏暑相连；秋处露秋寒霜降，冬雪雪冬小大寒"，代表的是立春、雨水、惊蛰、春分、清明、谷雨、立夏、小满、芒种、夏至、小暑、大暑、立秋、处暑、白露、秋分、寒露、霜降、立冬、小雪、大雪、冬至、小寒和大寒这二十四节气。请看下面的例子。

Today I'm going to talk about ways in which you can impress your boss and hopefully get the promotion. Well, obvious as it may sound, demonstrating leadership skills and the ability to work in a team are two of the main ways to get yourself noticed. Your manager will be impressed if you can collaborate with others on projects, especially if this maximises the company's profits or revenue. If you make sure your manager is aware of your strong points and the effort you have put into helping the company, you may be first in line for a promotion when your bosses decide to restructure a department or the company. Another skill you should try to demonstrate to your boss is that of being able to resolve problems or difficult situations. Many people naturally shy away from problems. If you can tackle them head-on, you make yourself valuable to your manager.

Promotion（升职）

Leadership/team work→profits（领导力/团队合作→利益）

Problem-solving（解决问题）

Promotion（升职）

根据这些关键词，我们基本可以对段落进行复述或翻译，也就是说，产出的语言可以是源语，也可以是译语，因为信息框架是相同的。如果不能将关键词写下来，而是在头脑中储存，就需要在它们之间建立联系，以便在复述或翻译时能够有效进行重新访问。比如，我们可以记录英文关键词的首字母"PLPP"，或者中文关键词"升/领导/问题/升"。

不论是上一章讲到的一般记忆法，还是本章讲到的口译相关记忆法，都各具优势。只有灵活使用，才能真正发挥记忆法对提升口译记忆及口译质量的不可替代的作用。交替传译中的记忆训练一定离不开对源语的理解和分析，因为不理解的内容是不能有效记忆的，何况交替传译还要在保持记忆的情况下对其进行回溯。因此，交替传译的记忆训练应该包含听力理解、积极分析、结构记忆等多个环节。只有较好地完成了这些环节，才可能有效地产出记忆成果。只要整个环节应对得比较自如，或者说一般长度的语段都可以在无笔记的情况下进行译述，笔记就可以真正地反映记忆成果，进而适当减轻记忆负担，辅助完成交替传译。

Guided Practice

🎧 Task A

Directions: Listen to the recording and fill in the charts with expressions that can best explain the given words. Then try to rebuild the paragraph, in English or Chinese, with the help of the chart, or just the words in the first column.

Paragraph 1

Aging process reversed?	American scientists		
	Experiment	Rats/health food	
		Memory/stamina	
	Result		
	Indication		

Paragraph 2

Chemical elements	109
	8
Compounds	Water
	Salt
Chemical reactions	Water
	Items e.g.
Magnetism	
Gravity	Earth
	Moon

Paragraph 3

Drug-resistant malaria	How serious?
	Where?
	How many people?
Factors	Poverty → funds → health projects
	Migrant workers/tourists
	Overuse of drugs/antibiotics
Vaccine	Genetic engineers:
	Scientists:
	Now:

Paragraph 4

Life expectancy	UK	
	Japan	
	South Korea	
Women/ men		
	1900	
	Now	
Reasons	Risks?	
	British scientists:	

🎧 **Task B**

Directions: Listen to the recording of different paragraphs on the same topic, and take down the main idea of each paragraph. You may compare your answer with that of your partner's. You may also try to reproduce the paragraphs, in English or Chinese, and ask your partner to comment on your performance.

The Effects of the Black Death

Paragraph 1

_____

_____

_____

_____

_____

_____

Paragraph 2

_____

_____

_____

_____

_____

_____

The Social Effects of Tourism in Developing Countries

Paragraph 1

_____

_____

_____

_____

_____

_____

Paragraph 2

_____

_____

_____

_____

_____

_____

Should Genetically Modified (GM) Foods
Have a Role in Future Agriculture?

Paragraph 1

_____

_____

_____

_____

_____

_____

Paragraph 2

_____

_____

_____

_____

_____

_____

|||||||||||||||||||||||| Summary Interpreting ||||||||||||||||||||||||

Consecutive Interpreting Without Notes（无笔记交替传译）

通常来说，口译话语具备一般话语的主要构成特点，即层层推进，信息级别各不同。因此，译员需要分辨并了解话语的推进方式和层次，并在此基础上记忆重要词汇及其表达的主要信息。同时，我们还要清楚，口译源语也跟一般话语一样转瞬即逝。信息的传达靠具体的字词句及其组织结构和方法，但是多少个句子构建哪些信息是多变和无常的。正如诺兰（Nolan）所说，成功的笔记技巧需要掌握一种方法，可以将词汇汇集为意思，再将意思用符号表现出来，接着用另外一种语言表达这种意思；译员不可能把所有的词汇都记下来，因为有时候多个单词表达一个意思，而有时候一个单词可能涵盖多层意思。

在无笔记阶段训练分辨并听懂主要信息，练习的是抛弃源语的词汇和结构，将意思筛选出来的能力。这样的练习到了记笔记阶段，之前反映在头脑中的主要信息就会一一反映在笔记上。这样的练习需要译员在只听一遍源语的情况下，边听边主动、积极分辨信息的构成和展开方式，甚至是话语未来发展的方向，也就是讲话人接下来可能会讲什么。

当然，不能指望交替传译训练一开始译员就能够将所有层次的信息都分辨得出，记忆得准，翻译得顺。最开始，需要训练译员分辨最主要或者第一层次的信息。然后，可以分辨哪些是次要信息或者说第二层甚至第三层信息，那么接下来就可以再将这些次要信息依层次加入记忆并产出。事实上，如果译员在无笔记的情况下，可以较好地分辨信息层次并依任务难度和能力限度进行记忆和产出，那么，加入笔记学习后，他们的笔记也是有层次的。

　　记忆训练及无笔记交替传译训练并不仅仅是交替传译的初级技巧或过渡性训练，两者应该贯穿整个交替传译的学习过程，不应该在学习了笔记之后就戛然而止。当然，其难度和训练方法需要有所进阶。记忆训练及无笔记交替传译训练对口译实践具有重要的指导作用，可以提升译员口译实践中的灵活程度，为他们成功进行口译实践打下坚实的基础。

Guided Practice

🎧 Task A

Directions: Listen to the recording of each paragraph and try to reproduce it, in English or Chinese, with the help of your memory only. You may ask your partner to comment on your performance. You may also read the paragraphs to your partner and ask him or her to reproduce them.

Paragraph 1

Studying Abroad or Online?

_____

_____

_____

_____

_____

Paragraph 2

China's Economic Growth

_____

_____

_____

_____

_____

Paragraph 3

Taking Notes in Lectures

_____
_____
_____
_____
_____

Paragraph 4

How to Get a Green Card?

_____
_____
_____
_____
_____

Paragraph 5

Tech to Help Tackle Ikea Flat Packs

_____
_____
_____
_____
_____

Paragraph 6

Gardening Tips

_____
_____
_____
_____
_____

🎧 **Task B**

Directions: Skim the following passages, with one or two sentences given in each paragraph. Based on the given information and your knowledge on the topic, try to produce the passage, in English or Chinese. Then you may listen to the recording and check how close your anticipation is to the original.

Passage 1

Where did Mobile Phones Come from?

Although mobile phones have been affordable for the masses only for the last several decades, they have in fact been around for more than sixty years in one form or another. _____

_____

_____

_____

The first mobile phones, referred to as first generation or 1G, were introduced to the public market in 1983 by the Motorola Company. _____

_____

_____

_____

They were more of a status symbol than a convenience.

During the 1990s, great improvements were made in mobile phone technology. _____

_____

_____

_____

Third generation (3G) technology is what many people still use in their mobile phones today. _____

_____

_____

_____

You could think that there is little more that you could do with cellular phone technology. This is, however, not the case. _____

_____

_____

_____

The mobile phone industry continues to grow by leaps and bounds, just as it has in the past few decades. _____

_____

_____

_____

Passage 2

High-speed Rail Network

The global high-speed rail network is one of the great feats of modern engineering, and proves to be the best form of transportation ever invented._____

_____

_____

_____

The global high-speed rail network is rapidly expanding across continents worldwide, delivering fast, efficient mobility to numerous nations every day. _____

_____

_____

_____

China's high-speed rail system, just a decade old, is now one of the biggest infrastructure projects in history. _____

_____

_____

_____

China's international reputation has also improved through building HSR and exporting HSR expertise. _____

_____

_____

_____

However, the prevalence of high-speed rail systems in Europe and East Asia does not mean that it is suitable for all countries to have their own high-speed rail systems._____

_____

_____

_____

Firstly, population density is an important factor to be considered for the construction of HSR. _____

_____

_____

Secondly, property rights also play an important role in the process of constructing HSR. ___

_____

_____

Another important facet of high-speed rail is the value of network effects. _____

_____

_____

_____

IIIIIIIIIIIIIIIIIIIIIIIIIIIIII **Information Link** IIIIIIIIIIIIIIIIIIIIIIIIIIIIII

Sight Interpreting（视译）

　　视译，顾名思义，就是边看边译。它是同声传译的一项准备练习，可以促进练习者的瞬时理解能力、双语转换能力和语言组织能力。视译可以帮助译员掌握视译文本相关的会议内容，快速进行重要概念的双语转换，并熟悉相关专业的术语表达。这些能力对交替传译同样重要。目前，由于其操作方式非常便捷，视译已经成为口译相关测试的必备环节。

　　视译的材料：会议中需要视译的材料主要包括讲话人的发言原稿，同时也可能包括发言的译语稿；有时，讲话人还可能提供讲稿的提纲或幻灯片，这些材料都可能需要视译。

　　视译的标准：由于中、英两种工作语言之间在句法和语法上差异较大，中英互译的视译中，更多时候需要进行断句和顺句驱动。判断视译质量的标准往往包括以下两点：第一，译员的译语产出自然流畅，没有过多源语句法和语法的痕迹，也就是没有"翻译腔"；第二，译员的译语产出尽量在阅读源语的时间内完成，这一点可以保障第一条标准的达成。

视译的练习：视译练习的语言组成可以根据译员的程度采用外语到母语、然后母语到外语的语言进阶。通过控制语段或话语的主题及语言难度调节整体训练难度。在主题和语言难度可以应对的情况下，计时视译（也就是在阅读源语的时间范围内完成视译）可以将这种练习的难度提升到较高的水平，进而提升训练效果。在计时视译练习的基础上，可以考虑将语段换为由多段组成的话语，在完整的话语之内，段落的语言采用母语和外语两种语言轮流进行，训练译员在保障话语正常推进的前提下，根据段落语言随时转换语言方向。比如，如果原文的段落为"英+中+英+中……"，则视译出来的段落应为"中+英+中+英……"。这种练习尤其适合训练译员快速准确地进行语言转换的能力，为他们进行双向的交替传译打下坚实的基础。

After-class Assignment

Directions: Listen to the following passage. Pause after each paragraph, and try to summarize the main idea of that paragraph. Then try to answer the multiple choice questions below.

The Effects of Stress

Paragraph 1

There is a famous expression in English: "Stop the world, I want to get off!" This expression refers to a feeling of panic, or stress, that makes a person want to stop whatever they are doing, try to relax, and become calm again. "Stress" means pressure or tension. It is one of the most common causes of health problems in modern life. Too much stress results in physical, emotional, and mental health problems.

Paragraph 2

There are numerous physical effects of stress. Stress can affect the heart. It can increase the pulse rate, make the heart miss beats, and can cause high blood pressure. Stress can affect the respiratory system. It can lead to asthma. It can cause a person to breathe too fast, resulting in a loss of important carbon dioxide. Stress can affect the stomach. It can cause stomach aches and problems digesting food. These are only a few examples of the wide range of illnesses and symptoms resulting from stress.

Paragraph 3

Emotions are also easily affected by stress. People suffering from stress often feel anxious. They may have panic attacks. They may feel tired all the time. When people are under stress, they often overreact to little problems. For example, a normally gentle parent under a lot of stress at work may yell at a child for dropping a glass of juice. Stress can make people angry, moody, or nervous.

Paragraph 4

Long-term stress can lead to a variety of serious mental illnesses. Depression, an extreme feeling of sadness and hopelessness, can be the result of continued and increasing stress. Alcoholism and other addictions often develop as a result of overuse of alcohol or drugs to try to relieve stress. Eating disorders, such as anorexia, are sometimes caused by stress and are often made worse by stress. If stress is allowed to continue, then one's mental health is put at risk.

Paragraph 5

It is obvious that stress is a serious problem. It attacks the body. It affects the emotions. Untreated, it may eventually result in mental illness. Stress has a great influence on the health and well-being of our bodies, our feelings, and our minds. So, reduce stress: stop the world and rest for a while.

Multiple choice questions

1. Which of the following is not a common problem caused by stress?

   A. Physical problems.   B. Anecdotal problems.

   C. Mental problems.   D. Emotional problems.

2. According to the essay, which of the following parts of the body does not have physical problems caused by stress?

   A. The arms.   B. The stomach.

   C. The lungs.   D. The heart.

3. Which of the following show how stress can affect the emotions?

   A. It can make people feel nervous.   B. It can cause panic attacks.

   C. It can make people feel elated.   D. It can make people feel angry.

4. Which of the following can result from long-term stress?

A. Bliss.　　　　　　　　　　　B. Depression.

C. Alcoholism.　　　　　　　　D. Whimsy.

5. Choose the best answer to explain how alcoholism is caused by stress.

A. Alcohol is used to relieve stress.　　B. Alcohol is popular.

C. Alcohol is a chemical.　　　　　　　D. Alcohol is similar to medicine.

6. Which of the following is not caused by long-term stress?

A. Bloating.　　　　　　　　　B. Addiction.

C. Anorexia.　　　　　　　　　D. Alcoholism.

7. Choose all of the answers that can complete this sentence: Stress can affect the respiratory system by _____.

A. causing stomach problems　　B. causing asthma

C. a loss of carbon dioxide　　　D. causing breathing problems

8. Symptoms of emotional stress include _____.

A. feeling joyous　　　　　　　B. feeling hungry

C. feeling thirsty　　　　　　　D. feeling tired

扫码获取本单元音频资料

Unit

15 Dialogue Interpreting

🎧 **Task 1: In this section, you are expected to interpret for both sides of the conversation about "how to sleep well". You may ask your classmates to act as the speakers, and others interpret for them.**

A: 最近我一直在考虑睡眠的问题，因为入睡很困难。生命三分之一的时间都用来睡觉，我们到底需要多少睡眠呢？究竟为什么需要睡觉呢？

B: Oh, you are not alone there. Many successful people barely sleep each day. I've always heard stories about so-called "super short sleepers". People like Bill Clinton, Martha Stewart and Napoleon that could function on around 4 hours of sleep per night.

A: 我想像他们一样。我曾经想象过，要是自己每天可以多几小时，可以多做多少事情啊！或者说，要是自己睡眠不足6小时，也可以不感觉累，可以多做多少事情啊！

B: Of course, it is difficult to answer the question, "Why do we sleep?" But according to an article in the *New York Times*, only about 5 percent of people are able to function at normal levels on about 4 hours of sleep per night, and it is not possible to train your body for less sleep. Nearly all of us need 8 hours of sleep per night to function at our highest level. Even dropping down to 7 hours harms our performance.

A: 他们如何做到了这一点呢？这个结论不容易得出来，不是吗？

B: The study had volunteers who spent two weeks at a sleep lab, where their sleep was carefully controlled as the performed tasks to measure their performance. There were three groups of sleepers, those who got 8 hours, 6 hours and 4 hours per night consistently over the two weeks. Most interestingly, while many of the 4 and 6 hour sleepers said that they "got used

246

to it" after a few days, tests they took showed that their actual performance had diminished substantially. So, even when people thought they were adapting to sleeplessness, it turned out they were unaware of its side effects.

A: 据我所知，Tesla（特斯拉）和SpaceX（太空探索技术公司）的CEO（首席执行官），埃隆·马斯克的睡眠就很少。他还在特斯拉工厂里边放上睡袋，就在生产线旁边，这样他可以在汽车生产出来之后更好地进行检查。难怪他可以成为美国排名第21位的大富豪。

B: Although the average person requires 7 to 9 hours of sleep, individuals may vary. While we may not know exactly why we sleep, most of us acknowledge that sleep makes us feel better. We feel more alert, more energetic, happier, and better able to function following a good night of sleep.

A: 我以前还能大概知道自己需要多少睡眠才够用，那时我还没有入睡困难的问题。曾几何时，我头一沾到枕头就睡着了，我觉得那个时候自己不缺觉。但是，不知从什么时候开始，我熬夜到越来越晚，忙着各种事情，可是没有一样跟睡眠有关系。毕竟，多看一集电视剧，多看一章书，多玩一个游戏，都比上床睡觉有趣多了，是吧？而且，即便是上床睡觉，也不是马上就能睡着啊。

B: I know it's not always easy to fall asleep right away. So what do you do when you're just staring at the ceiling, waiting for sheep to come? You know, any time someone mentions having trouble falling asleep, the suggestion to count sheep usually isn't far behind.

A: 我觉得自己得了失眠症。总是感觉很累，可是不困，甚至有些惧怕睡觉。就像是，头还没有沾到枕头，你就知道自己肯定睡不着觉。最后就是躺在那里，睁着眼睛，祈祷睡眠早点来到，可总是事与愿违。

B: Nowadays, my sleep isn't great, but it usually isn't terrible, either. There are many steps you can take to change behaviors and lifestyle to help you get to sleep and I have found a few things that help immensely.

A: 我尽量睡前不吃不喝，因为有人说晚饭吃得太晚或者睡前吃东西会刺激消化系统，让人难以入睡。我也尽量避免喝酒和咖啡，因为咖啡因的影响可以持续几小时，甚至24小时，所以它对睡眠的影响还是很大的。然而，这些方法好像对我都没有作用。你还有其他诀窍可以推荐吗？

B: We live in a world of screens, and heavy users of social media find it more difficult to fall asleep. Nowadays, they say that web surfing is the new second hand smoke. So I try to avoid digital distractions before bedtime and I find this is the most effective method that has worked on me. I also try to get all my worrying over with long before I go to bed. After dinner, I review the day and make plans for the next day. The goal is to avoid doing these things while trying to fall asleep.

A: 听起来很有道理。那么，我就睡前尽量减少接触电子设备。而且我觉得，睡前解决担心和焦虑对我更适用。我可以将它们写下来，留待明天解决。另外，或许我需要尝试一些放松疗法和减压手段，这样睡前身心都得到放松，看看是否奏效。

B: Healthy sleep habits can make a big difference in our quality of life. I hope these tips will help you sleep better at night and be more energetic and productive during your waking hours.

A: 谢谢！祈祷一夜好眠。

🎧 **Task 2: In this section, you are expected to interpret for both sides of the conversation about "school bullying". You may ask your classmates to act as the speakers, and others interpret for them.**

A: 我正在写一篇关于"校园欺凌"的文章，因为我觉得对这个问题的关注度不够。在对这个问题了解了更多之后，我发现应该在学校、教师、家长甚至学生们中间进行这方面知识的传播和分享。那么你的国家是怎么应对这个问题的呢？

B: Anti-bullying in Britain enjoys wide publicity. Bullying has taken on varied forms. It can be physical or verbal, like hitting, hair-pulling, kicking, teasing and name-calling. It can be emotional as well, like spreading rumours, frightening and intimidation, or exclusion at playtime or from social events. No child deserves to be bullied, and it can have a devastating effect on the victims. In most cases, bullying is viewed as an unfortunate but unavoidable part of school life. But in Britain, bullying is unacceptable behaviour and most schools have an anti-bullying policy.

A: 我觉得其他国家可以借鉴你们的做法。你刚刚说到，欺凌事件中的受害者应该得到保护，因为这可能对他们造成巨大的影响。心理学家们也发现，欺凌可能对儿童的个性发展和学业表现都造成不利影响。

B: Yes. Children being bullied will find it harder to trust others. They may lack self-confidence and often feel anxiety, anger, resentment or depression. These emotions will further undermine their ability to control their own life. And they may someday turn to bully others, which can form a vicious cycle.

A: 是的。预防总是胜于治疗。虽然说每个人都可能受到欺凌，但是有些群体更加脆弱，更容易成为被攻击的目标。调查也显示，普通学校的学生比重点学校的学生更容易经历欺凌事件；贫困家庭的孩子更容易在学校受到欺凌。实际上，欺凌他人的孩子首先自身就存在问题，了解造成这种行为的原因可能很有帮助。

B: Yes. Bullying can be subtle, so watching children's behaviour closely is important. Problematic children may be going through a difficult time, may feel overlooked, may be just copying someone else's behaviour. They may come from a family use aggression or force to get what they want. So teachers and parents should make sure that children understand that bullying is unacceptable. They should also encourage children to be friendly and kind to others.

A: 我的研究显示，有些情况下，孩子们不会告诉家长或者老师他们被欺凌。但是，他们的行为会发生一些改变，比如，他们可能不愿意上学，感到焦虑和急躁，与家庭成员发生争斗，夜里惊醒，甚至尿床。

B: That's true. I think publicity and government support are essential. In Britain, the National Curriculum covers bullying and relevant materials are widely used in schools by pupils for project work and by staff preparing lesson plans. Schools are asked to improve measures for preventing and handling bullying and establish an emergency plan for serious incidents.

A: 是的。研究者建议采取措施，比如，在教师、家长和学生中间加强沟通，开通欺凌事件报告热线，目的是在孩子们中间建立更加和谐的关系。

B: In Britain, organizations like "Bullying UK" and others provide anti-bullying support and advice all year round to anyone experiencing or suffering the effects of bullying. In schools, we have "Anti-bullying Month" and "Anti-bullying Week", when we help raise funds and awareness of anti-bullying. During the week schools will be undertaking their own awareness raising activities. I still remember we have "Wear Blue Day" in November each year.

A: 意思是那一天孩子们都穿蓝色衣服吗?

B: Yes. We ask schools, colleges, universities, individuals, organizations and businesses to wear blue and donate to "Bullying UK" and other organizations. We do this through our website, national support helpline, online resources and forums and through outreach in the community.

A: 公众的认识和参与非常有帮助。专家指出，教育是在学校环境下制止欺凌事件最好的方法。

B: I agree. And schools in Britain try to make the concept and idea of anti-bullying fun for children to take and remember. Students are asked to wear odd socks for anti-bullying awareness.

A: 这个听起来很"怪"。奇怪的袜子是什么呢?

B: Oh, on that day, children are encouraged to wear socks of different sizes or colors, or just oddly different socks! The idea is to make it easy to get involved with and there is no pressure to create an expensive costume. The "Odd Socks Day" is a national campaign, the aim of which is to help empower children and young people to celebrate what makes them unique, to help youngsters understand how important it is that they feel able to be themselves without fear of bullying.

A: 真是既有趣又有教育意义！这是个好主意，孩子们可以表达自己，学会欣赏个性和独特。我可以试着每天都穿奇怪的袜子！我现在可以在文章中加入新的想法了。

🎧 **Task 3: In this section, you are expected to interpret for experts from China and the US talking about "expansion of higher education". You may ask your classmates to act as the speakers, and others interpret for them.**

Host: Let's welcome our guests today, Dr. Hermans and Dr. Yang. Today's topic is expansion of enrollment of higher education. As we all know, policy makers around the world are considering large-scale reforms to increase the number of university students. Examples are "American's College Promise Act", which promises to grant all US students access to free community college. Another example is the 1999 Chinese reform that more than doubled university enrollment by increasing the size and number of public universities. What do you two think of the trend? What do you think are the causes for the expansion of enrollment of higher education?

杨博士：我认为诸多原因导致了扩招，比如，刺激国内消费，减轻劳动力市场的压力，公众对高等教育的兴趣和需求的增加，并且还可能仅仅是一个国家的政治意愿，需要发展高等教育。

Dr. Hermans: Exactly, the reasons can be varied and are usually based on demographic structure, social condition and even political need of a particular country. But generally, educational development is considered to be able to facilitate numerous favorable changes for individuals and nations. Some believe that expansion of enrollment is essential to national economic development, as better-educated citizens are more productive.

Host: Yes. Many scholars believe that enrollment expansion in higher education is an important method to expand domestic demand and stimulate economic growth. This is especially true for developing countries, right?

杨博士：是的。一些大的发展中国家，比如，金砖国家，已经是全球重要的力量。到21世纪中期，这些国家有望成为经济强国。它们是否能够达到那样的发展水平，一定程度上取决于这些国家是否可以成功造就高质量的高等教育。比如，印度的高等教育系统是世界上最大的，就读学生将近2,200万，高校数量超过46,000所。

Host: It is understandable that governments need educated labor force to develop the economy and citizens need to be better educated to enjoy better lives. But expansion of enrollment, in the short run, may lead to the decline of education level. How do you two think about this?

Dr. Hermans: After the university's enrollment is expanded, the rapid increase of the number of students and service workers and the frequent flow of teachers bring out many difficulties and problems to universities. For a particular university, it is always easy to construct buildings within a short period of time. Yet, it is not as easy to attract large number of professors to the university. In other words, betterment of software is always more difficult and takes more time. So, expansion of enrollment should always be a careful decision to make.

杨博士：我同意。过去几十年中，著名的大学，比如，哈佛、麻省理工、斯坦福等，招生人数基本维持在1.5万到2万人。

Dr. Hermans: There are many factors which come into play in determining the quality of university education, but one thing that many parents overlook is student-teacher ratio, which is the number of students who attend a school or a university divided by the number of teachers in the institution. For example, a student-teacher ratio of 10∶1 indicates that there are 10 students for every one teacher. The top 100 universities with the best student-to-staff ratios are predominantly US colleges, followed by Japanese institutions.

杨博士：生师比很重要，原因很多。首先，它是一个工具，可以用来衡量教师工作量以及资源分配情况。而更重要的是，它可以表明每个学生可能获得的关注程度。一所大学的生师比通常可以用来判断其教育质量。显然，扩招的同时，如果不在师资数量和质量上进行辅助提升，将导致生师比的恶化，长期就会导致教育质量的恶化。

Host: Anything that can be done to ensure the healthy development of higher institutions while providing more opportunities to students?

Dr. Hermans: Firstly, I think the expansion of enrollment should be moderate and steady. If it can be double enrollment over a three-year period, then it should not be five-fold in six years. Secondly, the study-aid policy, student loan policy, study-aid fund, and scholarship system should receive enough attention, which will support university students with financial difficulties.

杨博士：此外，大学扩招的同时，过时的教学材料和陈旧的教学方法等问题应该得到解决。这样，大学毕业生才可以成为社会需要的人才，也不会存在就业难的问题。

Host: Thank you two, Dr. Yang and Dr. Hermans for coming and sharing your ideas with us.

🎧 **Task 4: In this section, you are expected to interpret for experts from China and the US talking about "electric vehicles". You may ask your classmates to act as the speakers, and others interpret for them.**

Peter: Dr. Wang, thank you for having me here. We know that electric vehicles (EVs) have made huge technological strides since they were first introduced, and they're more popular than ever before now.

王博士：我们的国家与其他国家一道，认识到了电动汽车的优势。很多汽车生产大国已经跨越了传统的汽油和柴油技术。这也就是我们为什么要加速这种转变的原因，要尽快使电动汽车的优势能够惠及驾驶者、公众和环境。

Peter: Yes, we are giving financial help to drivers who choose cleaner vehicles through grants and the tax system, and supporting local authorities to provide incentives such as free parking and congestion charge exemptions. In the future, we want to make it easier and more convenient to recharge electric vehicles.

王博士：目前，对于驾驶者来说，选择一辆新车总是很难的抉择。如果在传统的汽油车和电动车之间做出选择，则是更难的事情。如今为人熟知的电动车包括日产聆风、福特福克斯电动车、特斯拉Model S等。

Peter: Yes, when choosing what car to buy, drivers will take the biggest benefit of electric cars into consideration, which is obvious: You no longer need gas. That's a big deal, since the average American spends between $2,000 and $4,000 on gas every year. With fully electric cars such as the Nissan Leaf, that cost is eliminated, though electricity isn't free.

王博士：除了省油，电动汽车的保养费用也比较低。因为电动汽车完全用电，不再使用发动机润滑油，这就意味着换机油已经成为历史。此外，电动车的刹车耗损也不像汽油车那么快，也就不必经常替换刹车片了。

Peter: And a plug-in hybrid can also eliminate a major portion of your gas bill, as well, but it still uses a gasoline engine as a range extender.

王博士：彼得，你讲到了电动车最大的弊端，就是里程有限。所谓的"里程焦虑"，就是还没有开到充电站就用光了电量的恐惧。这也是限制了潜在客户购买愿望的因素。

Peter: Indeed, to give an example, Nissan Leaf can travel up to 107 miles on a single charge. For most drivers, that's more than enough to get around. But, the thought of only being able to drive 100 miles on a charge worries a lot of potential customers, who think that the somewhat limited range of electric vehicles isn't enough to meet their needs.

王博士：与此相近，电动车另一大不足就是许多驾驶者需要在家里安装充电站。倒也不是必需，因为你可以在工作的地方为车充电，也可以使用许多公共场所的充电站。但是，大多数用户需要家里有一个充电站，这也符合他们最初购买电动车节省成本的初衷。

Peter: Yes, people who live in family houses can simply plug in their vehicles after they return home from work, and leave the next morning with batteries fully charged.

王博士：在充电基础设施方面，首先应该考虑的就是购物中心和其他类似的地方，人们一般会将车停在那里一段时间；而不仅仅是在加油站或是人们频繁进出的地方。另外，充电基础设施需要涵盖广泛的范围，这一点很重要。容易出现的情况就是，充电基础设施集中在主要线路和城市及郊区，一些小路和乡村的充电设施不足。

Peter: The government could consider going further and regulating so that all new houses with driveways for EV charging should have the electricity supply that is necessary for effective charging of EVs. All new workplaces should also have EV charging facilities on site or a provision to install charge points.

王博士：我认为拥有电动汽车的人应该被登记下来。在挪威，电动汽车车牌上会标上字母EL。我希望，使用电动汽车的人可以得到政府的奖励。这项技术令人兴奋，是未来的趋势。我很高兴我们两国的政府都抓住了这个机会。

Peter: Up to now, other technologies also have profound implications for the way we use our cars. Revolutionary new driver assistance systems are already delivering improvements that motorists now take for granted. Our parents could not have envisaged sat-nav, assisted parking or even cruise control, which would have seemed like science fiction just a generation or two ago.

王博士：从根本上说，电动汽车数量的增加，对我们如何使用汽车能源意义深远。

这不是科幻小说，而是科学事实。它们标志着更为重大的改变：我们这一代和下一代享用的各种技术，都将极大改变汽车产业。

Peter: Given all the facts, right now, introduction of comprehensive charging networks will make electric vehicles more practical for longer trips.

王博士：在电动车和汽油车之间进行选择是困难的，但我们依然希望，以上关于优点和不足的解释可以帮助您做出正确的选择。

Key to the Exercises

Unit 1

Warm Up

Task A

    （1）caught up   （2）deadly force   （3）dispossessed   （4）Trillions

    （5）fueling   （6）destabilized   （7）affects   （8）resolve

    （9）solidarity   （10）compromise

Task B

    （1）Asia-Pacific Economic Cooperation   （2）forum

    （3）Gross Domestic Product   （4）interdependence

    （5）Leaders' Meeting and Ministerial Meeting   （6）consensus

    （7）dynamic engine   （8）Residents

    （9）per capita income

    （10）climate change, anti-terrorism, health and energy

    （11）Australia, Mexico, Peru, Chile, Japan, the US and Vietnam

    （12）front

    （13）the benefits of growth are felt by all

    （14）all citizens have a real and fair chance to succeed

Listening Comprehension

Guided Practice

Task A

    （1）Monday, March the 13th

    （2）Food

    （3）"The Australian Week Cup" tennis tournament

    （4）Australian Investment Seminar

（5）Australian Painting Exhibition

（6）Australian Photographic Exhibition

Task B

Try This

（1）current or recent

（2）earlier

（3）borrow

（4）listen or watch

（5）typewriters

（6）copying machines

（7）Monday—Friday, 9 a.m.—6 p.m.

（8）Bank Holidays and University closures

（9）4:15 p.m.

（10）5:45 p.m.

（11）register

（12）contact in advance, make an appointment

（13）free or paid

（14）librarian

（15）download illegal things

（16）check availability

（17）put on hold

（18）order from other libraries

Task C

（1）Industry is the production of materials and goods

（2）An industry is a group of manufacturers or businesses that produce a particular kind of goods or services

（3）Industries can be classified in a variety of ways

（4）Manufacturing industry became a key sector of production and labour in European and North American countries during the Industrial Revolution

（5）manufacturing industries

（6）manufacturing industry

（7）Service industry is an industry that creates services rather than tangible objects

（8）all professional services

（9）all consumer services, and all government services

（10）A services-dominated economy is characteristic of developed countries

Try this

Manufacturing industries: 2, 3, 4, 8, 9, 10, 11, 13, 14, 19.

Service industries: 1, 5, 6, 7, 12, 15, 16, 17, 18, 20.

Try This

（1）the industrial sector

（2）industrialize

（3）emerging industries

（4）heavy industries

（5）light industries

（6）growth industries

（7）high-technology industries

（8）industrial robotics

（9）industrialists

（10）Ministry of Trade and Industry

Summary Interpreting

Guided Practice

Task A

东盟经济体的活力对欧洲来说是一个机遇。然而，许多这种机遇还只是潜在的，尚未成为现实。欧洲企业尝试在东南亚进行贸易或投资时，还是面临着关税和非关税壁垒，那里的市场有所倾斜，不利于国外的服务供应商，尤其在公共采购市场中更是如此。对外商直接投资亦是这样。欧洲企业还发现，他们的知识产权还是没有得到很好的保护，一些市场的总体透明度很低。这就要求我们制定一个自由贸易协定。

Task B

南北发展上极大的不均衡是世界经济不平衡的根本原因。最不发达国家是世界经济中的弱势群体。中等收入国家拥有全球贫困人口的60%，他们面临多重的外界影响和风险。如期实现千年发展目标，一个关键因素就是要为这些国家提供长久的资金支持，并且建立新型的全球发展伙伴关系，更加公平和均衡的关系。

Task C

非洲的发展是实现世界经济发展不可或缺的组成部分。中国呼吁国际社会要更加切实有效地支持非洲发展。

一是国际社会应该坚持决心不动摇，措施不减弱，帮助非洲实现千年发展目标；应该履行对非援助承诺，为非洲创造有利的外部国际经济、贸易和金融等条件。

二是国际社会应该深刻认识非洲国家的迫切需求——提高适应气候变化的能力，帮助他们更好应对气候挑战，同时提高其可持续发展能力。

三是国际社会应该更加理解非洲国家在解决全球问题，如粮食安全、能源安全和流行性疾病时面临的特殊困难。

Unit 2

Warm Up

Task A

（1）relentless

（2）unprecedented

（3）triple

（4）stable and secure

（5）innovative financing mechanisms

（6）China-Africa Development Fund

（7）eliminate extreme poverty

（8）uneven

（9）nutrition

（10）heights

（11）usher in

（12）coincide

Task B

（1）fairs　（2）communities　（3）historic　（4）permanent　（5）pressing

（6）forge　（7）employ　（8）concepts　（9）contribution　（10）dedication

Listening Comprehension

Guided Practice

Passage 1

（1）More attention has been paid to the serious and growing threat of cell phone use on roadways

（2）cell phone bans are simply not enforceable

（3）drivers do all sorts of distracting things while driving

（4）it is without a doubt that cell phone use while driving increases crash risk

（5）Talking on a phone while driving taxes the cognitive skills of your brain

（6）ban the use of cell phone while driving and the effect has been obvious

（7）once enforced, the ban should be further monitored, in order to guarantee its long-term effectiveness

（8）drunk driving, speeding, seat belts, child safety seats

（9）ban on cell phone use while driving can be enforced

（10）there is no scientific evidence

(11) drivers can safely talk on phones without getting into crashes

Passage 2

(1) Dress codes and appearance at work   (2) a uniform

(3) health and safety   (4) discriminatory

(5) comply with a dress code   (6) discomfort

(7) physical pain and even harm   (8) Consulting

(9) take into account   (10) give sexism the boot

Passage 3

(1) algebra teaches basic logic, but so does creating a budget and learning how to stick to it

(2) why personal finance should be taught in school are as enlightening as they are obvious

(3) money management is a learned skill

(4) a false one

(5) be exposed to financial planning concepts that they might otherwise not learn about

(6) important skills that need to be acquired as early on as possible

(7) know how to plan for a future that includes debt, rather than trying to cope with it once they've graduated

(8) make decisions about financial matters

(9) become capable of working with others to change things for the better

Try This

(1) account   (2) branch

(3) high-street banks   (4) current account

(5) debit card   (6) in the black

(7) go into the red   (8) overdraft

(9) interest rate   (10) deposit account

(11) credit card   (12) Buying with plastic

(13) pay it off   (14) emergency fund

(15) retirement plan   (16) investment account

(17) manage your money   (18) living from paycheck to paycheck

Summary Interpreting

Guided Practice

Passage 1

（1）circumstances

（2）Habitual

（3）helpful

（4）time and energy

（5）at some level

（6）focus

（7）goal

（8）keep

（9）avoid

（10）break

（11）building up

（12）regular

（13）add up to

（14）positive

（15）productive

（16）recharge

Passage 2

（1）a good diet

（2）plenty of exercise

（3）body and mind

（4）Studies

（5）an animal

（6）lower

（7）reduce

（8）pet owners

（9）people with dogs

（10）minutes

（11）reduces

（12）extends

（13）having a bond

（14）important

（15）isolated

（16）Loneliness

Passage 3

（1）decline

（2）interfere with

（3）Alzheimer's

（4）Dementia

（5）damage

（6）brain cells

（7）affected

（8）brain cell damage

（9）brain cells

（10）each other

（11）crisis

（12）public understanding

（13）less

（14）independently

（15）communities and businesses

（16）memory loss

（17）recalling

（18）affect

（19）symptoms

（20）problems

（21）struggling

（22）issues

(23) trouble   (24) problems

(25) difficulties   (26) Symptoms

(27) independent

Unit 3

Warm Up

Task A

(1) diagnosed   (2) World AIDS Day

(3) stigma   (4) have access to every level of society

(5) problematic   (6) alongside those communities

(7) claims   (8) solidarity

Task B

(1) awakening   (2) vulnerable

(3) unemployed   (4) fulfill

(5) poor mental health   (6) addressing

(7) taboo   (8) failing

(9) appalling   (10) outcry

(11) normalize   (12) minor

Listening Comprehension

Guided Practice

1. if we; if we; if we don't, we will both suffer

2. I say

3. optimism

4. used to; now

5. hundreds of thousands

6. bring in the skilled workers they needed; attract the best talent from around the world

7. opportunity; open their markets to China; welcome China in

8. continuity; Tony Blair; Gordon Brown; trade; investment; dialogue

9. threat; shared

10. We share an interest; we share an interest; we share an interest; political

Task A

　（1）H　　（2）G　　（3）D　　（4）C　　（5）I

　（6）F　　（7）B　　（8）A　　（9）E

Task B

　（1）K　　（2）E　　（3）I　　（4）L　　（5）B

　（6）H　　（7）G　　（8）F　　（9）C　　（10）J

　（11）A　　（12）D

Task C

　（1）G　　（2）E　　（3）D　　（4）C　　（5）B

　（6）F　　（7）A　　（8）K　　（9）I　　（10）L

　（11）H　　（12）J

Summary Interpreting

Guided Practice

Task A

　1. a temporary home for people who are traveling

　2. a swimming pool, a golf course, or a beach

　3. free space for the traveler's means of transportation

　4. the accommodations industry

　5. that were quite isolated

　6. to which people travel for recreation

　7. mountain scenery, the combination of sun and sea

　8. The first

　9. traveling on business

　10. The second category

　11. A third type of hotel

　12. The fourth category

Task B

　1. there is no requirement for food manufacturers to label their foods as containing GM ingredients

　2. GM foods are highly regulated

　3. "produced from genetically modified soybean"

4. "produced from genetically modified maize"

5. they vary on the amount of GM protein or DNA that can be present in a food before it has to be labeled as containing a GM ingredient

6. GM ingredients are no different to natural ones

7. whether that food ingredient came from a GM source

8. want to know the origin of all the ingredients

9. any potential risk is small and buy the food, or decide to avoid it

10. make a choice

Task C

You've probably been to lots of meetings and have seen them done well or badly. The key to **chair** any successful **meeting** is a competent chair person. If you were asked to perform the role, would you know what to do? If you don't, read on to learn how to make any meeting a success.

Firstly, the role of a chairperson is to keep control of the meeting, move it along and keep it on track. And, if you are chosen to be chairperson, you need to be **organised and authoritative**. The chairperson should be **a good timekeeper**. They should start the meeting on time, without waiting for latecomers.

Secondly, the chairperson should make sure the **agenda** (the list of things to be discussed) is **complete** by asking those involved what should be on it and then **distribute** it to everyone concerned. Also, the chairperson should make sure that everyone has the agenda well in advance. They should make sure each point on the agenda is allocated the time it deserves and should keep to the timetable. When the time allocated to one point is up, the chair should make sure that discussion moves on to the next point, even if the issue has not been completely covered. Also, the chair should make sure that the meeting discusses only what's on the agenda. Any other issues being raised can be noted for inclusion in the next meeting. In order to achieve this, the chair may need to be firm, so be prepared for this.

Thirdly, the chairperson should make sure that **participants** have the chance to **make their points**. Not only does the chairperson need to keep control of what is discussed at the meeting, he or she also has to decide how much time is spent on each topic, ensure that all those in attendance get the chance to contribute if they wish to do so, and keep the meeting from descending into a serious argument. It is the chairperson's job to ensure that everyone in the room feels able to comment if they want to, even those who may be shy. Meeting etiquette usually demands that any contribution from the chairperson comes last.

Last but not least, if the meeting is likely to be more than a couple of hours long, try to include **a break at the mid-point**; it acts as a marker and stops people getting restless.

Task D

It is truly a great pleasure to be here and it's inspiring to talk on the theme on **Corporate Social Responsibility**. It is also inspiring to lead **Ericsson**. And...eh...the fact that the...yes, and the fact that providing mobile telephoning to the world is...I think there are few products that have been invented, that has meant so much to people as **mobile phone**. It's fascinating to think about China today with 380 million people having their own phone and we can communicate in a better way. And, anyway, it is a great pleasure to be here; I'm very glad to be invited. For me it's a great opportunity to share with you our Ericsson's views on the importance and experience of Corporate Social Responsibility.

In recent years, and I would say, due to increasing **economic globalization and liberalization**, the pressing **environmental issues**, and a number of serious **corporate failures**, people are changing their view of the role of corporations in our society. Traditionally, the role of corporations has been understood primarily in economic terms. Now increasingly, **stakeholders**, like **shareholders**, **investors**, **communities**, **regulators**, **employees** and **customers**, are looking into corporate responsibility in a much broader perspective. And it includes not only economic performance, but also social and environmental performance factors, such as business ethics, corporate governance, environmental policies, corporate contributions, community development and also workplace issues.

Unit 4

Warm Up
Task A

（1）address （2）implications （3）urgency （4）innovation
（5）mentality （6）regeneration （7）solutions （8）phase
（9）facilitate （10）businesses

Task B

（1）concluded （2）reduction （3）praised （4）prevent
（5）complex （6）numerous （7）correlation
（8）The researchers say about one in six people over the age of 70 have problems with

mental operations

（9）Over time, the disease robs people of their memories. Finally, it takes away their ability to care for themselves

（10）The results did not show a difference in loss of abilities such as attention, language and memory

Listening Comprehension

Guided Practice

Task A

（1）The first one is that keeping a good mood can help you stay healthy

（2）moods and behaviors　　（3）liver　　　　（4）less

（5）Another reason is that with a good mood we can get on better with others

（6）a positive mood　　　　（7）nor　　　　（8）In all

（9）keeping a good mood　　（10）trying

Task B

（1）rich in　　（2）insufficient in　　（3）which are necessary

（4）that is why　　（5）easier　　（6）nutrition unbalance

（7）BPA　　（8）fast foods　　（9）harms　　（10）healthier

Task C

（1）The first　　（2）plastics　　（3）plastic　　（4）The next thing

（5）bottled water　（6）tap water　　（7）bottled water　（8）bottled water

（9）bottled water　（10）plastic　　（11）bottled water　（12）reusable

（13）water filters　（14）boiled water

Task D

（1）education level　　　　（2）education level　　　　（3）education

（4）The second thing that any country can do is in fact to invest in research and development

（5）ideas　　　（6）standard of living　（7）investment in research and development

（8）high-tech venture capital investments　（9）the United States　　（10）Asia

Summary Interpreting

Guided Practice

1. 我很高兴有机会来做欧委会最新的年度报告，报告欧盟成员国取得的进展，在实现教育和培训方面共同的欧洲目标方面的进展。

2. 结束演讲之前，我想再一次呼吁各成员国保持甚至增加教育经费，即便我们面临经济危机带来的限制。

3. 这就是为什么教育要摆在欧洲2020战略的核心，这一战略由欧盟提出，目的是应对前方的挑战，建立一个智能、包容和环保的社会。

4. 我坚信这一报告将帮助各成员国调集更好的资源，用于教育部门内最需投入的领域。

5. 他们必须愿意与高等教育机构合作，长期合作，帮助研发新课程，提供更多实习岗位等。

6. 电子商务在经济大环境恶化的背景下具有独特的吸引力：消费者可以对比价格，轻松快捷地货比三家。买家在网上购物，有时可以避开当地的营业税，而且通常免运费。

7. 在世界经济论坛上，瑞士高居最近公布的竞争力排行榜榜首，该国以其一年一度在达沃斯（瑞士的滑雪胜地）举行的经济论坛而闻名。紧随其后的是新加坡，芬兰略胜瑞典一筹，位列第三。在大的新兴经济体中，中国排名最高，巴西排名有所上升。

8. 日本人的医疗花费只是美国人的一半，却更长寿。平均寿命从1945年的52岁，上升到如今的83岁。很多人将其归因于他们价格低廉、覆盖广泛的医疗保险系统。日本是世界上新生儿死亡率较低的几个国家之一，然而其医疗支出只占GDP的8.5%。

9. 考虑到创新的历史，医疗保健行业却迟迟没有拥抱信息技术（IT）。其他大型的产业自20世纪80年代起就电脑化了，而世界大多数地区的医生仍旧在与笔和纸打交道。

10. 25年前，我来到香港，当时我还是个学生。那是1985年，邓小平和玛格丽特·撒切尔刚刚签署了历史性的联合声明。香港成功回归，自那以后获得巨大发展，这都向世界表明，两个国家信任合作，互相尊重，就可以互有所得。自那时起，中国发生了翻天覆地的变化。中国的国歌号召中国人民站起来。今天，中国人民不仅在自己的国家站了起来，还在世界上站了起来。人们说起全球经济，就要提及中国，因为它以每年10%的速度发展了30年；人们说起贸易，就要提及中国，因为它是世界上最大的出口国和第三大进口国；人们说起能源安全或气候变化，就要提及中国，因为它是世界上最大的能源消费国。中国正在重新获得世界最大经济体的地位，这个地位它在过去20个世纪的18个世纪中都一直拥有，这样的成就是中国人民应该引以为豪的。简言之，中国已经作为世界大国，重新崛起了。

Unit 5

Warm up

Task A

Microsoft is no longer the world's biggest company by market capitalization. Three other U.S. companies have overtaken the software giant in terms of stock market value. The firm's value has gone down sharply by 41% so far this year, from nearly $600 billion to $358 billion. Much of the reason for the fall has been the uncertainty prompted by the on-going anti-trust case. It has been overtaken by General Electric, now worth $506 billion, Intel, worth $441 billion and Cisco Systems, $436 billion.

Answers: 1. B   2. B

Task B

Paradise Lost is Milton's masterpiece. Its story is taken from the *Bible*, about "the fall of man", that is, how Adam and Eve are tempted by Satan to disobey God by eating the forbidden fruit from the Tree of Knowledge, and how they are punished by God and driven out of Paradise. In Milton's words, the purpose of writing the epic is to "justify the ways of God to men", but apparently, Milton is uttering his intense hatred of cruelness of the ruler in the poem. In the poem, God is no better than a cruel and selfish ruler, seated on a throne with a group of angels about him singing songs to praise him. He is cruel and unjust in punishing Satan. But Satan is by far the most striking character in the poem, who rises against God and, though defeated, still persists in his fighting.

Answers: 1. A   2. B   3. B   4. B

Task C

There are various ways in which individual economic units can interact with one another. In a market, transactions may take place via barter or money exchange. In a barter economy, real goods such as automobiles, shoes, and pizzas are traded against each other. Obviously, finding somebody who wants to trade my old car in exchange for a sailboat may not always be an easy task. Hence, the introduction of money as a medium of exchange eases transactions considerably. In the modern market economy, goods and services are bought or sold for money. An alternative to the market system is administrative control by some agency over all transactions.

Answers: 1. A   2. D

Listening Comprehension

Guided Practice

Try This

1. This pollution results mainly from the coal powered factories in developing countries, which produce inexpensive goods for North American and European consumers.

（1）This pollution results from the coal powered factories in developing countries.

（2）The factories produce inexpensive goods for North American and European consumers.

分译译文：

（1）污染源于发展中国家的煤电厂（发展中国家的煤电厂造成了污染）。

（2）这些工厂生产廉价商品满足北美和欧洲消费者（的需求）。

合译译文：

发展中国家的煤电厂为北美和欧洲消费者生产廉价商品，造成了污染。

2. This type of pollution reduces the amount of land suitable for agricultural production and contributes to global food shortages.

（1）This type of pollution reduces the amount of land suitable for agricultural production.

（2）(This type of pollution) It also contributes to global food shortages.

分译译文：

（1）这种污染减少了适合农业生产的土地数量。

（2）（这种污染）也造成了全球食物短缺。

合译译文：

这种污染减少了适合农业生产的土地数量，也造成了全球食物短缺。

3. Dumping of industrial and domestic waste produces much of the world's soil pollution, though natural disasters can also add to the problem.

（1）Dumping of industrial and domestic waste produces much of the world's soil pollution.

（2）Natural disasters can also add to the problem of (soil pollution).

分译译文：

（1）工业和生活垃圾的倾倒造成世界范围内的土壤污染。

（2）自然灾害也会加剧土壤污染（的问题）。

合译译文：

工业和生活垃圾的倾倒造成世界范围内的土壤污染，而自然灾害也会加剧土壤污染（的问题）。

4. People whose diet contains a high percentage of trans fats are at risk for heart disease

and stroke.

（1）Some people's diet contains a high percentage of trans fats.

（2）They are at risk for heart disease and stroke.

分译译文：

（1）一些人的饮食中含有较高比例的反式脂肪酸。

（2）这些人患心脏病和中风的风险较高。

合译译文：

饮食中含有较高比例反式脂肪酸的人患心脏病和中风的风险较高。

5. This concerns many health professionals who point out that many cancers take at least ten years to develop.

（1）This concerns many health professionals.

（2）They point out that many cancers take at least ten years to develop.

分译译文：

（1）很多健康专业人士为此担忧。

（2）他们指出，很多癌症至少需要10年才能形成。

合译译文：

很多健康专业人士为此担忧，他们指出，很多癌症至少需要10年才能形成。

Task A

（1）tone of voice, facial expression and body language

（2）non-verbally

（3）verbally

（4）the way we greet one another; how we stand, how we sit or walk; the way we position our arms and legs or use our hands and eyes

（5）discomfort or misunderstandings

（6）distance

（7）personal comfort zone

（8）embarrassment or apology

（9）potentially disastrous consequences

（10）overly afraid of using inappropriate body language in an unfamiliar culture

（11）advisable

（12）careful observation

Task B

(1) environmental concern   (2) premature deaths

(3) World Health Organization   (4) little or no access

(5) third world countries   (6) sewage and waste

(7) coal powered factories   (8) smog

(9) industrial and developing countries   (10) seep into

(11) land suitable for agricultural production   (12) global food shortages

(13) industrial and domestic waste   (14) natural disasters

Task C

(1) junk food   (2) semi-solid   (3) inexpensive

(4) margarine   (5) good cholesterol   (6) block

(7) Nutrition Fact   (8) daily recommendations   (9) all ingredients

(10) a labeling system   (11) unsaturated fats   (12) Labels

Try This

1. Trans fat is a semi-solid type of oil. It is made by adding hydrogen to liquid oil.

2. Because trans fat is inexpensive, makes food last longer, and improves the taste of food.

3. Trans fat became popular in the second half of the 20th century, when butter got a bad name and people started to use margarine made from trans fat.

4. Trans fat raises the bad cholesterol and lowers the good cholesterol that the body needs. Trans fat causes obesity, blocks blood flow to the heart, and causes higher risk for heart disease and stroke.

5. In US and Canada, food and beverage makers have to attach a Nutrition Fact label to their products. New York City banned trans fats from all restaurants. In Europe, food manufacturers have started using a labeling system.

6. They are saturated fats, trans fats, and unsaturated fats, and the last one is recommended.

Task D

(1) cancer

(2) mobile phone use

(3) impossible to study the long term exposure of mobile phone use

(4) many have been funded by those who benefit financially from the mobile phone industry

(5) Mobile phone antennas are similar to microwave ovens

(6) the lower frequency radio waves that mobile phones rely on may also be dangerous

(7) other types of wireless technology may also be dangerous to human health

(8) out of bedrooms

(9) six feet from your pillow

(10) use headsets or speaker phones

(11) use mobile phones only for emergencies

(12) tobacco

(13) lung cancer

Try This

1. C   2. C   3. A   4. B   5. B

Summary Interpreting

Guided Practice

Task A

1. The project is proceeding rather slowly because of his uncooperativeness.

His uncooperative attitude resulted in the project's slow progress.

2. Those of you who want to go on the spring outing are required to sign up and hand the payment before Friday.

If any of you wants to take part in the spring outing, please sign up and pay for it before Friday.

3. In my opinion, the dress in the shop is still too high-priced even if it is discounted.

The price of the dress in the shop is still more than I would pay even if a discount is offered.

4. If you should want to cancel the trip, please notify us in writing at least one month in advance.

One month's written notice should be provided prior to the cancellation of the trip.

5. It seems unlikely for him to grant such a request.

There is a strong possibility that he will turn down a request like this.

6. We analyzed the questionnaire responses and found that there were a number of differences between male and female subjects.

Differences between male and female participants were found through analysis of the questionnaire responses.

Task B

1. **Researchers**, between 2013 and 2014, tested (inspected) 14 provinces and municipalities, and the test included (covered) 46,000 adults 20 years old or older.

Researchers did a survey between 2013 and 2014. It covered 14 provinces and municipalities and 46,000 adults 20 years old or older.

Between 2013 and 2014, researchers tested more than 46,000 adults 20 years old or older in 14 provinces and municipalities.

A survey was done between 2013 and 2014, to cover 46,000 adults 20 years old or older in 14 provinces and municipalities.

A survey was done between 2013 and 2014, in 14 provinces and municipalities, and it covered 46,000 adults 20 years old or older.

2. **China's booming economy** has led to major dietary changes. People start to have high calorie diets and get less exercise; obesity therefore has been a problem on the rise.

China's economic development has changed people's diet. They start to have high calorie diets yet exercise less. Therefore, more and more people become obese.

China's economy has been developing, which has changed people's diet. More high calorie diets and less exercise have resulted in a rise in obesity.

The economic development of China has changed the diets of its people. More high calorie diets and less exercise have caused the increase of the number of obese people.

3. **Measures** have been taken to compel multinationals to enter in partnership with local investors. The purpose is to gain firm control over some of their important industries and products, as these industries and products are strategically significant (for the host countries).

In some developing countries, measures have been taken to compel multinationals to form partnership with local investors, with the aim of firmly controlling some of their important industries and products that may be strategically significant for the host countries.

4. **Auckland** is the biggest city in New Zealand in terms of population. Its diversified industries include: manufacturing, services, finance, entertainment and education. It is also a city with a variety of ethnic background. The industrial diversity and ethnic variety make the city a mirror of New Zealand as well as a window on the wider world.

In New Zealand, the most populous city is Auckland. It boasts of its diversified industries such as manufacturing, services, finance, entertainment and education. Its industrial diversity, coupled with its variety of ethnic background, makes Auckland both a typical city of New Zealand and a window on the wider world.

5. **To improve education**, my government will train more teachers, build more schools, provide more scholarships, help families in rural areas lacking schools, publish affordable

textbooks, and improve educational television programs.

My government's education plans include more teacher training, more school construction, more scholarships, helping rural families far from schools, publication of affordable textbooks, and educational television improvement.

6. **Jane saw a deer in the road**, so she swung her car around to miss the animal. Her car headed for the trees. Her mind flooded with images of her family, and she wondered if she would die today. As the front of the car crunched into the tree, she lost consciousness for a moment, though she thankfully survived the crash with just a few bumps.

While out driving, Jane hit a tree because she swerved to miss a deer. She thought about how her family would miss her if she died as the car slammed into the tree. She sustained minor injuries, though the impact knocked her out for a bit.

Unit 6

Warm Up

Task A

(1) empowerment   (2) advocate   (3) advancing   (4) pillars

(5) enhancing   (6) Genuinely   (7) theme   (8) exploitation

(9) overturning   (10) quality

Task B

(1) eating less of the foods rich in cholesterol

(2) meats, milk products and eggs

(3) deaths from heart disease

(4) Food and Nutrition Board of the United States National Academy of Sciences

(5) no evidence to link

(6) heart attacks

(7) heart attack deaths

(8) the amount of cholesterol in a person's blood

(9) the number of deaths

(10) settle the cholesterol dispute

(11) low cholesterol foods

(12) anticholesterol drugs

(13) private groups, government agencies and several popular books

（14）no good scientific evidence

（15）false hopes

（16）unnecessary fears

Listening Comprehension

Guided Practice

Task A

Paragraph 1

（1）so　　（2）dog　　（3）the brindle Staffie　　（4）the first and the last animal

（5）Max　（6）He　　（7）he　　　　　（8）his

（9）he　　（10）his　　（11）Animal Rescue Live

Paragraph 2

（1）body clocks　　　　　　　　　（2）waking up refreshed

（3）bed at a suitable time　　　　　（4）sleeping rhythm

（5）irregularity　　　　　　　　　（6）sleeping pattern

（7）constant stream of light　　　　（8）blue light

（9）TV, tablets or mobile phones　　（10）technology

Paragraph 3

（1）the supply　　　　　　　　　（2）the demand

（3）electricity　　　　　　　　　（4）power companies

（5）energy　　　　　　　　　　　（6）dependent

（7）supply of electricity　　　　　（8）alternative energy sources

（9）independence　　　　　　　　（10）power companies

（11）energy　　　　　　　　　　（12）fossil fuels

（13）these fuels　　　　　　　　　（14）oil and gas

Task B

Passage 1

Getting Things Done

Everyone puts things off until the last minute sometimes, but procrastinators chronically avoid difficult tasks and deliberately look for distractions, and they put things off until the last minute. And in order to meet deadlines, procrastinators would burn the midnight oil for three consecutive days, drink Red Bull and a whole lot of coffee, and even smoke cigarettes to get the so-called inspiration. Procrastinators may say they perform better under pressure, but more often than not that's their way of justifying putting things off. Procrastination in large part reflects our struggle with self-control.

Actually, those who don't procrastinate seem to get loads of work done. And they don't have any innate gift in that. They just know techniques and strategies that you don't. You'll probably find it hard work incorporating all of the techniques and strategies into your life simultaneously. Then you may pick out the most promising-looking ones to start with, or the easiest ones, or perhaps the ones that you need most. Here are a few tips that may help you become more organized, to achieve "effortless accomplishments" that others admire.

First, learn to say no. If you're someone who finds it hard to say no, it's much harder to keep the workload down when you're taking on extra just because you can't find the words to say no. You may in fact be able to say no that still sounds helpful, if you give an explanation why you can't take the extra, or suggest an alternative solution that may also be of some help.

Second, visualise the finished thing. Once you're daunted by a task, think about how you'll feel and what you'll enjoy once it's complete. Also, you may give yourself a treat or a reward once you finish the whole task, or at the end of each smaller chunk of the task if the task is a long one. It's an effective way to push yourself get onto the task if you imagine beautiful things you can do afterwards. And always, it won't be long before you suddenly realise you're over halfway and can see the light at the end of the tunnel.

Third, streamline your workload. If you want to get through your workload faster, it makes sense to put your tasks into related groups. It's always quicker to do things that belong to the same category because you have the same resources to hand, and your mind doesn't have to make so many leaps. Even you can multitask some of those tasks, especially those which are relatively mindless. For example, you can get some general reading done during ad breaks on TV. You can plan your meals for the week while you're shopping in the supermarket.

Everyone can get more done if they decide to make it happen, and that includes you. Stick with it, and you'll find that not only are you achieving far more, you're also making less effort and your life is more relaxed.

（1）Procrastinators   （2）put things off   （3）pressure

（4）self-control   （5）innate gift   （6）techniques and strategies

（7）promising   （8）easy   （9）needed

（10）effortless   （11）workload   （12）an explanation

（13）an alternative solution　（14）visualise　　（15）treat

（16）reward　　　　　　　（17）streamline　　（18）category

（19）resources　　　　　　（20）multitask

Passage 2

Walking

Traditionally well-known cardiovascular exercises like slow jogging, bicycling, or swimming can effectively improve circulation. And current recommendations suggest adults make time for at least 20 minutes of moderate to vigorous physical activity and it can make them more active, lose weight and become healthier.

Today, we talk about the easiest and simplest form of exercise — walking. Walking is a basic movement we use every day, but it can require discipline to walk enough to gain health benefits. As to the best time of day to walk, actually anytime is fine as long as it fits with your schedule. Many people prefer a brisk morning walk to get the blood moving, while others prefer an after-dinner walk to aid with digestion. And the good amount of time to walk? About 45 to 60 minutes would be good. If you aren't used to walking that much, start with whatever you are comfortable with, then add an extra 5 minutes of walking each day.

It's recommended that individuals take at least 10,000 steps each day for exercise, which can be easily measured by a pedometer. Sometimes overlooked as a form of exercise, walking briskly can help you build stamina, burn excess calories and make your heart healthier. You don't have to walk for hours. A brisk 10-minute daily walk has lots of health benefits.

So, now walking is a popular sport, and more and more people have joined the ranks of walking. A recent survey by social networking app QQ has unveiled that fast walking topped all exercise activities in China due to its accessibility and low cost. Fast walking, or brisk walking, sometimes also referred to as speed walking, is a type of exercise where a person walks quickly in order to increase the heart rate and get in shape. It can be a great way to lose weight and increase physical fitness, and is very easy to do. There are many benefits to incorporating such an exercise routine into everyday life. Fast walking can be a great exercise for people of all ages. There are a few different ways for individuals to tell if they are walking quickly enough for physical benefits; these are perceived exertion, heart rate, and a measure of distance versus time. The perceived exertion when walking briskly should cause the walker to begin to sweat and to breathe slightly more heavily, but he or she should still be able to talk easily.

In Europe, also, walking has become one of the fastest growing sporting activities springing up in local parks up and down the country. And the more popular kind of walking in Europe now is Nordic Walking. Invented in the 1930s, Nordic Walking started in Finland after super-fit cross-country skiers began using poles in their off-season training when there was no snow on the ground. They soon found that this was giving them a competitive edge. It wasn't until the 1980s however that Nordic Walking began to catch on as a general recreational activity.

But what's so special about Nordic Walking? Why not just — well, go for a walk instead? Advocates of the technique point to evidence which suggests that it burns up to 46% more calories than ordinary walking and that the poles enable people to work the upper body at the same time as the legs. It exercises muscles and joints we wouldn't normally use. The poles also act as a support, reducing the pressure on the knees and the joints and aiding balance and coordination — all increasingly important elements of physical well-being as we age.

As well as the physical benefits of walking, there's another side to the sport that is equally important, and that's the opportunity of meeting other people. The regular sessions are the perfect opportunity to share and discuss anything and everything — almost like walking therapy. Walking is such a sociable activity. Of course people can do it on their own too, but the benefits of spending time with others exercising outdoors are huge.

（1）slow jogging （2）bicycling （3）swimming
（4）20 （5）(a brisk) morning walk （6）(an) after-dinner walk
（7）45 to 60 （8）10,000 （9）brisk walk
（10）brisk walking （11）speed walking （12）perceived exertion
（13）heart rate （14）a measure of distance versus time
（15）Nodic （16）Finland （17）1930s
（18）recreational activity （19）calories （20）poles

Summary Interpreting

Guided Practice

Task A

Sentence 1

Best companies from around the world choose Britain to base their investments in Europe, and to help in their global research effort. How can all this help Chinese companies? First, we know how important it is to choose the right country to invest in on the basis of objective criteria. The most important criterion is the judgment of international business, and international business has shown clearly its own reference for Britain as the location of choice in Europe. Second, we have an enormous and vibrant ICT community. A new generation of technology companies like Cambridge Display Technology or Cambridge Silicon Radio are pioneering new advances in displays and in radio technologies, and in semiconductor design. These technologies will help China to develop and manufacture new leading edge high value products. Third, global companies find they need to do R&D in Europe, and most of that work is in Britain. Microsoft and Bell labs put their first overseas R&D operation into Britain. IBM's software development facility in Hampshire is the largest of its kind in Europe. We are committed to helping Chinese companies explore all the opportunities available in Britain. That will help to build long-term partnerships between Britain and China.

Sentence 2

London unveiled a plan to help hundreds of rough sleepers who use buses in Britain's capital as a temporary home during the night. Increasing numbers of homeless people in London are using all-night buses and underground trains as a place to sleep during the twilight hours. This reflects a trend of rising homelessness seen more widely across the capital in recent years. Special funding is to be provided for a team to help provide accommodation and support services for these people. The team would also help reconnect people with family and friends to prevent them from ending up sleeping on the streets. Even one person ending up in this position is too many, and the capital is determined to make sure homeless people get the support they need. Continued efforts will be made by councils, homeless organisations, and government to make sure there is a way off the street for every rough sleeper in London.

Sentence 3

Once you've delegated a chore to someone else, don't under any circumstances do it yourself. This applies at home and at work, and anywhere else. Once someone discovers that if they don't do their own tasks, you'll do them instead, why would they ever bother to do them? So you have to be firm and stick to your guns. If that means your children end up with nothing clean to wear at the weekend because they haven't put their dirty clothes in the laundry, that might teach them something. Or your assistants can't find the website they want because they didn't make a note of it when you asked them to. Don't relent because the longer it takes before you relent, the longer they'll hang on next time, waiting for you to step in. So you have to say no and mean it. If you've already fallen into this trap, then tell everyone that you won't be doing their jobs any more and stick to it. They may not believe you at first, but they pretty soon will when the thing just doesn't get done.

Task B

Passage 1

Conflict Management

Nowadays, the silent hidden problems could easily burst out and become conflict, causing a lot of damage. For one thing, people feel a bit more secure behind their computer screens and are more prone to raising issues, challenging inappropriate behaviors and defending their rights. For another, in today's environment of rapid change, an over-dependence on electronic rather than face-to-face communication encourages conflict.

Conflict happens at work can cause enormous damage to staff morale, performance and customer confidence. Four types of conflict management style have been identified.

1. Avoider. For these people conflict is something to be feared, they feel frustrated and hopeless, as they cannot achieve their goals. For avoiders it is easier to withdraw (physically and psychologically) from a conflict than to face it.

2. Controller. These people chase their aims without considering relationships. They think that one side winning and the other losing settles conflicts. They feel that they achieve higher status by winning. Losing makes them feel weak, inadequate and a failure.

3. Accommodator. Some people have a strong need to maintain relationships. When conflict happens they think that their own goals are unimportant. They want conflicts to be resolved quickly to create harmony. They worry if conflict continues, someone will get hurt and that will ruin the relationship.

4. Collaborator. These people view a conflict as a problem to be solved. They are good at seeing other people's point of view, without forgetting their own goals. They are not satisfied until solutions have been found and the tensions and negative feelings have been resolved.

So, be alert when working with people, as disputes can very often be predicted. Don't wait for them to happen and be caught napping. Of those outlined a more collaborative approach to conflict management and dispute resolution is probably best. If you take a proactive approach you are much more likely to get better ideas for solutions to conflict.

Passage 2

Moving into Retirement

The world is rapidly aging. A whopping two billion people will be 60 years and older by

2050, more than triple the number in 2000, according to the World Health Organization. This demographic change has major implications for the global economy. Countries are facing rising health-care costs, a shrinking workforce, higher pension costs and diminishing fertility rates. Many countries have already begun adapting to their increasingly aging populations by raising the retirement age, reducing pension benefits and spending more on elderly care.

Population is aging, so providing good elderly care becomes increasingly important. Countries should be prepared for a future when more of their elderly need social facilities for retirement care. Under this backdrop, retirement village has become an increasingly popular concept.

Retirement villages are also known as retirement communities and care villages. Retirement villages were first developed in the US where they are also called a senior village, adult retirement community or retirement living community. These are a large group of retirement or sheltered housing schemes for seniors. Such communities offer independent living, in modern housing that is designed for the elderly, and with care readily at hand. The communities often have organized activities, in addition to shopping trips during the day. In many cases the residents organize their own clubs and activities, so there is no feeling of restriction, and can still lead an active life.

What is the development of retirement care like in China? China's one-child policy has skewed its population toward the grey end, presenting a demographic opportunity for the eldercare industry. According to UN data, by mid-century, China could have nearly 500 million people aged over 60, more than the population of the US.

With the Chinese population aging, there is a growing need for good retirement solutions. As many elderly Chinese only have one child that may not be able, or prepared, to take care of them, retirement communities are becoming increasingly popular. In some of these luxury high-end retirement communities, residents enjoy barrier-free facilities, fingerprint locks in every apartment, theater and hobby classes and the support of nutritionists that can recommend appropriate diets. However, all the services come at a very high price, tens of thousands of RMB each month. Therefore, affordable retirement care is a long-term project for both government and communities.

What's more, in their traditional idea, Chinese people enjoy elderly care at home, and many people believe it is not filial to send an elder to a place such as eldercare home. In a word, going somewhere for care is still a foreign concept, and it takes time for more people to accept and welcome the concept. It is without a doubt however, eldercare industry is a thriving one.

Unit 7

Warm Up

Task A

（1）People do not analyze every problem they meet

（2）the last time they had a similar problem

（3）act without thinking

（4）six stages in analyzing a problem

（5）recognize

（6）define

（7）the gears, the brakes, or the frame

（8）possible solutions

（9）his bicycle repair book and read about gears

（10）suggestions

（11）put oil on the gear wheels; buy new gear wheels and replace the old ones; tighten or loosen the gear wheels

（12）the thinker suddenly sees something new or sees something in a new way

（13）a piece of chewing gum

Task B

（1）treatment	（2）informed	（3）enrolled
（4）progress	（5）tapping into	（6）lack
（7）cycle	（8）obtain	（9）perspectives
（10）equality	（11）affirm	（12）oppressed
（13）violence	（14）ideals	（15）humility
（16）old-fashioned	（17）claim	（18）behalf

Listening Comprehension

Guided Practice

Task A

How to Fight Your Fitness Fears

Many people feel uncertain or fearful about stepping into a gym. Feeling inept or embarrassed in front of other people isn't something that any of us enjoy and it's usually the fear of this that keeps us from trying new things. We've all had that similar feeling; your self-confidence drains and the feelings of insecurity start to take hold. But don't let that stop you from exercising! Here are some top tips on how to drop the gym anxiety and make exercise something you really want to do.

Tip 1

Some people say why they don't want to come into the gym or join an activity class is because everyone there will be better, fitter, thinner, muscle-ier...than them. Many believe they are not in the right shape for the gym, class or activity. But this just isn't true. People of all ages, abilities and body shapes exercise and they all exercise for different reasons.

Tip 2

It's important to choose somewhere you feel safe, supported and comfortable. It's worth taking the time to explore different venues before you sign anything to find out what you prefer. Some people prefer a traditional gym, whereas others may want somewhere that offers lots of classes, or has courts and pitches for team games.

Tip 3

We're always more confident when we have a friend to support us, and this is no different when we exercise. Find a friend or family member who has the same fitness goals and you'll find exercising is more sustainable. If you start to feel unconfident or anxious, share your experience and laugh about it with your friend.

Tip 4

If you're struggling at the gym and it's affecting your motivation, consider employing the services of a personal trainer. Set your goal with your trainer and explain your reason for employing them, they can be that voice of support when your anxiety kicks in. Most gyms have in-house trainers who can be booked for one-off or multiple sessions.

We all suffer from anxious feelings from time to time, but don't let it get the better of you. Remember, just getting up off the sofa and moving is amazing, so be confident, keep an eye on your goals and remember to tell yourself just how great you are. The more you exercise, the more confident you'll feel.

Answers

Tip 1

Drop your misconceptions

Tip 2

Choose the right venue

Tip 3

Buddy up

Tip 4

Buy in the confidence

Task B

早上好，欢迎参加新西兰旅游论坛，我们非常高兴你们能参加这次展示新西兰旅游业的盛会。与别国相比，我们的国土面积相对较小，但就景色和活动的多样性来讲，我们比任何国家都毫不逊色。旅游业是新西兰最大的出口产业。它对整个新西兰，对新西兰各个地区，以及新西兰的城镇，乃至于偏远地区的经济都起着至关重要的作用。我们每年接待的游客人数超过230万，他们每年在我国的消费高达60多亿美元。近年来，本地区的旅游市场营销已经越来越富有创意。我们有一些很好的例子，比如一些地区充分发挥它们的独特之处，推出文化旅游、葡萄酒旅游线路和其他一些活动来吸引游客。你们带回美好的回忆和愉快的体验，并与他人分享，就是我们新西兰最好的使者。良好的口碑千金难买；而一次不愉快的经历则可能影响游客的整个假期。所以，我们的一个非常重要的目标就是，不断为游客带来更好的体验。

Task C

Rainbows are often seen when the sun comes out after or during a rainstorm. Rainbows are caused when sunlight shines through drops of water in the sky at specific angles. When white sunlight enters a raindrop, it exits the raindrop a different color. When light exits lots of different raindrops at different angles, it produces the red, orange, yellow, green, blue, indigo, and violet that you see in a rainbow. Together, these colors are known as the spectrum. These colors can sometimes be seen in waterfalls and fountains as well. Did you know that there are double rainbows? In a double rainbow, light reflects twice inside water droplets and forms two arcs. In most double rainbows, the colors of the top arc are opposite from those in the bottom arc. In other words, the order of colors starts with purple on top and ends with red on bottom. In addition, rainbows sometimes appear as white arc at night. These rainbows are called moonbows and are so rare that very few people will ever see one. Moonbows are caused by moonlight shining through drops of water.

Summary Interpreting

Guided Practice

Task A

Hi, I'm April and I'm a university lecturer. I chose this profession because I wanted to do something rewarding. Years ago, when I started my career, I enjoyed it: preparing and giving lectures, discussing with students their presentations and projects. However, the workload made me stretched. I knew of course that work could sometimes be difficult, but that it was stimulating and challenging, in a word, difficult, but in an enjoyable way.

Hi, my name is Buster and I'm a software engineer. Lately, I began to feel overwhelmed by work and the pressure was building up. I have the feeling that work is too competitive. I know lifestyles less stressful are difficult to possess. So I need to be able to deal with the stresses and strains of my job. I don't want to become so stressed out because of overwork, or to have nervous breakdown. These days, in my profession, burnout is an increasingly common problem among colleagues.

Hi, I'm Carroll and I'm a freelance designer, a freelancer. That means I work for myself and I'm self-employed. To use the official term, I'm a sole trader. Deciding what you want to do for a living is the biggest vocational decision you can make, the second is deciding how you'll do it. Becoming a freelancer is a serious lifestyle decision that should not be made lightly. I've made my living for the past years solely as a freelancer and plan on continuing to do so for years to come. This by no means makes me any sort of guru on the subject, but it does mean that I've experienced many of the joys and disasters that come with the territory.

Hi, my name is David and I'm a volunteer working for non-profit organizations, also called not-for-profit organizations. Organizations of such kind are also called charities, and form the voluntary sector, and they rely heavily on volunteers. They are usually managed by paid professionals, and they have social aims such as helping those who are sick or poor, or encouraging artistic activity. They put a lot of effort into fund-raising, getting people to donate money to the organization in the form of donations. Non-profit organizations are not to be confused with loss-making companies. Voluntary sector employees earn five to ten percent less than they would in the private sector. Research shows that volunteers give the most needed service to people, so I'm proud of my job.

Name of the Person	His/Her Profession	Words Used to Describe His/Her Profession (As many words as you can take down)
April	university lecturer	rewarding, stretched, difficult, stimulating, challenging, enjoyable
Buster	software engineer	overwhelmed, pressure, competitive, stressful, overwork, nervous breakdown, burnout
Carroll	freelance designer	self-employed, sole trader, vocational decision, guru, joys and disasters

续表

Name of the Person	His/Her Profession	Words Used to Describe His/Her Profession (As many words as you can take down)
David	volunteer	non-profit organization, not-for-profit organization, charities, voluntary sector, professionals, fund-raising, donations, loss-making companies, private sector

Task B

(1) Time is money

(2) they never have enough time

(3) how to manage time

(4) expressions

(5) timescale or timeframe

(6) lead time

(7) schedule or timetable

(8) on schedule

(9) delay

(10) procrastination

(11) Victor Hugo

Try This

(1) Time management

(2) diary

(3) calendar

(4) realistic plan

(5) prioritize

(6) To-do lists

(7) urgent

(8) important, but not urgent

(9) low-priority

(10) productive

(11) the bulk of your work

(12) energy peaks

(13) workflow

(14) work mode

(15) occasional distraction

(16) multitasking

(17) quality

(18) perfectionism

Unit 8

Warm Up

Task A

(1) 25 million

(2) 1.2 billion

(3) perception of the world

(4) estimated

(5) thrill

(6) Accessibility

(7) market potential

(8) universal accessibility

(9) industry stakeholders

(10) enriching and compelling

Task B

"Tourism for All" was chosen to bring awareness to accessibility issues facing many travellers whether they be disabled, a family with children or senior citizens. Accessibility is an issue many people don't even consider but for others it dictates their journeys, preventing them from reaching the full experiences others enjoy and often take for granted. Everyone needs travel, but not everyone can travel.

Tourism is important. It cleanses the mind from a hectic work week; it can expand the soul to new beliefs and most importantly; it can mature the individual through cultured experiences.

Tourism is a massive industry for Bangkok, Thailand, bringing in $44.6 billion in revenue and 30 million international tourists. Our company operates with a passion for travel and a strong belief that the more people travel, the better they become through growth, life experience and enjoyment. Our intention is to find ways to use technology to make travel attainable to the general population. Since the year 2000, we have revolutionized the travel space, applied affordable and accessible world-class technology, made it easy for people to book flights and hotels through a mobile device, and built bigger airports, and these have all made travel and tourism a more inclusive activity.

Accessibility concerns include problems such as hotels in areas with no requirements for wheelchair access, no room for walkers, difficult terrain for the elderly, size requirements for families with kids or even airlines with limitations for disabled passengers. Accessibility can even mean including handicap stalls in public restrooms to highly trafficked tourism areas. Bringing awareness to this important subject will push governments to enforce regulations for accessibility and convince private tourism business to make these accommodations as well.

Travel is important for everyone, whether young or old, average or special, abled or disabled. Everyone deserves the same opportunities to be able to go anywhere in the world and witness the beauty of each destination. Not all hotels, landmarks, sights, activities, transportation services or airlines are equipped to handle the variety of tourists they might receive.

Bringing attention to this issue, and the many other issues World Tourism Days have addressed in the past is a step in the right direction. Tourism is important. For travellers, tourism expands the mind, creates cross-cultural dialogue, introduces new ways of thinking and incites adventure. Bringing attention to issues like accessibility opens the dialogue to discuss ways to improve this dilemma.

Travel should be enjoyed by anyone and everyone. It's a shame that so many people are limited in visiting the cities they only hear about in movies or seeing the sights they only see on postcards. Everyone should have access to these experiences and everyone should be able to travel wherever they like. Tourism should not just be available to all; it should be experienced by all.

Lastly, accessibility isn't just a human rights concept, it's important for business as well. Providing access like this would open the doors to include another 1 billion visitors, and it sounds like a no-brainer.

Answers

1. It means that accessibility might prevent some people from reaching the full experiences others enjoy and often take for granted.

2. It cleanses the mind from a hectic work week, it can expand the soul to new beliefs, and most importantly, it can mature the individual through cultured experiences.

3. Tourism is a massive industry for Bangkok, Thailand, as it brings in $44.6 billion in revenue and 30 million international tourists.

4. They have revolutionized the travel space, applied affordable and accessible world-class technology, made it easy for people to book flights and hotels through a mobile device, and built bigger airports.

5. It will bring convenience to travellers, help improve the service of the travel destinations, and promote business revenue.

Listening Comprehension

Guided Practice

Task A

Paragraph 2

Shared parking takes advantage of the fact that most parking spaces are only used part time, and many parking facilities have a significant portion of unused spaces, with utilization patterns that follow predictable daily, weekly and annual cycles.

Paragraph 4

Unlike shared bikes, shared parking space has both market demand and policy support. Shared parking can be advantageous for developers, businesses and governments, but takes time and careful investment.

Paragraph 6

In Arbor, Michigan, USA, Downtown Development Authority coordinates parking availability, location and price as part of the larger transport system that is essential to the urban core's vitality and growth. The city makes an effort to satisfy parking demands with existing public spaces.

Paragraph 8

The biggest hurdle to shared parking is uncertainty and lack of information. Technology gives us new ways to think about how to make shared parking more efficient. Apps or other technological platforms should help match supply with demand, and facilitate payments between the two. When we can all start to understand how much parking we really need, and the minimum amount of parking we need, we can then make better decisions about the best use of our valuable land. And the big empty parking lot downtown will become a thing of the past.

Task B

Paragraph 1

Modern technological innovations have made deep-sea mining more realisable. China miners plan voyage to bottom of sea. Chinese companies have three of the 27 licences awarded by the International Seabed Authority for deep-sea mining in the Pacific Ocean. China supplies 95 percent of the world's rare earth — metals used in making nearly all today's electronics products. But global demand for green-tech products such as wind turbines and solar panels, which depend on rare earth metals, may outstrip even China's land-based supply. Meanwhile, anticipation of rising demand for electric vehicles has pushed up prices for metals used in batteries such as copper, manganese, nickel and lithium. While countries such as Japan and South Korea have developed maritime mining technology, much of it adapted from deep-sea oil drilling and diamond mining, China is particularly keen on tapping into a wealth of maritime resources.

Paragraph 2

After decades of turbulence, the world order led by the United States has begun to change. On the global front, the strength of developing countries has greatly increased. And the International Monetary Fund has predicted the share of high-income countries in the global purchasing power parity-based GDP will drop from 64 percent to 39 percent, with Asian emerging powers' share increasing from 12 percent to 39 percent, with China taking 21 percent. A multipolar world order and globalization will be the highlights of the new era. Countries across the world are willing to compete and cooperate on the basis of fairness and justice, yet the deadlock between emerging powers and the established ones will continue for some time.

Paragraph 3

Summer is the season for internships, and many college students are interning in companies or government departments. However, some online shops are reportedly selling internship certificates to students who never do an internship. Why are there people selling fake certificates? The answer is simple. There is demand for them. First of all, the majority of colleges require their students to attend internships as a prerequisite for graduation, yet they seldom check the internship certificates the students hand in. Second, some college students falsify their internship experiences to make their resumes look better, in the hope of getting a better job on graduation. However, the practice has devalued internships, and led to more students opting to purchase a certificate as they do not see the need for an internship to prove their abilities and advantages.

Paragraph 4

Ministry of Industry and Information Technology of China lately launched a technical inspection of smartphone apps. It is found that 80% of these apps are illegally collecting users' information, promoting third-party apps and charging users for no good reason. It is not enough to simply expose the malicious smartphone apps and warn people to delete them. Effective supervision is needed to root out these apps. This is a daunting task as people profit from the apps and there are no specific laws and regulations to deter them from producing and selling the apps. Nor is there any guideline with which cyberspace managers can impose needed sanctions on app developers. China's top internet watchdog, Cyberspace Administration of China, regulates that an app must be a single application not a bundle. However, there are no punishments specified that can hold irresponsible developers and app stores accountable.

Summary Interpreting

Guided Practice
Task A

The Causes of Floods

Floods are second only to fire as the most common of all natural disasters. They occur almost everywhere in the world, resulting in widespread damage and even death. Consequently, scientists have long tried to perfect their ability to predict floods. So far, the best that scientists can do is to recognize the potential for flooding in certain conditions. There are a number of conditions, from deep snow on the ground to human error, that cause flooding.

When deep snow melts it creates a large amount of water. Although deep snow alone rarely causes floods, when it occurs together with heavy rain and sudden warmer weather it can lead to serious flooding. If there is a fast snow melt on top of frozen or very wet ground, flooding is more likely to occur than when the ground is not frozen. Frozen ground or ground that is very wet and already saturated with water cannot absorb the additional water created by the melting snow. Melting snow also contributes to high water levels in rivers and streams. Whenever rivers are already at their full capacity of water, heavy rains will result in the rivers overflowing and flooding the surrounding land.

Rivers that are covered in ice can also lead to flooding. When ice begins to melt, the surface of the ice cracks and breaks into large pieces. These pieces of ice move and float down the river. They can form a dam in the river, causing the water behind the dam to rise and flood the land upstream. If the dam breaks suddenly, then the large amount of water held behind the dam can flood the areas downstream too.

Broken ice dams are not the only dam problems that can cause flooding. When a large human-made dam breaks or fails to hold the water collected behind it, the results can be devastating. Dams contain such huge amounts of water behind them that when sudden breaks occur, the destructive force of the water is like a great tidal wave. Unleashed dam waters can travel tens of kilometres, cover the ground in metres of mud and debris, and drown and crush every thing and creature in their path.

Although scientists cannot always predict exactly when floods will occur, they do know a great deal about when floods are likely, or probably, going to occur. Deep snow, ice-covered rivers, and weak dams are all strong conditions for potential flooding. Hopefully, this knowledge of why floods happen can help us reduce the damage they cause.

Task B

Make a Good First Impression

It goes without saying that first impressions are limiting in many ways. Sure, we can get either a positive or negative vibe about a person, but more often than not, it really limits our ability to get to know someone beyond a superficial level. After all, people are complex creatures who often surprise us in more ways than expected. In a word, the first impression may not always be reliable. Yet, many times, first impressions are so important that it is to our benefit to think about how to make a good first impression.

As the proverb goes, first impression is the last impression. Whether you meet someone at a party, go out on a first date or become acquainted to your new boss, first impressions are a guiding point in getting a "feel" for what a person is all about. Sometimes, a first impression can speak more truth through the person's actions than words. It can be an effective way for us to predict people's trustworthiness at first sight. As a basic human quality, trustworthiness plays an important role in social communications.

In a job interview, first impressions are extremely important. The first few minutes of an interview are crucial and can be a make-or-break factor. And recognizing the impact of first impressions is a step in the right direction. Learning how to make a memorable impact in a few minutes is a powerful tool. Here are some useful tips that you should pay special attention to, on how to impress a potential boss, in order to leave a good first impression in a job interview and walk away with a job.

First, plan ahead. This will boost your confidence and shows the interviewers that you did your homework and care enough to learn more. Read the company website and press releases, and use the Internet to find news articles. Prepare answers to predictable questions, such as the introductory "Tell me about yourself", and questions about your abilities, career history, personality and goals. Rehearse well beforehand. Arriving to your interview on time is essential for locking in a good impression. It is imperative that you'll be able to show up at the interview location a few minutes early. This may mean doing a test drive or walk to the location a couple of days before the interview. If you need to arrange a ride, make sure you're using a reliable source. If for some reason you're unable to attend due to an unexpected emergency, make sure you notify your interviewer as soon as possible.

Second, be mindful of your appearance. People make first impressions not only by what you say, but by what you wear. Make sure your attire is appropriate for an interview. It's smart to invest in a business suit that you'll be able to wear for interviews. You want your appearance to look professional, including making sure you're properly groomed and don't wear anything too distracting. If it's appropriate, try adding some color to your outfit to make yourself stand out among the drab grays and blacks. Your whole outfit doesn't have to be bright red, but you can choose a cute scarf to stand out.

Third, be considerate. You should be polite and friendly to each and every person you meet before and after your interview. In an organization or company, you never know who knows the hiring manager or your interviewer and will tell them if there are unpleasant encounters. Always greet your interviewer with a handshake and a smile, and you should do the same as you leave the interview. When you first meet the interviewer, shake his or her hand firmly. A firm handshake is highly impressive and always leaves a lasting impression. But, do wipe your hands before the interview, and be sure to do it without the interviewer looking.

Fourth, don't forget eye contact. Making eye contact with the interviewer is a good way of increasing your likelihood of success. You don't need to maintain eye contact with your interviewer while you're answering their questions. However, various studies of interviewee body language have shown that candidates who engage in eye contact are thought to be more alert, more assertive, more dependable, more confident, more responsible, and more creative.

Fifth, follow up with a memorable email. Your interviewer may be interviewing dozens of candidates, so a follow-up email will be a nice reminder of who you are. Personalize your email, bring up something you really enjoyed talking about during your conversation, and maybe even allude to what makes you different from the other candidates. And you'll be surprised how much a follow-up email can help with scoring the job.

To sum up, once you understand the importance of how you present yourself at the very start of the interview, you'll be able to preemptively control factors that leave a good impression and give you a better chance of landing the job.

1. a   2. b   3. b   4. c   5. c   6. b

7. a   8. a   9. b   10. a   11. b   12. a

Task C

(1) c   (2) f   (3) j   (4) a   (5) k   (6) g

(7) d   (8) h   (9) i   (10) e   (11) b

1. Marketing is the process of teaching consumers why they should choose your product or service over your competitors.

2. So, marketing is doing everything to satisfy customer needs, so as to make a profit.

3. Marketing is best identified using what are called the four Ps or a mix of marketing: Product, Price, Promotion, and Place.

4. Starting with products, companies have many procedures they must undertake to ensure their products are ready for selling.

5. Price is also tested through focus groups and surveys.

6. Promotion is deciding how the product will be supported with brochures, advertising, special activities, and information which companies use to generate interest in their products.

7. Place in marketing is deciding how the product will be distributed and where people will buy it.

8. All distribution decisions are part of the overall marketing process.

9. Do you know the different types of marketing?

10. More recently, social media marketing is becoming a type of marketing that smart companies can't avoid when it comes to reaching potential buyers, whether it's advertising on Facebook or posting advice on Twitter with links to a website.

11. All told, marketing is anything that informs, interests and gets people to make purchase decisions.

Unit 9

Warm Up

Task A

(1) personally and professionally

(2) renovation

(3) gratifying

(4) taken its toll on this national treasure

(5) companies and developers

(6) strategize the best approach to restore it to its full potential

(7) ultimately

(8) vibrancy

(9) tangible validation

(10) siblings and me

(11) I pledged our commitment to this project and to ensuring its successful execution

(12) exceeding

Task B

(1) qualities　(2) turbulent　(3) models　　(4) aspiration　(5) compassion

(6) spark　　(7) nurture　　(8) formative　(9) charities　　(10) exceptional

Listening Comprehension

Guided Practice

Task A

(1) interactive games　(2) many　　(3) real-life　　(4) vision

(5) virtual reality　　(6) see　　　(7) socialise　　(8) encourages

(9) aids　　　　　　(10) risks　　(11) upsetting　(12) violent

(13) try to exclude them from the game

(14) try to steal and destroy their virtual possessions

(15) skills and knowledge　　　　　(16) hard　　(17) concerns

(18) parents and carers　(19) understand　(20) appropriate

(21) agreement　　　　(22) screen　　(23) varied

Task B

(1) many inventions　(2) delivery　　(3) a shop

（4）not （5）collected （6）our shopping

（7）fruit and veg （8）delivery robot （9）zeroes

（10）worries （11）drones （12）commercial

（13）hinder （14）safety and reliability （15）thieves

（16）customer （17）thief （18）delivery drones

（19）delivering （20）everyone

Summary Interpreting

Guided Practice

Task A

Greener Hospital

Ladies and gentlemen,

There is a new trend in today's health care: greening hospitals to reduce toxins and provide a healthier healing environment. Hospitals and health centers today are using innovation and investment to transform the health sector, in order to foster a healthy future for people and the planet. Our aim is to accelerate the use of environmentally preferable products, practices and construction of green buildings in hospitals and medical practices worldwide.

In this, we want to collaborate with all interested parties in the green hospital area from hospitals, healthcare leaders, hospital suppliers, green building vendors, universities and governmental entities who can bring valuable resources in how to build or even convert existing hospitals to become more sustainable.

At the same notion, we want to provide first hand insight on the many benefits of becoming green hospitals of the future. Although initial cost to adopt green practices might be higher, they are the best investment in your facility. Green hospitals have been shown to reduce long-term energy costs. In addition, there is a growing consensus among the health care profession that pollutants generated by medical facilities must be reduced. Moreover, green hospital design has been linked to better patient outcomes and staff retention.

So, what kind of hospital can be called a green hospital? We believe there are at least seven elements that we should focus on: food at the hospital, water use at the hospital; waste at the the hospital, alternate energy at the hospital; green building design at the hospital, energy efficiency at the hospital; transportation in and around the hospital. The Green Hospital is defined as a hospital that has taken the initiative to do the one or more of the following: choose an environmentally friendly site, utilize sustainable and efficient designs, use green building materials and products, think green during construction and keep the greening process going.

Then I would like to share with you something about the hospital I am from. We aspire to provide health care services in a manner that protects and enhances the environment and the health of communities now and for future generations. Our Environmental Priorities are as follows: climate & energy, safer chemicals, sustainable food, waste reduction, and water conservation. We believe all these have a lot to do with the living quality of human beings, and it is our responsibility to do our share promoting it. Then it comes to the question, why clean energy in health care so important? Actually, sustainability is in itself a health issue. And greenhouse gas, according to research, contributes to climate change and the rise of pollution and disease. So, what we are doing in health care sector supports renewable energy and creates solutions to environmental problems.

I think it is already known to most of us that climate change poses a lot of effects to the world, be it food and water shortage, international conflict, heat stress, and injuries from extreme weather, and all these are intertwined with health effects of climate change, for example it may lead to mental health problems of people. And we shouldn't neglect two direct effects that climate change can cause to our lives, that is vector, food & water-borne disease and respiratory disease. Therefore, we believe green hospital construction and operation can do a lot of contribution to the improvement of our environment, so that human beings can enjoy a more sustainable life, so that our children, and their children can expect to have a better world.

We share a vision of a health care sector that does no harm, and instead promotes the health of people and the environment. To that end, we are working to implement ecologically sound and healthy alternatives to health care practices that pollute the environment and contribute to disease. For example, the incineration of medical waste is a leading source of dangerous air pollutants such as dioxin and mercury, and the use of hazardous chemicals indoors may contribute to the high rates of asthma among health care workers. The huge scale of the health care sector worldwide means that unhealthy practices — such as poor waste management, use of toxic chemicals, unhealthy food choices and reliance on polluting technologies — have a major negative impact on the health of humans and the environment.

The good news is that the health care sector can play a leading role in solving these problems. The health care sector can help shift the entire economy toward sustainable, safer products and practices. Our work will be able to transform the health care sector worldwide, without compromising patient safety or care, so that it is ecologically sustainable and no longer a source of harm to public health and the environment.

Task B

Co-working

Honored leaders, professors, businesspeople and other guests, it's my pleasure to speak to you today.

I'm going to share with you some of my experiences and research in studying creative business ecosystems around the world. As I define it, co-working is part of the trend of globalization, as co-living, incubators, creative communities, and other forms of new economy innovation and entrepreneurship. Co-working as a new working style is extremely important because many of the newest high-value adding industries depend on a strong, educated workforce.

Let me start with some simple definitions. Co-working is a style of work that involves a shared working environment, often an office, and independent activity. When I speak about a traditional office and workplace, I think everyone understands. We all probably know the concept of service office as well, this is a well established business model and many large companies use serviced offices. But about ten years ago, a new labor trend started to happen. After many people in the US and Europe lost their jobs due to the global financial crisis, many decided not to go back to traditional work. They opened their own companies and became entrepreneurs or freelancers. But when these people started, they usually worked at home. But working at home has too many distractions and it's not professional. So, many of these people started opening small offices with other people and called it not a serviced office, but a shared office.

And later, co-working became popular. Usually these co-working spaces were flexible. They included small offices and even desks in open areas, so you could sit, interact with people, have fresh coffee, and meet your clients in a meeting room. And co-working is different from traditional service offices because often it is community-driven and even community-managed. So when I talk about co-working, I mean a shared office between generally younger, entrepreneurial and freelance workers who want to work in a creative space with fewer rules. Co-working is a social gathering of a group of people who are still working independently, but who share values, and who are interested in the synergy that can happen from working in the same place alongside each other. Co-working offers a solution to the problem of isolation that many freelancers experience while working at home, while at the same time letting them escape the distractions of home.

Do you notice some of the differences here between the traditional offices, and the creative co-working offices? Which place would you rather work? Most young people want to work in these kinds of places, not in a traditional office, which they find boring. A survey found most coworkers are currently in their late twenties to late thirties, with an average age of 34 years. Two-thirds are men, one third are women. Four in five co-workers started their career with a university education. The majority of co-workers work in creative industries or new media. Slightly more than half of all co-workers are freelancers.

Now, as I just mentioned, co-working as a trend started happening in the US and Europe because many more people were becoming entrepreneurs and freelancers. This same thing is happening in Asia and in China today, when many of the talents come back from overseas, they are also becoming entrepreneurs.

Co-working in Asia has become popular since space is limited in major cities. In Hong Kong for example, dozens of co-working spaces have been set up to foster the rapidly growing startup community. In fact, co-working spaces also exist in other cities of China. Shanghai and Beijing have hundreds of them! Now I can tell you that some of the bigger co-working spaces in China, such as WeWork in Shanghai, have enough seats in just one location for 1000 people. Co-working is very closely connected to entrepreneurship and small companies, freelancers and creative workers. So, if we want more people to work on things like 3D printers, virtual reality, Internet and apps, the new service industries, and so on, we need more co-working spaces.

Co-working is not only about the physical place, but about establishing the co-working community first. It is actually recommended to start with building a co-working community first before considering opening a co-working place. However, some co-working places don't build a community. We need to have a team of people to create interaction in the community, events and so on. We need them to support the life and work issues of co-workers. That's why some co-working places are built but they are badly managed and they fail.

In this perspective, we can have the government to support existing local spaces to get bigger. I prefer this option because it improves indigenous economic development. But we can also encourage some of the bigger brands, the global ones like WeWork, and the bigger Chinese ones like URWork and others, to set up more locations in cities that welcome innovation and entrepreneurship.

Today we've talked briefly about features of the future style of working, co-working spaces.

And I think everyone knows this: many of those technologies will add great improvement to our lives. But they will also require less work, and less people to do the work. If we use robots to make a product, what happens to the workers that used to make that product? So I believe, we should start getting ready for having people working much less overtime, having them working part-time instead of full-time, having them working for four days a week instead of five, and then three days a week. And with the rest of their time? They can enjoy great community that we have built for them.

Unit 10

Warm Up

Task A

（1）greener　　（2）agenda　　（3）momentum　　（4）informed

（5）extend　　（6）objects　　（7）lifestyles

（8）Then, we will come to the ways on how to properly dispose of the rubbish

（9）Then, a system of collecting these sorted materials needs to be established

（10）Give the public information they can grasp, and then you will increase your chances of gaining followers

Task B

Thirty-five years since the emergence of AIDS, the international community can look back with some pride but we must also look ahead with resolve and commitment to reach our goal of ending the AIDS epidemic by 2030.

There has been real progress in tackling the disease. More people than ever are on treatment. Since 2010, the number of children infected through mother-to-child transmission has dropped by half. Access to HIV medicines to prevent mother-to-child transmission is now available to more than 75 percent of those in need. Fewer people die of AIDS-related causes each year. And people living with HIV are living longer lives. The number of people with access to life-saving medicines has doubled over the past five years, now topping 18 million. With the right investments, the world can get on the fast-track to achieve our target of 30 million people on treatment by 2030.

While there is clear progress, gains remain fragile. Young women are especially vulnerable in countries with high HIV prevalence, especially in Sub-Saharan Africa. Globally, people who are economically disadvantaged lack access to services and care. Criminalization and discrimination foster new infections each day. Women and girls are still especially hard hit.

The 2030 Agenda for Sustainable Development was adopted with a promise to leave no one behind. Nowhere is this more important than in tackling AIDS. Supporting young, vulnerable and marginalized people will change the course of the epidemic. The UNAIDS strategic framework is aligned with the SDGs, which highlight how the work against HIV is linked to progress in education, peace, gender equality and human rights.

During its first decade, affected groups refused to accept inaction, mediocrity and weakness in the AIDS response. Their courage drove progress on securing women and children's health, lowering the costs of lifesaving drugs and giving voice to the voiceless. We must all join together in that same uncompromising spirit. On World AIDS Day, I salute the tireless effort of leaders, civil society, colleagues in the UN and the private sector to advance this cause.

Answers

1. F   2. F   3. T   4. T   5. T   6. F

Listening Comprehension

Guided Practice

Paragraph 1

(1) the most significant   (2) access more   (3) various subjects

(4) anytime   (5) everywhere   (6) learning information

(7) being made available   (8) communicate with others   (9) the Internet

(10) the older

Paragraph 2

(1) hungry shoppers   (2) in different places   (3) time

(4) spending more money   (5) easy   (6) basket or trolley

(7) waiting in the queue   (8) expensive items   (9) more

(10) money off   (11) spending   (12) more

(13) what you buy and when   (14) more   (15) half of it

(16) entrance   (17) checkout counter   (18) more money

(19) more things

Paragraph 3

(1) end   (2) economic recovery   (3) downturn

(4) encouraging signs   (5) good jobs   (6) our economy

(7) employment   (8) more jobs   (9) cutting people's taxes

（10）a quality education　　（11）clean energy　　（12）patient

（13）economic plan　　（14）benefits

Paragraph 4

（1）four decades

（2）extremely rapid economic growth

（3）per capita GDP growth rate

（4）miraculous growth

（5）inequality

（6）coastal and inland provinces

（7）central and western

（8）Opening-up and Reform

（9）The eastern coastal region

（10）ideal hubs

（11）the east coast grew faster than the rest of the country

（12）grew more rapidly

（13）coastal, central and western regions

（14）geography, policy and transportation

（15）the coastal regions and western China

（16）building the infrastructure

（17）Western Development

（18）One Belt, One Road

（19）silk road

（20）Central Asia

Summary Interpreting

Guided Practice

Task A

Speech 1

Many of us don't know the best ways to look after our eyes. Could you share your ideas on this?

Eye care organizations and health professionals are joining together to promote the importance of eye health and the need for regular sight tests for all. Sight is the sense people fear losing the most. Fight for sight. Here are top tips for healthy eyes.

1. Have regular check-ups. You should have your eyes tested every two years even if you think your vision is fine. An eye test can spot some eye conditions and other illnesses not related to sight. Regular check-ups are vital even if you have no symptoms. You may also talk to your relatives about your family eye health history. Some eye conditions have genetic links which increase your risk of developing them. And you should share this information, if any, with your eye health professional.

2. Wear protective glasses. Protect your eyes when it is sunny or when you're in high glare areas such as near snow or water. Sunglasses provide a safe level of protection from the sun's damaging rays. Also, wear safety glasses or protective goggles to protect your eyes from injury if you work with hazardous materials. This applies to home too if you are doing DIY, gardening or setting off fireworks.

3. Take care of your contact lenses. Nowadays, people wear contact lenses to improve poor vision, or to improve the quality of vision for those who wear high power glasses. Some people wear contact lenses that can enhance or change the eye color, known as cosmetic contact lenses. If you wear contact lenses, make sure you look after them properly. Thoroughly wash and dry your hands before inserting or removing your contact lenses. Your lenses and their case should only be cleaned with the lens solution recommended by your optometrist. Serious sight threatening infections can occur with contact lens wear and one should be aware of these. The important point to note with any contact lenses is not to share the lenses with friends as this can increase the risk of infections in the eye. Always follow the instructions given to you by your optometrist or the lens manufacturer. This way, you should be able to be comfortable with lens wear with good vision.

4. Limit the use of digital devices. For most of us, digital devices have a strong and growing presence in our lives. Computers, tablets, smartphones and other electronic devices with visual displays can all cause tired eyes and digital eye strain, or what's known as "computer vision syndrome". Computer vision syndrome is the name for a group of eye and vision symptoms that might be experienced as a result of extended periods of viewing digital devices.These symptoms include eye strain, red or tired eyes, irritation, blurred vision, double vision and headaches. For most of us, our eyes prefer to focus further than six metres away, so viewing a computer screen forces our eyes to work harder. Often the type we are viewing on a digital device can be small or unclear, and glare is emitted off the screen from the blue light. Also, while it's normal for us to blink about 15 times a minute, studies have shown that we blink far less often while using digital

devices. Follow these tips to help minimise computer vision syndrome. Sit at least an arm's length from the computer screen, and try not to hold your tablet or smartphone too close to your eyes. Take regular breaks using the 20/20/20 rule: every 20 minutes, shift your eyes to look at an object at least 20 feet away (six metres), for at least 20 seconds. Use lubricant eye-drops or artificial tears to refresh your eyes when they feel dry. Avoid using screens in an otherwise dark room and set up computer screens so there are not reflections from windows on the screen. Apps and programs like Apple Night Shift can help reduce blue light from LED screens, particularly helpful for those using devices late at night.

Speech 2

To what extent has information technology reduced social inequality? Give reasons for your answer and include any relevant examples from your own knowledge or experience.

People who live in highly developed countries often take access to information technology for granted. They find it hard to imagine a world in which this technology does not bring greater prosperity. However, as the IT revolution moves forward in some parts of the world, in other parts of the world the poor are falling further and further behind. Indeed there are many barriers to wider IT access and its potential benefits.

In many parts of the world, illiteracy remains obstacles to IT access. In some countries, less than 50 percent of the population is able to read. Women and the poor are especially likely to be illiterate and therefore at a disadvantage when it comes to IT access and its potential benefits.

Another major barrier is inadequate infrastructure. In some countries, the electricity supply is irregular. In addition, broadband may only be available in major cities, rendering many rural areas off the map as far as IT access is concerned. In these circumstances, the Internet may actually be increasing rather than decreasing social inequality between urban and rural areas.

Even where IT access is available, governments are often fearful of a well-informed public. In fact, government censorship of the Internet is widespread. The use of blocking software and firewalls is common, even in countries such as Australia, which are commonly regarded as free and democratic. Those who are well-educated and sophisticated may be able to find a way around such obstacles. However, those who are less advantaged may remain unable to access some information freely.

In short, where unequal access to infrastructure, education and free information exist, the IT revolution is unlikely to reduce inequality. Unless fundamental inequalities are addressed, the Internet may, in fact, increase social divides.

Task B

Speech 1

Should we return to natural methods of food production instead of having convenience food?

Some people strongly agree that we should return to more natural methods of food production, such as organic farming, even if this means that we produce food less efficiently. They believe this because of the following reasons.

1. It is better for the environment to produce food using fewer chemicals such as pesticides and herbicides.

2. Naturally produced food tastes better than food produced using more artificial methods.

3. Man-made chemicals used in modern methods of food production could be harmful to human health.

4. Convenience foods are bad for the planet because of excess packaging, use of petroleum based products, as well as fossil fuels in their factory production, polluting the land, the air and the seas.

5. Convenience foods are bad for humans emotionally. Cooking and eating foods prepared from scratch has long been part of human culture, losing that interaction is a loss to humans on a psychological level.

Some people strongly disagree that we should return to more natural methods of food production, such as organic farming, even if this means that we produce food less efficiently. They believe this because of the following reasons.

1. More people will need to be employed on farms, and fewer people will be available to do work that will help the country develop economically.

2. It is a great help to busy people as they have a lot to do, and they have to make pragmatic choices on how they feed themselves and their children.

3. Producing food less efficiently could lead to food shortages.

4. Organically produced food is no more nutritious than food produced using pesticides and artificial fertilisers.

5. Food that has been produced without preservatives is less likely to stay fresh, so more food may be wasted.

Speech 2

What influences our purchasing decisions? Do we mainly buy things because we need them, or are other factors involved?

1. It is often the case that consumers buy products on impulse because of the way they are

displayed. In supermarkets, for example, snacks are often situated by the checkout to tempt those who are tired and bored with queuing. Another good example of this is when necessities such as clothes are displayed with matching accessories, such as jewellery. In fact, shoppers are often surprised at how much more they spend than they had intended.

2. Some people buy products that they do not really need because they feel empty and unhappy. For instance, people often consume alcohol, cigarettes or sugary foods because these enhance mood. At the same time, we are hoping that possessing certain things will make us happy, and for a short time they do, but the novelty wears off quickly, and then we are onto the next thing. Real, lasting happiness comes from good and meaningful relationships, stimulating and fulfilling lives, friendships, enjoyable activities — and none of these can be bought. We can buy temporary comfort, some stimulation and a bit of excitement, but these don't last.

3. People often buy products they do not really need because they want to display their status or wealth. A good example of this is when people dispose of perfectly good items (clothing, furniture, electronic goods) simply to buy a more up-to-date model. Another example is when shoppers choose high-value brands that prominently display their logos over anonymous brands that are equivalent in quality but cheaper. Going deeper to this mindset, we hope that other people will look at our possessions and be impressed with us. We are buying things for esteem-related reasons. We are trying to display our wealth and our financial success, and we do it by buying and showing off expensive things we don't really need or use. But the really wealthy often don't need to show off their money.

4. Some people buy things they don't really need because they believe they should own these things only because others have got them. They try to keep up with the Jones, want to keep up with their friends and family. However, they don't understand that everyone is different and therefore has different needs. What your friends and family needs isn't necessarily what you need. Individuals compare themselves with others to evaluate themselves. When an individual cannot find objective or non-social ways to assess him/herself, he/she will find a way of comparing him/herself with others in order to evaluate his/her opinions and abilities. For example, consumers want to possess luxury goods to impress others with the desirable status that the luxury goods represent.

5. Sometimes people are more likely to buy products because celebrities have been employed to advertise them. The famous people used in these advertisements make these products more attractive. In buying the products, consumers may feel closer to the persons they admire. Celebrities are social symbols who represent the values and ideas in a particular

culture. By watching stars and celebrities' latest fashion, people find similar ways to dress to show similar tastes in order to gain self-confidence and self-esteem through others' appreciation. An example of this is when famous sportsmen or women endorse a particular brand of trainer or sportswear, people would follow and buy these products. Indeed, the powerful influence of this type of advertising on consumer behaviour is reflected in the large sums of money such celebrities are often paid for their advertising work. Therefore, the influence of celebrities can be a powerful reason for some purchasing decisions.

Speech 3

As increasing number of unique, and potentially useful plants and animals come under threat, people have a growing awareness of the importance of preserving the world's biological diversity. But how can this be done?

1. Extensive agricultural and industrial activities have resulted in a massive loss of natural habitat, which is threatening the nation's biodiversity and socioeconomic sustainability. One possible approach is to regulate agricultural and industrial activity so that pollution and disruption to natural habitats is kept to a minimum. People argue that economic prosperity must be curtailed if it comes at the expense of the environment. However, businesses affected are unlikely to comply with such a strategy. It may even generate hostility to conservation efforts generally if the economic costs are perceived to be too high.

2. An alternative approach would be to protect and expand nature reserves so that complete ecosystems can be kept intact. If possible, we can acquire new sites to be returned to wildlife rich reserves. This would ensure that a minimum number of wild plants and animals would survive. China protects giant pandas by expanding nature reserves and forbidding all kinds of construction and development in their habitats and surrounding areas. This measure would have immediate positive consequences for those areas by preserving delicate ecosystems. However, this strategy also has limitations. It does not protect from phenomena such as acid rain and water pollution, which can cross boundaries and affect large areas.

3. Governments could promote greater understanding of plants and animals by investing in the research and preservation efforts of universities, zoos, and botanical institutes. This may ensure the survival of individual species and produce tangible benefits in the form of new medicines and products. Both the public sector and the private sector should be encouraged to look for funding or launch fundraising appeals for the preservation of natural habitats.

4. A more effective approach is to educate the public about the benefits of biodiversity. Once people understand that there are real benefits to exploiting natural resources in a sustainable way, they are more likely to make the short-term sacrifices necessary to preserve natural habitats. Also, our children should be more connected with nature. Nowadays, fewer than one in ten children play in wild places. In fact, children are far more likely to recognise television characters than our most common wildlife. This is highly important as it matters for their physical and mental health and it matters because today's children are tomorrow's wildlife guardians. They will be able to protect nature if they care enough.

Unit 11

Warm Up
Task A

（1）tackle the challenges facing the global opportunity

（2）seize the opportunities that lie ahead

（3）expand new opportunities for business owners

（4）trade barriers

（5）business-friendly regulations

（6）technology and infrastructure

（7）thrive

（8）the expert deployment mechanism for trade and development

（9）fair and equitable

（10）from negotiation to ratification

（11）convention

（12）the Republic of Peru

（13）benefit from their pensions

（14）redoubling efforts

（15）equal participants

（16）marginalized

（17）vulnerable

（18）Indigenous communities

Task B

1. And when you encounter obstacles — because I guarantee you, you will, and many of

you already have — when you are struggling and you start thinking about giving up, I want you to remember something that has carried us through every moment of our lives, and that is the power of hope — the belief that something better is always possible if you're willing to work for it and fight for it.

2. It is our fundamental belief in the power of hope that has allowed us to rise above the voices of doubt and division, of anger and fear that we have faced in our own lives; our hope that if we work hard enough and believe in ourselves, then we can be whatever we dream, regardless of the limitations that others may place on us; the hope that when people see us for who we truly are, maybe, just maybe, they, too, will be inspired to rise to their best possible selves.

3. That is the hope of students like Kyra who fight to discover their gifts and share them with the world. It's the hope of school counselors like Terri and all these folks up here who... who guide those students every step of the way, refusing to give up on even a single young person. It was the hope of many ordinary working class people, that one day their kids would go to college and have opportunities they never dreamed of.

4. That's the kind of hope that every single one of us — politicians, parents, preachers — all of us need to be providing for our young people. Because that is what moves this country forward every single day — our hope for the future and the hard work that hope inspires.

Listening Comprehension

Guided Practice
Task A
Paragraph 1
Could we be cared for by robots? In Japan, for example, where 26% of the population is aged 65 years or older, scientists are developing a robot capable of lifting patients out of beds and into wheelchairs. It's called Robear, and is designed to look like an approachable white bear. If tests are successful, it would do a job that would normally involve several care workers. Also, an EU-funded project is investigating ways technology can improve the day-to-day care of elderly people, the robot is designed in part to combat loneliness, and to offer reminders for tasks such as taking medicine. The care home which is being used in the experiments is equipped as a smart home. There are more than 60 sensors in the home, multi - directional cameras that can identify and track people, also various sensors, such as ones for temperature, attached to all the hot and cold water taps, so they know when someone is in the bathroom and using the taps or

flushing the toilet.This all sounds like something out of a science fiction scenario but in the light of the care crisis it may be a solution worth considering. What do you think: are we ready for this revolution? Can it solve our care problems? (19 errors)

Paragraph 2

Hunger is still one of the most urgent development challenges, yet the world is producing more than enough food. Up to one third of all food is spoiled or squandered before it is consumed by people. It is an excess in an age where almost a billion people go hungry, and represents a waste of the labour, water, energy, land and other inputs that went into producing that food. Food loss and food waste refer to the decrease of food in subsequent stages of the food supply chain intended for human consumption. Food is lost or wasted throughout the supply chain, from initial production down to final household consumption. The decrease may be accidental or intentional, but ultimately leads to less food available for all. This may be due to problems in harvesting, storage, packing, transport, infrastructure or market/price mechanisms, as well as institutional and legal frameworks. Reducing food losses and waste is gathering increasing global interest and action. Governments, research institutions, producers, distributors, retailers and consumers have all different ideas about the problem, the solutions, and the ability to change. The FAO-led Save Food initiative is partnering with international organizations, the private sector and civil society to enable food systems to reduce food loss and waste in both the developing and the industrialized world. (19 errors)

Paragraph 3

There's a lot to consider when weighing the pros and cons of farm-raised vs. wild-caught fish, from nutrition to sustainability to cost to contaminants. Everyone is trying to eat more fish these days. Eating at least two servings of fish or shellfish per week appears to reduce the risk of heart disease, delay the onset of Alzheimer's and dementia. Although meat, poultry, and fish are all good sources of protein, seafood boasts the healthiest fatty acid profile: it's low in saturated fat and high in those omega-3 fats we hear so much about. When you get to the fish counter, should you buy wild-caught or farm-raised fish? Actually, the nutritional differences between wild and farmed fish are not as great as you might imagine. Farmed and wild-caught rainbow trout, for example, are almost identical in terms of calories, protein, and most nutrients. There are some minor differences: wild-caught trout have more calcium and iron. Farm-raised trout have more vitamin A and selenium. But for the most part, they are nutritionally equivalent. Also, are farm-raised fish higher in contaminants? The contaminant that most people worry about with fish

308

is mercury. The fish that present the biggest concern (swordfish, king mackerel, tilefish, shark, and tuna) are all <u>wild-caught</u>. The most common farm-raised fish (catfish, tilapia, and salmon) all have low <u>or very low</u> mercury levels. Finally, there are concerns about environmental impact <u>and sustainability</u>. However, these are just as likely to apply to wild as to farmed fish. Wild-caught fish are sometimes <u>harvested</u> using practices that do a lot of <u>collateral</u> damage to the <u>ecosystem</u> and other fish. Fish-farming practices, on the other hand, can pollute the water <u>and threaten local flora and fauna</u>. Once again, it depends a lot on who is doing the fishing and/or farming. (23 errors)

Task B

Passage 1

Street Markets and Shopping Malls

Going shopping is a part of people's daily routine because they need to meet the demands of their everyday life. People consume various necessities. Therefore, they need to buy foods, clothes, newspapers and some other necessary goods every now and then. There are different places such as street markets and shopping malls where customers can go and do their shopping. Although the consumers' aims are basically similar, there are significant differences between street markets and shopping malls.

The first noticeable difference between them is about their locations. Street markets are open-air bazaars which are settled in particular streets of a neighborhood on certain days. They are open temporarily. Different from that, shopping malls are complex buildings mostly located in the suburbs of the city. They are permanent shopping centers with covered areas and parking lots. They are open from 10:00 a.m. to 10:00 p.m. every day.

Another difference between street markets and shopping malls is the prices they offer. First of all, the goods in a shopping mall are very expensive when compared to street market prices. But if there is something wrong with what you buy, the shop will replace it, or give you a refund. To the opposite, food and clothes are usually cheapers in street markets. Sometimes you can try to agree a lower price for something you buy in a street market; we call this haggling or bargaining. Of course, if you don't like what you buy in a street market, you can't normally take it back and get a refund.

Last but not least, street markets and shopping malls represent different parts of culture and heritage. People prefer going to street markets because they like the atmosphere that they get from the different stalls. Street markets can be limited to selling only one kind of thing, or it can sell a variety of goods as well. In street markets, sale people bring goods from all over the places and can even sell exotic merchandise from foreign countries. The stall vendors usually have nearby places where the stalls can be locked up and covered for the night, some even rent out locations nearby to keep their cart and goods so that they would not have to waste time transporting it. Many places maintain street markets, in addition to malls and supermarkets, as it is considered a part of the culture. While some people like modern shopping malls because everything is under one roof and it is convenient. A shopping mall is that one gives you access to all the stores through one entrance. Once you get into the mall you can go to any store in that mall without ever going back outside. The concept of the mall has not been a new one; they have been around since ancient Rome. The malls gained popularity around the 1920s, following World War II, when people started shifting to the suburbs from the city. In order to make it easier for the people to shop, many stores were opened in one bigger store that allowed easier access to the various stores in the same place.

(1) street markets　　　(2) shopping malls　　(3) different

(4) locations　　　　　(5) temporarily　　　(6) permanent

(7) prices　　　　　　(8) expensive　　　　(9) refundable

(10) the goods are cheaper but not refundable　　(11) culture and heritage

(12) atmosphere　　　　(13) convenient　　　(14) Ancient Rome

Passage 2

Time Measurement

A large variety of devices has been invented to measure time. The study of these devices is called horology. The measurement of time has come a long way since ancient times. It began with such devices as the sundial, where the position of the sun's shadow marked the hour. Daylight was divided into twelve "temporary hours", and these temporary hours were longer in the summer and shorter in the winter, simply because the amount of daylight changes with the seasons.

The earliest sundial we know comes from Egypt. It was made of stone and is thought to date from 1500 BC. Sundials were used throughout the classical world, and with time, evolved into more elaborate devices that could take into account seasonal changes and geographical positioning and reflect the hours accurately, no matter what the time of year. This was quite an achievement in technology. Today, sundials can be seen as decorative pieces in many gardens.

An hourglass (or sandglass, sand timer, or sand clock) is a device used to measure the passage of time. It comprises two glass bulbs connected vertically by a narrow neck that allows a regulated trickle of material (historically sand) from the upper bulb to the lower one. The hourglass uses the flow of sand to measure the flow of time. There are many factors that contribute to the ability of an hourglass to accurately measure time. The type and quality of sand is key. It must have a rate of flow that does not fluctuate. Sand that is too coarse will wear away the glass, eventually making the neck too large. Other factors affecting the time interval measured include bulb size and neck width. Hourglasses may be reused indefinitely by inverting the bulbs once the upper bulb is empty.

An alarm clock (or sometimes just an alarm) is a clock that is designed to alert an individual or group of individuals at specified time. Alarm clocks first appeared in ancient Greece around 250 BC with a water clock that would set off a whistle. The primary function of alarm clocks is to awaken people from their night's sleep or short naps; they are sometimes used for other reminders as well. Most use sound; some use light or vibration. To stop the sound or light, a button or handle on the clock is pressed; most clocks automatically stop the alarm if left unattended long enough. A classic analog alarm clock has an extra hand or inset dial that is used to specify the time at which to activate the alarm. Alarm clocks are also found on mobile phones and watches.

In the eleventh century, the Chinese invented the first mechanical clocks. They were large and expensive, and certainly not intended for individuals. However, this is the type of clock we are familiar with today. There have been many developments in clocks and watches since then, and they have been greatly improved, but if your clock or watch makes a ticking sound, then it could well be based on the mechanical movements the Chinese developed a thousand years ago!

However, timekeeping has moved on from the mechanical clock. The most accurate timekeeping devices are atomic clocks, which are accurate to seconds in many millions of years, and are used to calibrate other clocks and timekeeping instruments. Atomic clocks use the frequency of electronic transitions in certain atoms to measure the second. Time has become so important that there is a series of atomic clocks around the world which measure International Atomic Time. Even though many countries have their own calendars, globalisation has made it essential that we measure time uniformly, so that we know, for example, that when it's 6 a.m. in the United Kingdom, it's 2 p.m. in Beijing. This standard was set in 1958. Now these atomic clocks are situated in over seventy laboratories all over the world.

（1）horology　　　　　（2）The measurement of time　　（3）Sundial

（4）temporary hours　　（5）Egypt　　　　　　　　（6）stone

（7）decorative　　　　（8）classical　　　　　　（9）seasonal changes

（10）geographical positioning　（11）technological　　（12）glass bulbs

（13）the type and quality of sand　（14）bulb size　　（15）neck width

（16）inverting　　　　（17）alert　　　　　　　（18）ancient Greece

（19）sound, light or vibration　（20）mobile phones and watches

（21）mechanical clocks　（22）ticking　　　　　（23）atomic clocks

（24）calibrate　　　　（25）International Atomic Time　（26）seventy

Summary Interpreting

Guided Practice

Task A

（1）cognitive　　（2）consumption　　（3）markedly　　（4）decline

（5）elderly　　　（6）compelling　　（7）consistent　　（8）trials

（9）establish　　（10）prevalence

After-class Assignment

Answers

1. D　2. D　3. B　4. C　5. C　6. B　7. D　8. C　9. C　10. D

Unit 12

Warm Up

Task A

（1）the first International Conference on the Illegal Wildlife Trade

（2）severity of the crisis

（3）against a very different backdrop

（4）halt the destructive trade

（5）saving the wild animals from extinction

（6）warrants

（7）demonstrate our collective confidence

（8）remarkably uncontroversial

（9）a great loss for humanity

（10）relatively straightforward

（11）from killing field to marketplace

（12）fueling the demand

（13）rising to the challenges of our age

（14）natural heritage

Task B

（1）inspired　（2）reflection　（3）amateur　（4）critical　（5）regulating

（6）availability （7）enthusiasts （8）auspicious （9）immersed （10）resilient

Listening Comprehension

Guided Practice

Task A

Passage 1

Working in Austria

I think working in Austria is quite different to working in the UK. Um, I've done both. When I started my career, working in Austria in an office, where we produced, uh, manufactured computers, basically. And so basically the main difference, I found is, I mean the office where I worked in Austria was literally my hometown, so my commute was...um...walkable... cyclable, and it was literally just like, five minutes down the road. Um, so in the end it made the day a lot longer...um...because you know, you just finished work at five or something and then you were back home at ten past five or you meet, you were meeting friends...um...in the city center. It's not, you don't have to plan as much. Now I work in London and you know, my commute is about an hour cycling or forty-five minutes on the tube. And that actually takes two hours off your day. You know, you're getting out of the office and it takes you another hour to get back home. So the day's a lot shorter and the evenings are a lot shorter as well. Apart from this, the attitude towards work in Austria is really a funny in-between...um...the Italian, you know, we really "work to live" attitude...um...and the German, you know, "life is all about work" attitude. So in Austria you have a kind of funny mix about both.

（1）different　（2）walkable　（3）cyclable　（4）longer　（5）tube

（6）shorter　（7）work to live　（8）life is all about work　（9）in-between

Passage 2

Weddings in India

In India, weddings are a big thing. Um, it's like a carnival. Uh, people, lots of people come over attend the wedding. Uh, you have all your relations, sisters, brothers, cousins, uncles, aunts are coming and staying with the family for a couple of days at least because the wedding takes such a long time. And generally for, I think even now, most of the weddings are arranged, um, by the bride and groom's father, parents. And the boy and the girl will not know each other before the wedding, and that's how it happens mostly. But things are changing in India at the moment so people tend to fall in love and get married, uh but still the majority of the weddings are arranged in India.

And then the kind of ceremonies would also be different, depending on the region, but uh, usually it's never a one-day affair, it can go on for several days. And uh, you know, all this while, all the relatives and all the friends should be there at your home. And there's always celebration happening, a lot of music and dance, and you know, some meals being organized and it's like a very big affair. And the rich families, uh spend a lot of money, they're very lavish. Uh, sometimes they do tend to waste lot of money, the kind of wastage...uh...in terms of food and other things...uh...considering all that, a lot of money is being wasted. They have their weddings...uh...children's weddings at the five star hotels, blow up a lot of money, very expensive gifts are being exchanged. So it happens at all scales, at all levels. But...uh...no matter if you're rich or poor, you end up spending more money than you can actually afford to do on your wedding in India.

（1）carnival　　（2）days　　　（3）arranged　　（4）region

（5）celebration （6）lavish　　　（7）waste　　　（8）money

Task B

Passage 1

Family Relations

From my experience, the family relations in the UK, in many cases are good between the son and the father, the mother and the daughter. But there is no obligation for the person to live all the time with his mother and father. Um, it's slightly different in Saudi Arabia, where religiously you are encouraged to stay with your parents, especially if they need your help. Then the first option for them is to come over to your house. I'm sure this is in many cases still existing in Britain, but it is not from what I have seen, it's not the norm. Um, there are houses for elderlies, elderly people and all around the country, which is not the case in Saudi Arabia. Although in the recent years there has been some change in the attitudes toward elderly people but is still, they still within the family in most cases, from my experience.

（1）family relations good, but no obligations to live with parents

（2）religiously encouraged to live with parents

（3）house for elderlies more accepted

（4）most elderlies cared by families

Passage 2

Fishing Nets to Carpets

Our organization is an international conservation charity...um...working in fifty countries worldwide, and one of the projects we work on and, and one of the places we've done a lot of work is in the Philippines...um...where we run a project called Net-Works. Um, Net-Works is a really exciting initiative...um...very different and a lot of fun for us to all work on. Um, and the objective of Net-Works is to...um...turn old, discarded fishing nets in the central Philippines eventually into carpet tiles, which we put on the floors of people's houses and offices in different parts of the world.

Um, so discarded fishing nets are made from nylon, which is a form of plastic...um...that is very high grade plastic. So it's an engineering plastic and it has a lot of uses, it's quite valuable. It's used in fishing nets, particularly, in its purest form, and also in carpets in its purest form. But it's also used in computers...um...car tyres, all sorts of different things. Um, when it's used in fishing nets, then those fishing nets are often mono-filament fishing nets, which means that they are, they catch on things very easily, so they catch the fish very easily. But the trouble is they get damaged after a bit of time, and after two to three months these nets are damaged and ripped and they don't catch fish as well as they used to. So at this point, the fishermen often throw the nets away. In places like the central Philippines, um, which are in rural, remote communities...um...very poor communities, they don't have access to the same sort of recycling and waste management services that we do. So most of the time people just throw them on the beach or just dump them in the sea, which is a real problem for the environment. The plastic can last for up to six hundred years before it degrades...um...and then during that time if it's in the sea or on the beaches then it can continue to catch and ensnare marine life, which is a process called ghost-fishing. So it's called ghost-fishing because these nets catch the fish and the fish die, the crabs die, and they rot but they don't actually have any benefit for any of the people. So it's reducing the fish catches of the local people and really having a negative impact on their income.

And the thing that really makes our project different is that we have set up community-based supply chains, to be able to collect nets off the beaches and out of the environment, and also to get nets from the fishers after they have finished using them so that they don't throw them into the sea. So the fishers can sell their nets to community groups that we set up, and then the community groups aggregate all of those nets, make sure they're clean and nice. And then they sell them to us as one group, and we help them or facilitate them reach a market. And those nets actually go to Slovenia, where there's the only recycling plant in the world for nylon. So that's not something they can easily sell their nets to directly without our help. So we set up these kind of community groups who can do the buying within the communities.

（1）international conservation charity, working in fifty countries

（2）Net-Works

（3）to turn old discarded fishing nets into carpet tiles

（4）nylon

（5）plastic

（6）thrown away by the fishermen, on the beach or in the sea

（7）ghost-fishing

（8）six hundred

（9）marine life

（10）community-based

（11）collected and bought

（12）slovenia

（13）recycling plant in the world for nylon

Summary Interpreting

Guided Practice

Task A

Paragraph 1

Can we achieve the economic growth rate target of 7.5% set by the government this year? Actually, economy is very complex with forces that cannot be predicted. Nobody, not even the greatest economists, can predict what the growth rate is going to be. Therefore, it is not reasonable to expect the growth rate to be exactly 7.5%.

Paragraph 2

The world population is now 7 billion, and we produce food enough for 9 billion. However, one third of the food is wasted during transportation and cannot be properly sent to consumers, due to inadequate infrastructure and sometimes bureaucracy.

Paragraph 3

Chinese workers are demanding higher wages as the country's wealth rises and as production becomes modernized. At the same time, employers are going to resist the trend by, for example, automating the production. So China will loose its low-cost labor advantage until equilibrium between workers and employers in terms of wages is reached.

Paragraph 4

British and American English are different. Different from British English, American English, more like Canadian English, enunciates every sound. You can also listen for "end R" or vowels to tell the difference. It is sometimes difficult to understand people from different English-speaking regions.

After-class Assignment

Answers

1. T 2. F 3. T 4. T 5. F 6. F 7. F 8. F

Unit 13

Warm Up

Task A

(1) 12 weeks unpaid leave   (2) dependent on   (3) back to normal

(4) practical reality   (5) One in four   (6) can't afford to

(7) motherhood penalty   (8) advancement   (9) unpaid and underappreciated

(10) sole breadwinner   (11) privileged

(12) in order to liberate women, we need to liberate men

Task B

(1) psychological disaster   (2) worthlessness and lack of self-esteem

(3) an associate professor of health   (4) translates

(5) 20,000   (6) 7,500

(7) family breadwinner   (8) unemployment

（9）depression and anxiety

（11）Nine months

（13）hopelessness

（15）contagious disease

（10）psychotic behavior

（12）at epidemic rate

（14）rejection

Listening Comprehension

Guided Practice

Task A

Paragraph 1

Obesity occurs in many cultures, but it is predominant in Western societies. However, the causes are probably lifestyle choices rather than genetic predisposition. Many westerners can control their weight and remain a manageable size; the amount of weight a person carries is usually proportional to what foods they eat and how much exercise they do. People often find going to the gym a monotonous task, involving hours at the treadmill or doing repetitive exercises, but there are other forms of exercise more compatible with a person's disposition. Swimming, cycling and tennis are all good forms of exercise. Even if a person is slim, they should still do exercise. Being slim doesn't make a person immune to health problems which come from a lack of exercise. The optimum amount of time to spend exercising per day is just one hour. Surely, that's manageable for everyone!

Paragraph 2

An ecosystem is a geographical area of a variable size where plants, animals, the landscape and the climate all interact together. Plants are essential for any ecosystem. They provide all the energy for the ecosystem because they can get energy directly from sunlight. They use a process called photosynthesis to use energy from the sun to grow and reproduce. They must also get nutrients from the soil. These nutrients get into the soil when decomposers break down waste and dead materials. Plants require space to grow and reproduce. All other organisms in the food chain get energy from plants by eating them directly, as herbivores do, or by eating plant eaters, as carnivores do. Omnivores can get energy either by eating plants directly or by eating herbivores. Since all the energy in your ecosystem comes from plants, you'd better have a lot of them.

Paragraph 3

I'm from Jakarta, the capital city of Indonesia. The country comprises more than 17,500 islands, but only about 6,000 are inhabited. The population of Indonesia is more than 240 million, and about 26 million live in Jakarta. Can you imagine what it's like? There are many wonderful animals in Indonesia. The most beautiful for me is the Sumatran Tiger, but unfortunately there are not many living now, and you can only see them on the island of Sumatra. My father is a farmer. Actually, about 45% of Indonesian workers are engaged in agriculture because the country possesses vast and abundant arable fertile soils. We have large farm on the outskirts of Jakarta, where we cultivate a wide variety of agricultural tropical products including palm oil, natural rubber, rice, peanuts, cocoa, coffee and tropical spices.

Paragraph 4

Think about the two sports: swimming and running. What equipment does each one require? In swimming, you need wetsuit and goggles. You can buy quite cheap wetsuits these days, but the problem is that they tend to be made of thick material and are not very flexible, making body movement quite difficult. More expensive wetsuits give you a better body fit and different thickness of rubber in areas such as the shoulders. This gives you greater flexibility of movement when you are swimming. Goggles are really important, but the shape is up to you. Decide which style you feel most comfortable with. Small goggles simply cover your eyes, while wider mask-type goggles cover your eyes and some of the face. In running, you need shoes and heart-rate monitor. You need to be properly measured and fitted for running shoes as everyone's feet and running style are different. The more expensive shoes tend to have greater cushioning and stability; some triathletes prefer racing flats, or ultra-lightweight trainers. Heart-rate monitors (HRMs) are good for working out your training programmes and help you work within your limits. Basic ones tell the time and your heart rate. The most advanced ones can also measure speed and distance.

Paragraph 5

Throughout history, adventurers have risked their lives crossing strange countries and seas in search of new lands, fame and fortune. For many, however, death was the only reward. Marco Polo: In the early Middle Ages, Europeans knew little about China and the Far East, except through travellers' tales brought back by traders. In 1271, however, the Venetian merchant Marco Polo set off with his father and uncle on an epic expedition that was to open people's eyes. After they had crossed Turkey, Iran, Afghanistan, India and most of China, the Polos spent 17 years as guests of the Mongol emperor Kublai Khan, visiting places never seen before by Europeans. The New World: Exactly which European first discovered the Americans is still a subject which is hotly debated. Leif Ericsson from Iceland, who landed on the North American continent in AD

1000 at a place he named Vinland because of the wild grapes he found growing there. However, the man most commonly credited with discovering both North and South America is Christopher Columbus, who was born in Italy. Columbus set sail across the Atlantic in August 1492, and after a perilous voyage he reached the Caribbean in October. He continued on to Cuba and Haiti, and then returned home.

Paragraph 6

Our science programme today concentrates on something we all take very much for granted, but which we cannot do without. And that is water. So, what exactly is water? Water is the liquid form of the chemical H_2O. There are two atoms of hydrogen (that's the H_2) and one atom of oxygen (that's the O) in every molecule of water. There's a lot of liquid water and it covers about 70 percent of the Earth's surface. But water can also be a solid or a gas, so it's not always wet. About 97 percent of the water on earth's surface is in the world's oceans. The other 3 percent is in lakes, rivers, at the Polar ice caps, in the clouds, falling as rain or stored in rocks. And don't forget sea icebergs! such as icebergs! If we don't get enough water, we become dehydrated. This can cause serious health problems such as kidney damage, but even mild dehydration can be unpleasant, you might get tired, headachy and unable to concentrate. Then how can we make sure we get enough water? The best thing to do is to make drinking water part of your routine, so that you do it without thinking about it. Drink a glass of water when you wake up, and carry a bottle of water with you when you go out. Eating fresh fruit and vegetables will help too.

Summary Interpreting

Guided Practice

Task A

Paragraph 1

数字娱乐

信息水平/综合国力

定义：基于数字技术的文化产业

创新性，高科技，日常，带动，增长，潜力，媒体习惯；

未来：＄电影，音乐，游戏，电视

科技支撑（手机，宽带，网速，移动设备）

家庭电视：个人电视（依然主角）：实例/好处

移动性（新风尚）：平台/服务

Paragraph 2

后发效应

后工业化国家速度超越先工业化国家

英，美，日，韩，中

经济增长一倍用时：

58/47/34/11/9

原因（后工业化国家可以）：

1. 利用经验技术等；

2. 劳动力和资源优势；

3. 新兴产业，没有旧工业负担。

Paragraph 3

Learning styles:

interesting/important

Everybody has

The way you prefer to learn

Intelligent/skills ×

Good/bad ×

Important: to understand your own

Main types: e.g. remembering a phone number

auditory: hear it as it is being recited

visual: picture it in your minds

kinaesthetic: dial it without looking at the phone

Paragraph 4

Plastic:

molded substance better than pottery and glass

1905: invented by Baekeland, a Belgian

named as Bakelite

do not soften easily: material of a thousand uses

Now: we rely on it

But: it uses oil (last for decades)

So: renewable or alternative needed

Solution: bioplastic (made from crops)

e.g. biodegradable bags

but, expensive/melt easily

Task B

Paragraph 1

运动：

不寻常的运动：

        1. 水下球类：1954/英国/水下曲棍球

                       俄罗斯/水下橄榄球/冰球

                       更复杂、更有趣

                       水下摄像机

        2. 骑 鸵 鸟：非洲→美国

                       速度70千米/一步5米

        3. 掷金枪鱼：澳大利亚

                       冷冻金枪鱼/10千克

                       仿真鱼替代/∵浪费+鱼碎

Paragraph 2

南极：

      最冷：年均–25℃/最低–90℃

      冰封/大风/干燥

      最孤独：无人/停留短<6个月

      日出一次/日落一次

宝地：资源

      困难！（勘探和开采/领土主权/环境污染）

      战略！未来唯一宝库

Paragraph 3

New tech: Xeros

      Clean clothes with plastic chips + a cup of water

      Just as clean as water-washed

Advantages:

      1. Clothes dry; tumble dryer not needed;

      2. Remove all everyday stains;

      3. No sorting is needed for mixed colors;

4. No detergents, so linen more lasting;

5. Less energy, more environmentally friendly;

It is hoped: used in commercial washing/dry cleaning.

Paragraph 4

Digital age: 1970s, PC

Things are digitised:

　　changed into digits and numbers/electronic language

　　e.g. words, numbers, photos, X-rays, sounds, objects

　　anything!

　　bits of info.

　　e.g. photos: dots→lines/shading

With info. digitised, you can: store/transmit/enhance

Pros: 1. paper use ↓

　　　2. info. dissemination ↑

　　　3. preservation of heritage/library, archive, museum, gallery ↑

Cons: 1. easily edited, not trustworthy

　　　2. more complex to preserve

After-class Assignment

Answers

1. B 2. A 3. C 4. C 5. B 6. A

Unit 14

Warm Up

Task A

(1) Peer pressure, media influence, and personal expression

(2) sign

(3) Gangs

(4) identify

(5) wear green army jackets and have large "Xs" tattooed on their arms

(6) brand-name clothes

(7) the popularity of tattoos in North America

（8）commercials

（9）Famous sports heroes

（10）Fashion models

（11）wealth, success, and status

（12）their artistic nature, their beliefs, or their feelings

（13）individuality

（14）guitar

（15）endangered animals

（16）each others' names

（17）public sign

Task B

（1）human civilization

（2）agricultural, fishery and forestry products

（3）it is most critical to provide food and employment

（4）flourishing agribusinesses

（5）a long-term sustainable economic growth

（6）mobilization of international and domestic financing for agriculture

（7）developing countries and countries in transition

（8）financing agencies

（9）funding commitments

（10）urgency of committing their own resources to agriculture

（11）Debt forgiveness programmes

（12）remains to be done

（13）volume of public investment in agriculture

（14）promoting profitable partnerships

（15）public and private sectors

（16）farmers and consumers

（17）from farm to fork

（18）Precision agriculture

（19）livestock production

（20）Refrigeration and modern packaging technologies

Listening Comprehension

Guided Practice

Task A

Paragraph 1

A team of American scientists may have found a way to reverse the aging process. They fed diet supplements, usually found in health food shops, to elderly rats, which were then tested for memory and stamina. The animals tended to display more active behaviour after taking the supplements, and generally their memory improved. In addition, their appearance became rather more youthful and their appetite increased. The researchers believe that this experiment is quite a clear indication of how the problem of old age may be overcome. They claim that in a few years' time many people may be able to look forward to a fairly long and active retirement.

Paragraph 2

The world around us is made up of a limited number of chemical elements. Scientists have discovered 109 of these and each one has different properties. But 98% of the Earth's crust is made up of just eight elements, including oxygen, iron, aluminum, sodium and calcium. Elements often combine to form new substances, called compounds, of which there are millions. Water is a compound of hydrogen and oxygen, while salt is a compound of sodium and chlorine. Chemical reactions occur all around us and are the means by which new substances are created from existing ones. For example, water is created when hydrogen and oxygen are ignited together. Reactions are used to produce many items, including soap, cosmetics, paint and plastic. Magnetism plastic something that pushes or pulls an object in a particular direction. If an object exerts a force on another, it receives an equal and opposite force in return. Objects exert a force of attraction towards each other, which is known as gravity. The larger the object's mass, the greater the attraction. Earth's is so huge that it pulls everything nearby towards it. The moon's gravity pulls the water in the Earth's oceans around, causing tides.

Paragraph 3

Can malaria be controlled? Drug-resistant strains of malaria, already one of the world's major killers, are steadily spreading across the globe. The deadly strains have established themselves in South East Asia and South America, and have recently begun to spread across India and Africa. Formerly under control in many areas, the disease now threatens two billion people living in more than 100 countries. Estimates suggest that there are now more than 350 million cases of malaria a year — a total four times the level of the early 1970s. In Africa alone the disease kills one million children each year. Several factors are responsible for this disturbing development. Spreading world poverty has deprived nations of funds for sanitation, so that many health projects have been stopped, while increased movements of migrant workers and tourists have carried infections more rapidly from one country to another. At the same time, the overuse of drugs, especially antibiotics, has led to the establishment of resistant strains of diseases. As well as this, hopes that genetic engineers might soon develop the world's first malaria vaccine, a long-sought goal, have been questioned recently by several scientists. There are so many strains of malaria parasite, and each is able to alter its chemical surface and trick its way past the body's defense. We'd need a remarkable vaccine to cope with that. However, a malaria vaccine is now undergoing human trials and may be valuable for use if proved successful.

Paragraph 4

For the past centuries, we have seen in all countries in the world achieved impressive progress in health that lead to increases in life expectancy. In the UK, life expectancy doubled and is now higher than 80 years. In Japan, health started to improve later, but the country caught up quickly with the UK and surpassed it in the late 1960s. In South Korea, health started to improve later still and the country achieved even faster progress than the UK and Japan; by now life expectancy in Japan and South Korea has surpassed life expectancy in the UK, reaching about 85. Despite the overall increase in the expectancy over the past century, women still live significantly longer than men. In fact, in 1900 men could expect to live to 49 and women to 52, a difference of three years, while now the figures are 74 and 79, which shows that the gap has increased to five years. Various reasons have been suggested for this situation, such as the possibility that men may die earlier because they take more risks. But a team of British scientists have recently found a likely answer in the immune system, which protects the body from diseases. The thymus is the organ which produces the T cells which actually combat illnesses. Although both sexes suffer from deterioration of the thymus as they age, women appear to have more T cells in their bodies than men of the same age. It is this, the scientists believe, that gives women better protection from potentially fatal diseases such as influenza and pneumonia.

Task B

The Effects of the Black Death

Paragraph 1

The Black Death landed in Europe by sea in 1347. People gathered at the docks waiting to greet the trading ships that had gone through the Black Sea. The people waiting were in for a big surprise; the sailors aboard the ships were all dead from the plague except for a few stragglers that were alive but greatly ill. It was a serious pandemic that infected Europe and nearly wiped out 60% of its population during its two year spread all across Europe. A rough estimate of about 60~200 million people were claimed as victims of the Black Death. At the time, there was no way to cure the sickness and if you had it, you most likely were left to die in the streets. It took 150 and in some areas more than 250 years for Europe's population to recover, which had an economic impact. Price of labor skyrocketed in the face of worker shortage, and the cost of goods rose. The plague recurred occasionally in Europe until the 19th century, and was one of the most devastating disasters in human history. (The Black Death landed in Europe via ships and caused huge population loss. Labor and goods costs skyrocketed, which damaged the economy. It is a devastating disaster.)

Paragraph 2

The Black Death entered the harbor of Europe carrying the disease. Actually, the ships contained rats infected by flea that transmitted the tiny bubonic bacterium to the people on land. When the ships arrived at the harbor, it took only twelve months for the pandemic to kill a third of the population. The Black Death had many drawbacks but then again there were multiple pluses. The Plague brought forth the Renaissance. It helped us advance our medicine. It brought the end of the serfdom because labor force was down. The role of women became more important because of labor shortage. There was major growth in activism and religion. The Hundred Years War between England and France was put off when the English found that 40% or so of the fighting men in the population were dead because of the sickness. (The Black Death was caused by the bacterium brought to Europe by ships. Despite population loss and many other drawbacks, the plague brought forth the Renaissance, helped advance medicine, ended the serfdom, empowered women, enhanced activism and religion, put off the Hundred Years War.)

The Social Effects of Tourism in Developing Countries

Paragraph 1

When countries begin to provide facilities for mass tourism, such as hotels and leisure complexes, there is an immediate demand for labour. Work is created for cleaners, waiters, gardeners and drivers on a scale which may significantly boost the local economy. Such work may provide opportunities for the locals to learn valuable new skills, and to open new businesses. For many, these semi-skilled jobs provide an attractive alternative to subsistence agriculture or fishing, while at the same time the tax revenues from their earnings increase the national income. (Tourism facility development demands labour, with locals learning skills and opening businesses, therefore boosts economy. Tourism is a new way, other than agriculture and fishing, to increase tax revenues and national income.)

Paragraph 2

One inevitable feature of tourism's growth is the creation of badly-paid, seasonal jobs in holiday resorts. Much of this work combines insecurity with long hours of work in poor conditions. In Thailand, for example, there are cases of hotel maids working 15 hour days for less than $4. Moreover, the combination of wealthy tourists being served by exploited waitresses is likely to increase social tensions in these areas. Another risk is that natural or human disasters such as wars and earthquakes may drive visitors away without warning, leaving tens of thousands unemployed. (Seasonal jobs in holiday resorts are badly paid, which increases social tension. Resorts vulnerable to natural or human disasters may end up having more unemployed.)

Should Genetically Modified (GM) Foods
Have a Role in Future Agriculture?

Paragraph 1

Genetic modification (GM) is the most recent application of biotechnology to food, which can also be called genetic engineering or genetic manipulation. The phrase "Genetically Modified Organisms" or GMOs is used frequently in the scientific literature to describe plants and animals which have had DNA introduced into them by means other than "natural" process of an egg and a sperm. New species have always evolved through natural selection by means of random genetic variation. Early farmers used this natural variation to selectively breed wild animals, plants and even micro-organisms such as yogurt cultures and yeasts. They produced domesticated variants better suited to the needs of humans, long before the scientific basis for the process was understood. Despite this long history of careful improvement, such procedures are now labelled "interfering with nature". (GM process is similar to natural selection and such procedures should not be labelled "interfering with nature".)

Paragraph 2

Genetic modification (GM) is in fact far more than a mere development of selective breeding techniques. Combining genetic material from species that cannot breed naturally is interference in areas which may be highly dangerous. The consequences of this kind of manipulation cannot be foreseen. It seems undeniable that these processes may lead to major benefits in food production and the environment. There is no doubt, for example, that some medical advances may have saved millions of lives. However, this level of technology can contain a strong element of risk. Our ignorance of the long-term effects of releasing GM plants or even animals into the environment means that this step should only be taken after very careful consideration. (GM process is quite different to traditional processes of selection. Crossing the species barrier is a dangerous step and there is insufficient knowledge of the long-term results of such developments.)

Summary Interpreting

Guided Practice

Task A

Paragraph 1

Studying Abroad or Online?

Every year large number of students travel abroad to study at university. Most of them spend thousands of pounds on their degree courses. The cost of travel and accommodation adds significantly to their expenses. But they could save a lot of money by studying their courses online, using the Internet and email. Increasing numbers of universities are offering tuition by the Internet, and this has many advantages for students. In the future most students are likely to stay at home and study in front of a computer.

Paragraph 2

China's Economic Growth

Now, most people would agree that the massive economic growth China has enjoyed in the last decades represents perhaps the most significant geopolitical event of the 21st century. It started with the economic reforms back in the late 1970s, before which time China's economy was largely rural. Since the 1970s China's economy has grown on average 10% a year. Since 2001, China has doubled its share of global manufacturing output. In fact, China is second only to the US, and most forecasts suggest it will overtake the American economy within the next ten years. The huge population resource of China means not only is China the world's largest market, but it also underpins the main reason for its economic rise, a large workforce. Many would also argue that the growing middle class is the backbone of China's success.

Paragraph 3

Taking Notes in Lectures

I'd like to begin by giving you a few pointers on taking notes in lectures. Taking notes in lectures is a vital skill. Most important of all is that you shouldn't try to make a note of everything you hear. A lecture is not a dictation. You have to decide what is important and what is not. Second, when you make notes, don't write everything in full. Use abbreviations, symbols, numbers, anything to help keep pace. Also, try to be an active listener. By that, I mean you need to try and predict what the speaker is going to say. So before the lecture, ask yourself what you already know about the topic, and during the lecture think about where the talk might be heading.

Paragraph 4

How to Get a Green Card?

Having a green card, or permanent residence status, gives you the ability to legally live and work in the United States, and it's a step toward becoming a US citizen. There are three main ways you can get permanent residency, or a green card. If you are coming to work in the US and you have a permanent job, then you can get an employer-based green card. In applying for this type of green card, your US employer must complete forms for you and both the Department of Labor and the Department of State must approve, and then you will be given an immigrant Visa Number. If you have family here who are citizens or already have a green card, then you can apply for a family-based green card. Finally, you can win a green card through the Diversity Visa Lottery programme. 50,000 green cards are given away every year to people from countries with low rates of immigration to the US.

Paragraph 5

Tech to Help Tackle Ikea Flat Packs

If you've ever opened the Ikea flat pack and found yourself helpless, a simple solution may soon be at hand. Ikea, the furniture giant, has teamed up with a London start-up that could allow people to scan a product code with a smartphone and receive information, such as instructional videos, which could show people how to make a bed or how to assemble it in an easy-to-follow, step-by-step way. The idea of the app is to co-create with Ikea to make its services more accessible. Ikea believes that service like this has a big potential in creating a better everyday life at home for everyone, which is just the motto of the company. This case is a successful demonstration of how big businesses can gain a competitive edge by collaborating with start-ups to gain better local presence and greater social good.

Paragraph 6

Gardening Tips

With a wealth of research suggesting that gardening is beneficial for wellbeing and mental health, we are happy to share some top horticultural tips for small outdoor spaces. 1. Grow Herbs. Herbs are the perfect plant to cultivate on a balcony, patio, or even in a window box. Not only are they relatively easy to grow, they can also liven up your cooking and add that extra punch of flavour. 2. Hanging baskets. Hanging baskets are a great way to maximise on limited space and add some variation and colour to your outdoor balcony or patio. Make sure you use a good lining material for your basket. 3. One-pot container vegetable gardens. There are a variety of different one-pot containers that can be used to create your own mini-garden in a smaller space. A steel tub or wooden planter can allow you to grow salad plants, chili plants or herbs. Tomato grow bags are also really convenient solutions to help grow your own tomatoes with ease. Runner beans and squashes are also very easy to grow in pots and containers. Do you have a small garden or just a balcony? Let us know what you grow.

Task B

Passage 1

Where did Mobile Phones Come from?

Although mobile phones have been affordable for the masses only for the last several decades, they have in fact been around for more than sixty years in one form or another. The technology that would later be used in today's mobile phones was created in the late 1940s and the idea of a mobile phone was introduced then. This technology was first used mainly in taxis, police cars and other emergency vehicles and situations.

The first mobile phones, referred to as first generation or 1G, were introduced to the public market in 1983 by the Motorola Company. These first mobile phones used analogue technology, which was much less reliable than the digital technology we use today. The analogue phones also had a great deal more static and noise interference than we are now accustomed to. The first mobile phones during this era were confined to car phones, and they were permanently installed in the floor of cars. After a few years, they became mobile and users could take the phones with them outside of the car. However, they were the size of a large briefcase and very inconvenient. Also, these new mobile phones were expensive, many of them costing hundreds of dollars. They were more of a status symbol than a convenience.

During the 1990s, great improvements were made in mobile phone technology. These phones used second generation (2G) technology, which was faster and much quieter than its analogue predecessor. As a result, mobile phones became even more popular. The new technology also used smaller batteries and other technology that made the phones more energy-efficient, helping to contribute to their smaller size and their popularity.

Third generation (3G) technology is what many people still use in their mobile phones today. It was created very soon after the excitement created by 2G technology. The new technology is not only capable of transferring voice data (such as a phone call), but is also able to transfer other types of data, including emails, information and instant messages. These capabilities have helped to increase the number of sales and the popularity of these new phones. Many users prefer to use the instant messaging capabilities to text other users rather than call them in the form of a traditional phone call.

You could think that there is little more that you could do with cellular phone technology. This is, however, not the case. We are currently using fourth generation (4G) technology. This mainstream set of standards includes a combination of technologies that can make information transfer and Internet capabilities faster and more affordable for mobile phones.

The mobile phone industry continues to grow by leaps and bounds, just as it has in the past few decades. Even though the phone revolution started a mere 30 years ago, manufacturers have created an abundance of new technologies that keep mobile phone users coming back for more. Users today enjoy live video chat, mobile payment, on their smartphones, which mobile phone users of the past could have never ever imagined. Developers of mobile phones continue to increase the number of capabilities and services to accommodate the growing needs of today's "on the go" culture. Waiting anxiously is the only way to find out what they will think of next.

Passage 2

High-speed Rail Network

The global high-speed rail network is one of the great feats of modern engineering, and proves to be the best form of transportation ever invented. High-speed rail is rail transport that operates significantly faster than traditional rail traffic. The first such system began operations in Japan in 1964 and was widely known as the bullet train. HSR has been in operation in Japan for more than 50 years carrying more than 9 billion passengers without a single fatality. HSR is powered almost exclusively by electricity, not diesel. Compared to driving, flying, or riding conventional rail, it is the fastest way to travel between two points that are a few hundred kilometres apart and reduces carbon emissions up to 90 percent. Over time, its energy source is likely to get cleaner as renewables generate a greater share of electricity.

The global high-speed rail network is rapidly expanding across continents worldwide, delivering fast, efficient mobility to numerous nations every day. Many countries have developed high-speed rail to connect major cities, including Austria, Belgium, China, France, Germany, Italy, Japan, Poland, Portugal, Russia, South Korea, Spain, Sweden, Turkey, United Kingdom, United States and Uzbekistan. Only in Europe does HSR cross international borders. China has 22,000 kilometres of HSR at the end of 2016, accounting for two-thirds of the world's total.

China's high-speed rail system, just a decade old, is now one of the biggest infrastructure projects in history. The government has spent an estimated 2.4 trillion yuan building 22,000 kilometres of high-speed rail lines, more than the rest of the world combined. China is continuing to expand its high-speed rail network as fast as it can to meet people's growing transport needs and support the country's industrial development and economic restructuring. With ever more passengers riding the speedy trains, many of the rail lines are now profitable in China.

China's international reputation has also improved through building HSR and exporting HSR expertise. In 2014, World Bank researchers lauded China's trains as "world-class" and described the development of the railway network as "remarkable". China is pushing forward with high-speed railway projects in Russia. China is also actively seeking high-speed railway deals in Malaysia, Britain and the United States as it looks to export its expertise around the world.

However, the prevalence of high-speed rail systems in Europe and East Asia does not mean that it is suitable for all countries to have their own high-speed rail systems. Varied factors such as population density, property rights, and network effects shall be taken into consideration in making the economics of high-speed commuter rail.

Firstly, population density is an important factor to be considered for the construction of HSR. HSR is expensive and requires high ridership to break even, or to be economically viable. After all, HSR doesn't scale for very long distances. That is why only certain places in the world have sufficient population density to support HSR. China has by far the most HSR lines, with Japan and Western Europe behind. Where adequate density exists, HSR can be an important component of a sustainable transportation system.

Secondly, property rights also play an important role in the process of constructing HSR. One of the most expensive parts of building new rail lines is securing land along a relatively straight path as trains cannot run at highspeeds along too sharp a curve. Countries that have strong property rights make securing land exceedingly expensive. Plus, private property owners will be affected by the construction of the high-speed rail system. In light of this fact, authorities have to be committed to do everything they can to educate, inform, and work collaboratively with affected property owners.

<u>Another important facet of high-speed rail is the value of network effects.</u> It is a far more attractive proposition to build an HSR system that looks more like a web instead of a point-to-point line. This is because webs tend to result in much higher utilization than point-to-point systems. And utilization is the most important determinant behind the economics of high fixed-cost businesses like high-speed rail.

After-class Assignment

Answers

1. B 2. A 3. ABD 4. BC 5. A 6. A 7. BCD 8. D

Unit 15

Task 1

A: You know, I've been thinking about sleep a lot lately because I've been really struggling to go to sleep. We spend a third of our lives sleeping. I wonder how much sleep people really need, and why people need to sleep anyway.

B: 哦，很多人跟你有同样的想法。很多成功人士每天几乎不睡觉。我总是听说"超级短眠者"的故事。有些人，比如比尔·克林顿、玛莎·斯图尔特、拿破仑，他们每晚睡4小时就够了。

A: I wish I could be like them. I've imagined how many more things I could get done if I had a few more hours each day. Or how much more I could get done if I wasn't so tired when I got less than six hours of sleep.

B: 当然，要回答"我们为什么需要睡眠?"这样的问题非常困难。但是，根据一篇《纽约时报》的报道，只有5%的人每晚睡4小时就可以正常生活。而且，训练我们的身体适应缺乏睡眠的状态是不可能的。几乎所有人都需要每晚8小时的睡眠才能达到最好状态。即便只是降到7以下，都会影响我们的表现。

A: I wonder how they could have done that. It's a difficult conclusion to draw, isn't it?

B: 这个研究中，志愿者们在一个睡眠实验室里生活两周的时间。在实验条件下控制他们的睡眠和需要完成的任务，以衡量他们的表现。一共有三组睡眠者，在两周之内每晚的睡眠分别达到8小时、6小时和4小时。最有趣的是，很多4小时和6小时的睡眠者，实验开始几天后表示，他们"已经适应了"。然而，测试结果表明，他们出现表现大幅降低的情况。因此，即便人们认为自己已经适应了睡眠缺乏的状态，实际上他们只是没有意识到其副作用而已。

A: As far as I know, Elon Musk, CEO of Tesla and SpaceX, sleeps little and even keeps a sleeping bag in Tesla's factory, next to the production line, so he can better inspect vehicles as they come off it. No wonder he is now the 21st wealthiest person in America.

B: 一般人需要7到9小时的睡眠，但这也因人而异。我们不知道究竟为什么要睡觉，但是我们大多数都认识到，睡眠可以使我们感觉更好。一夜好眠之后，我们感觉更有精神和精力，更有幸福感，更有能力应付工作。

A: I used to be able to work out how much sleep I need to feel well rested, when I had no difficulty falling asleep. There were those days when I could fall asleep immediately after my head hit the pillow. I think at that time I was able to get enough sleep. But I don't know since when, I started to stay up later to engage in a variety of activities that had nothing to do with sleep. After all, finishing one more episode of TV series, reading one more chapter of a book, or playing one more game is way more fun than going to bed, you know? Besides, if you go to bed, it's not like you're going to fall asleep immediately.

B: 我知道，不会总是可以马上睡着。那么，盯着天花板，等待绵羊的到来，你都做点什么呢？你知道，只要有人说入睡困难，往往人们就会提出数绵羊的建议。

A: I think I'm suffering from insomnia. I'm always tired, but not sleepy. I even dread going to sleep. It's like you know that you won't be able to sleep before your head even hits the pillow. You'll just lie there with your eyes open, begging for sleep. But it just won't come.

B: 现在我的睡眠也不太好，但也一般不太坏。你可以采用几个步骤，改变一下行为和生活方式有助睡眠，我发现几个方法特别好用。

A: I try not to eat or drink right before going to bed, as they say that eating a late dinner or snacking before going to bed can activate the digestive system and keep you up. Also I try to avoid alcohol and coffee, as the effects of caffeine can last for several hours, perhaps up to 24 hours, so the chances of it affecting sleep are significant. But those don't seem to work for me. Do you have other tips to recommend?

B: 我们生活在屏幕的世界中，严重依赖社交媒体的人更是难以入睡。现在，有人说上网已经成为新时代的二手烟。因此，我尽量睡前避免电子干扰，我发现这对我来说是最有效的方法。我还尽量在睡前早早解决掉烦恼。晚饭后，我就回顾当天的事情，并为第二天做好计划，目的就是避免入睡的时候还在想这些事情。

A: Sounds reasonable. So, I will try first to have less digital contact before sleep. And I think resolving worries or concerns before bedtime might be more relevant to me. I can try to jot them down and set it aside for tomorrow. Besides, maybe I need to take a number of relaxation therapies and stress reduction methods, to relax the mind and the body before going to bed, and see how it works.

B: 健康的睡眠习惯可以极大改变我们的生活质量。希望这些方法可以帮助你睡个好觉，白天可以更有精力和创造力。

A: Thanks. Fingers crossed for a good night's sleep.

Task 2

A: I am now writing an article about school bullying because I feel that not enough attention has been paid to this issue. When I dig deeper into this area, I find that more knowledge about this should be spread and shared among schools, teachers, parents, and even school children themselves. How is it tackled in your country?

B: "反对欺凌" 在英国宣传广泛。欺凌的形式很多，可能是身体上或者语言上的，比如，打人、揪头发、踢人、取笑人、骂人；也可能是情感上的，比如，传播谣言、惊吓和恐吓，或者在游戏及社会活动中加以排挤。任何孩子都不应该受到欺凌，因为欺凌可能对受害者造成巨大影响。大多数情况下，欺凌被视为不幸事件，是学校生活中不可避免的部分。但在英国，欺凌是不能被接受的行为，大多数学校都执行反欺凌政策。

A: I think other countries can learn from the practice of your country. As you mentioned, victims in bullying should be protected as bullying may have devastating effect on them. Psychologists have found that being bullied can have an adverse impact on a child's personal development and academic performance.

B: 是的。受到欺凌的孩子会更加不容易相信他人，他们可能缺少自信，经常感到焦虑、愤怒、怨恨或者抑郁。这些情感会继续破坏他们控制自己生活的能力，他们可能某一天转成欺凌他人，进而形成恶性循环。

A: Right. Prevention is always better than cure. While anyone has the potential to be bullied, some groups are more vulnerable and at greater risk of being targeted. The survey also found that students from ordinary schools experienced more bullying than peers from key institutions, and children from poor families are more likely to be bullied at school. Actually a child who is bullying others often has problems of his or her own in the first place. Try to understand what may be causing this behaviour may be helpful as well.

B: 是的。欺凌事件难以被人觉察，因此密切关注孩子们的行为非常重要。问题孩子可能在经历艰难时期，可能感觉受到忽视，可能只是在模仿他人的行为。在他们的家庭中，可能就需要通过攻击和武力才能够得到想要的东西。因此，教师和家长应该确保孩子们明白，欺凌是不能够被接受的；他们也应该鼓励孩子们，对他人友好、善良。

A: From my research, in some cases, children may not tell their parents or teachers that they are being bullied. However, you may notice some changes in their behaviour, for example, when they are unwilling to go to school, feeling anxious or irritable, becoming aggressive towards family members, waking in the night, or even bedwetting.

B: 确实是。我认为宣传和政府支持非常重要。在英国，欺凌和相关材料被纳入国家课程，在学校中被广泛使用，孩子们用于作业设计，教师们用于备课计划。学校也被要求改善措施，更好地预防和处理欺凌事件，针对严重事件设立应急计划。

A: Yes. Some scholars also suggest measures like boosting communication between teachers, parents and students and operating a hotline for reporting of bullying, with the aim of establishing more harmonious relationships among children.

B: 在英国，一些组织，如"欺凌在英国"等，全年提供反欺凌方面的支持和建议，帮助任何正在经历或遭受欺凌影响的人。在学校，我们有"反欺凌月""反欺凌周"等活动，帮助筹款或提升反欺凌意识。在一周的时间内，各个学校都举行提升反欺凌意识的活动。我还记得，我们每年11月份都有"蓝衣日"。

A: Does it mean that all children wear blue on that day?

B: 是的。我们要求学校、学院、大学、个人、组织和商界人士穿着蓝色衣服，通过网站、国家支持服务热线、网上资源和论坛、社区推广等形式，为"欺凌在英国"等组织捐款。

A: Public awareness and participation will be very helpful. Experts say that the best way to curb bullying in a school environment is through education.

B: 我同意。英国的学校试图将反欺凌的概念和理念变得有趣，这样孩子们能够更容易接受并记住。学生们还需要穿奇怪的袜子来提升反欺凌的意识。

A: Oh, this sounds "odd" to me. What are odd socks?

B: 哦，那一天，学校鼓励孩子们穿不同大小或不同颜色的袜子，或奇奇怪怪不一样的袜子。这个想法让参与变得简单，没有任何压力，不必穿着昂贵的服装。"怪袜子日"是全国性的活动，目的是赋予孩子们和年轻人力量，让他们为自己的独特之处引以为豪。同时帮助年轻人明白，他们有能力做自己，不惧怕欺凌十分重要！

A: This is both interesting and instructive, a good idea for children to express themselves and appreciate individuality and uniqueness! I may try to wear odd socks every day. I can now add new ideas to my article.

Task 3

主持人：让我们欢迎今天的嘉宾，赫曼斯博士和杨博士。今天的主题是高等教育扩招。我们都知道，全世界范围内的决策者都在考虑进行大规模改革，增加大学就读学生的数量。比如，美国的"学院承诺法案"就做出承诺，美国学生可以免费进入社区学院学习。另一个例子是，1999年中国的改革，通过增加公立大学的规模和数量，将大学扩招两倍。两位对这种趋势是怎么看的？是什么原因促成了高校扩招呢？

Dr. Yang: I think a variety of factors have led to the enrollment expansion, to stimulate domestic consumption, to ease the pressure on the labor market, the high public interest in and demand for higher education, and it could be just the political will of a country to develop higher education.

赫曼斯博士：是的。原因是多样的，通常基于一个国家的人口结构、社会情况甚至是政治需要。但通常来说，教育的发展可以给个人和国家带来很多有利的变化。一些人认为，扩招对国家经济发展非常重要，因为受教育程度更高的国民具备更高的生产力。

主持人：是的。许多研究者认为，高校扩招是扩大内需和刺激经济发展的重要方法，对发展中国家尤为如此，对吗？

Dr. Yang: Yes. Some large developing economies, like the BRICS countries, are already important players globally, and by mid-century, they are likely to be economic powerhouses. Whether they reach that level of development will depend partly on how successfully they create quality higher education. For example, India's higher education system is one of the world's largest, enrolling nearly 22 million students in more than 46,000 institutions.

主持人：我们可以理解，政府需要受教育程度更高的人力资源以发展经济，国民需要受到更好的教育以获得更好的生活。但是，短期来看，扩招可能导致教育水平的下降。关于这一点，两位是怎么看的？

赫曼斯博士：大学扩招之后，学生和服务人员的数量激增，教师流动更加频繁，这些都给大学带来了许多困难和问题。对一所大学来说，短期之内新建高楼往往很容易，但是吸引大量教授就不那么容易了。换句话说，软件的提升往往更难、更费时。因此，扩招应该是非常慎重的决定。

Dr. Yang: I agree. For the last decades, well-known universities like Harvard, MIT, Stanford, have kept their enrollment at about 15 to 20 thousand.

赫曼斯博士：很多因素可以决定大学教育的质量，但是很多家长忽略生师比这个因素。生师比指的是，一所学校或大学的学生数量除以该机构的教师数量所得的值。比如，生师比10：1表示每个老师负责10名学生。生师比排名前100的大学大部分都在美国，其次是日本。

Dr. Yang: Student-teacher ratio is important for a number of reasons. For one thing, it can be used as a tool to measure teachers' workload as well as the allocation of resources. More importantly, however, it can be an indicator of the amount of individual attention any single student is likely to receive. The student-teacher ratio of any given university is frequently used to judge the quality of the education provided by that university. Obviously, expansion of enrollment without supportive increase of both number and quality of teachers will lead to the deterioration of the student-teacher ratio, and in the long run, the quality of education.

主持人：那么我们可以做什么来保证更多学生获得机会的同时，大学又能够健康发展呢？

赫曼斯博士：首先，我认为扩招应该比较适度、稳健。如果可以是三年扩招两倍的速度，那么绝不要六年扩招五倍。其次，助学政策、助学贷款、助学金和奖学金体系应该得到足够重视，可以支持经济困难的学生。

Dr. Yang: Apart from that, while universities are expanding enrollment, problems of outdated teaching materials, and antiquated teaching methods should be tackled. This way, college graduates can be expected to become the talents demanded by society, leading to no difficulty finding employment.

主持人：感谢杨博士和赫曼斯博士来到这里分享你们的观点。

Task 4

彼得：王博士，感谢邀请我前来。我们知道，电动汽车自面世以来已经获得了巨大的技术进步，现在也更加受到欢迎了。

Dr. Wang: Our countries are not alone in recognising the benefits of electric vehicles. Many major car-producing countries are looking beyond conventional petrol and diesel technology. That is why we want to accelerate the transition and bring the benefits of electric vehicles to drivers, the public and our environment as soon as we can.

彼得：是的，我们通过资助和税收制度对选择清洁汽车的驾驶者提供经济助力，还支持当地机构提供激励政策，比如，免费停车和免收拥堵费等。未来，我们想要使电动汽车的充电变得更加简单及便捷。

Dr. Wang: Nowadays, choosing a new car is always hard for drivers. And it's even harder if you're trying to make the decision between a traditional gas-powered car or an electric car such as the Nissan Leaf, Ford Focus Electric or Tesla Model S.

彼得：是的，在选择买什么车的时候，驾驶者往往会考虑电动汽车最大的优点，也是很明显的：不需要加油。这确实是大事，美国人在加油上的花费是年人均2,000到4,000美元之间。使用全电动汽车，比如，日产聆风，这部分的费用就省去了，当然充电也不是完全免费的。

Dr. Wang: Beyond the fuel-saving benefit, EVs offer another major cost savings: maintenance. Since an EV is fully electric, it no longer uses oil to lubricate the engine. That means oil changes are a thing of the past. Plus, brakes won't wear as quickly, either, so you won't need to replace pads as often as you do on a normal car.

彼得：当然，插电式混合动力汽车也可以节省大部分的油费，但是它仍然使用汽油发动机，可以起到续航的作用。

Dr. Wang: Peter, you talked about the biggest perceived negative of electric cars, which is their limited range. The so-called "range anxiety" is the fear you'll run out of power when you're nowhere near a charging station. This is a factor now holding back potential buyers.

彼得：确实。举个例子，日产聆风充电一次可以行驶107英里。对大多数驾驶者来说，足够用了。然而，一次充电只能行驶100英里，大多数潜在客户还是有所担心，认为电动汽车有限的里程还不能满足他们的需求。

Dr. Wang: Along the same lines, another big disadvantage is that many drivers will have to install a charging station at home. It's not necessary, however, as you can simply charge your EV at work or at various public charging stations. But most users will want a charging station at home, cutting into the cost savings from owning an EV in the first place.

彼得：是的，住在整套房子里的人们，下班回家之后，可以将车插上电，第二天早上离开家时，电池就已经充满了。

Dr. Wang: On the priorities for the charging infrastructure, will be the focus on shopping centres and other places where people naturally leave their cars for a considerable time, not just petrol stations and places where they want to nip in and out. It is also very important that the charging infrastructure is spread. There is a risk that charging infrastructure becomes focused on major routes and in urban and suburban areas, and that smaller roads and rural parts are under-provided.

彼得：政府应该进一步加以管理，让所有新房子的车道都可以配电，以更有效地为电动汽车充电。所有新建的工作场所也应该设有电动汽车充电设施，或者预留出充电桩的安装位置。

Dr. Wang: And I think those who have electric vehicles should be identified. In Norway, such vehicles have the identifying letters EL on their licence plates. I hope that people can be rewarded by the government for turning to electric vehicles. It is an exciting technology. It is the future, and I am glad that our governments are grasping it by the horns.

彼得：目前为止，其他技术也对我们如何使用汽车产生了深远的影响。革命性的新型辅助系统已经为驾驶者提供了崭新的驾乘体验，我们已经对这些习以为常了。我们的父辈不能想象卫星导航，辅助停车，甚至巡航控制，这些对上一代或之前一代的人们来说，更像是科幻小说。

Dr. Wang: In essence, the increase in electric vehicles has big implications for the way we power our cars. And this is not science fiction; it is science fact. They merely mark the way towards a much more significant change: the combination of technologies we will enjoy in our lifetime, and certainly in our children's, will change motoring profoundly.

彼得：基于这些事实，现在我们需要引入广泛的充电网络，使电动汽车也可以用于长途旅行。

Dr. Wang: While it can be difficult to decide between electric vehicles and gas-powered models, we hope our explanation of the benefits and disadvantages can make the choice a little easier.

References

柴明颎. 英语口译——公共演讲与复述 [M]. 上海：上海交通大学出版社，2014.

常俊跃，邹德艳. 同声传译 [M]. 北京：国防工业出版社，2013.

陈明瑶. 论语篇连贯与话语标记语的汉译 [J]. 上海翻译，2005（4）：20-23.

戴惠萍. 交替传译实践教程 [M]. 上海：上海外语教育出版社，2014.

东尼·博赞. 思维导图——大脑使用说明书 [M]. 北京：外语教学与研究出版社，2005.

东尼·博赞. 博赞记忆术 [M]. 北京：化学工业出版社，2014.

高彬，柴明颎. 释意理论的历史性解读 [J]. 解放军外国语学院学报，2009（3）：71-76.

龚龙生. 商务英语口译教程 [M]. 上海：上海外语教育出版社，2011.

桂诗春. 心理语言学 [M]. 上海：上海外语教育出版社，1998.

哈里·洛拉尼. 哈佛记忆课 [M]. 北京：北京联合出版公司，2014.

胡壮麟等. 系统功能语法概论 [M]. 长沙：湖南教育出版社，1989.

胡壮麟等. 系统功能语言学概论 [M]. 北京：北京大学出版社，2008.

剑桥大学考试委员会外语考试部. 剑桥雅思考试全真试题 [M]. 北京/伦敦：外语教学与研究出版社/剑桥大学出版社，2013.

刘和平. 口译技巧——思维科学与口译推理教学法 [M]. 北京：中国对外翻译出版公司，2001.

刘宓庆. 口笔译理论研究 [M]. 北京：中国对外翻译出版社，2004.

刘志华. 超级记忆力训练法 [M]. 北京：中国纺织出版社，2015.

卢信朝. 英汉口译技能教程——听辨 [M]. 北京：北京语言大学出版社，2012.

屈承熹，潘文国. 汉语篇章语法 [M]. 北京：北京语言大学出版社，2006.

谭载喜. 新编奈达论翻译 [M]. 北京：中国对外翻译出版公司，1999.

王斌华. 口译即释意？——关于释意理论及有关争议的反思 [J]. 外语研究，2008（5）：72-76.

夏雅君等. 浅谈复述在英语教学中的运用 [J]. 景德镇高专学报，2007（1）：89-90.

徐赳赳. 现代汉语篇章语言学 [M]. 北京：商务印书馆，2010.

徐然. "专注听力"——口译听力培训方法之我见 [J]. 中国翻译，2010（3）：43-47.

杨承淑. 口译教学研究：理论与实践 [M]. 北京：中国对外翻译出版公司，2005.

杨帆. 李显龙在2014年国庆群众大会上演讲的口译实践报告［D］. 大连外国语大学，2016.

张德禄等. 功能语言学与外语教学［M］. 北京：人民教育出版社，2005.

张今，张克定. 英汉语信息结构对比研究［M］. 郑州：河南大学出版社，1998.

张文，韩常慧. 口译理论研究［M］. 北京：科学出版社，2006.

仲伟合等. 口译研究方法论［M］. 北京：外语教学与研究出版社，2012.

仲伟合，詹成. 同声传译［M］. 北京：外语教学与研究出版社，2009.

邹德艳. 口译教学与教学口译［J］. 长春理工大学学报，2011（5）：162-164.

邹德艳. 社会表征视阈下的释意理论解读［J］. 云南民族大学学报（哲学社会科学版），2013（6）：113-116.

邹德艳. 口译的记忆训练——理论与实践［M］. 北京：中央编译出版社，2016.

邹德艳. 交替传译工作记忆能力的差异研究［M］. 北京：中央编译出版社，2017.

邹申，陈春华. TEM 8 听力理解［M］. 上海：上海外语教育出版社，2013.

Aish F. & Jo Tomlinson. *Listening for IELTS* [M]. London: HarperCollins Publishers, 2011.

Al-Rubai'i, Alya' M. H. Ahmad. Instructing novice consecutive interpreters: Steps to improve the performance of memory [J]. *Babel*, 2009, 55(4): 329-344.

Andres, D. & M. Behr. *To Know How to Suggest-Approaches to Teaching Conference Interpreting* [M]. Berlin: Frank & Timme Verlag fur wissenschaftliche Literatur, 2015.

Badger, I. *English for Life: Listening* [M]. London: HarperCollins Publishers, 2014.

Bailey, S. *Academic Writing: A Practical Guide for Students* [M]. London: Nelson Thornes Ltd, 2003.

Baker, M. *In Other Words* [M]. London: Routledge, 1992.

Callis, S. *Working with People* [M]. Coventry: Hodder Education, 2010.

Chaudron, C. & J. C. Richards. The effect of discourse markers on the comprehension of lectures [J]. *Applied Linguistics*, 1986 (7): 113-127.

Chernov, G. V. *Inference and Anticipation in Simultaneous Interpreting* [M]. Shanghai: Shanghai Foreign Language Education Press, 2011.

Cohen, A. Measuring intelligibility in foreign language learning [A]. In A. J. van Essen & J. P. Menting (Eds.). *The Context of Foreign Language Learning* [C]. Assen, 1975.

Craven, M. *Real Listening and Speaking* [M]. Cambridge: Cambridge University Press, 2008.

Cruse, A. *Meaning in Language: An Introduction to Semantics and Pragmatics* [M]. Oxford: Oxford University Press, 2002.

Dam, H. V. On the option between form-based and meaning-based interpreting: The effect of source text difficulty on lexical target text form in simultaneous interpreting [J] . *The Interpreters' Newsletter*, 2001 (11): 27-55.

Davison, A. & G. M. Green. Introduction. In A. Davison & G. M. Green (Eds.). *Linguistic Complexity and Text Comprehension: Readability Issues Reconsidered* [C] . Hillsdael, NJ: Erlbaum, 1988: 1-4.

Eisenberg, A. M. *Living Communication* [M] . New Jersey: Prentice Hall, 1975.

Flowerdew, J. & S. Tauroza. The effect of discourse markers on second language lecture comprehension [J] . *Studies in Second Language Acquisition*, 1995 (17): 435-458.

Fraser, B. What are discourse markers? [J] . *Journal of Pragmatics*, 1999 (30): 931-952.

Gile, D. The processing capacity issue in conference interpretation [J] . *Babel*, 1991 (37): 115-127.

Gile, D. *Basic Concepts and Models for Interpreter and Translator Training* [M] . Amsterdam: John Benjamins Publishing Company, 1995.

Gillies, A. *Note-taking for Consecutive Interpreting: A Short Course* [M] . Shanghai: Shanghai Foreign Language Education Press, 2009.

Halliday, M. A. K. & R. Hasan. *Cohesion in English* [M] . London: Longman, 1976.

Halliday, M. A. K. *Spoken and Written English* [M] . Victoria: Deakin University, 1985.

Halliday, M. A. K. *An Introduction to Functional Grammar* [M] . London: Edward Arnold, 1994.

Halliday, M. A. K. *An Introduction to Functional Grammar* [M] . Beijing: Foreign Language Teaching and Research Press, 2000.

Halliday, M. A. K. Things and relations: Regrammatizing experience as technical knowledge [A] . In Jonathan J. Webster (Eds.). *The Language of Science, Volume 5 in the Collected Works of M. A. K. Halliday* [C] . London: Edward Arnold, 2004.

Jones, R. *Conference Interpreting Explained* [M] . Shanghai: Shanghai Foreign Language Education Press, 2008.

Lebauber, R.S. *Learn to Listen: Listen to Learn* [M] . Beijing: Pearson Education Asia Limited and Beijing Language and Culture University Press, 2006.

Levelt, W.J.M. *Speaking: From Intention to Articulation* [M] . Cambridge: MIT Press, 1989.

Liu, M. & Y. Chui. Assessing source material difficulty for consecutive interpreting: quantifiable measure and holistic judgment [J] . *Interpreting*, 2009 (2): 244-266.

Lucantoni, P. *English as a Second Language* [M] . Cambridge: Cambridge University Press,

2009.

Mascull, B. *Business Vocabulary in Use* [M] . Cambridge: Cambridge University Press, 2002.

Nida, E. *Language, Culture and Translation* [M] . Shanghai: Shanghai Foreign Language Education Press, 2001.

Nida, E. & C. Taber. *The Theory and Practice of Translation* [M] . Leiden: E. J. Brill, 1982.

Nolan, J. *Interpretation: Techniques and Exercise* [M] . Shanghai: Shanghai Foreign Language Education Press, 2008.

Pöchhacker, F. *Introducing Interpreting Studies* [M] . London: Routledge, 2004.

Rezaf. Information Theory [A] . *Encyclopedia Americanna* [Z] . Beijing: Foreign Languages Press, 1990.

Templar R. *How to Get Things Done Without Trying Too Hard* [M] . Harlow: Pearson Education Limited, 2011.

Tudhope, Simon. *Usborne London Quiz Book* [M] . London: Usborne Publishing Ltd., 2017.

Ure, J. Lexical density and register differentiation [A] , In G. Perren & J. L. M. Trim (Eds), *Applications of Linguistics: Selected Papers of the Second International Congress of Applied Linguistics* [C] . London: Cambridge University Press, 1971: 443-452.

Weber, W. K. *Training Translators and Conference Interpreters* [M] . Orlando: Harcourt, 1984.

Williams, A. *Writing for IELTS* [M] . London: HarperCollins Publishers, 2011.

Yule, G. & G. Brown. *Discourse Analysis* [M] . Beijing: Foreign Language Teaching and Research Press, 2000.

http://www.mbalib.com/

https://www.englishclub.com/

https://www.eslgold.com/

https://www.english-magazine.org/

http://www.studyez.com/cet/mnst/

http://www.englishbus.net/

http://web2.uvcs.uvic.ca/elc/studyzone/

http://www.en84.com/

http://media.unwto.org/

http://www.wikihow.com/Paraphrase-a-Paragraph

http://www.wikihow.com/Start-a-Paragraph

https://www.itdp.org/wp-content/uploads/2014/12/Shared-Parking_ITDP.pdf

http://www.pressreader.com/china/china-daily-usa/20170803/textview

https://www.thebalance.com/what-is-marketing-2296057

http://www.lansingstatejournal.com/story/money/business/2015/07/31/first-impression-interview-lasting-impact/30824309/

http://www.maturetimes.co.uk/

https://integrity.mit.edu/handbook/academic-writing/summarizing

https://blog.mint.com/planning/3-reasons-why-personal-finance-should-be-taught-in-high-schools-1113/

http://www.acas.org.uk/index.aspx?articleid=4953

http://www.childnet.com/parents-and-carers/hot-topics/gaming

http://hospital2020.org/agreenhospital.html

https://www.greenbiz.com/news/2006/03/14/americas-top-10-green-hospitals

http://big5.news.cn/gate/big5/news.xinhuanet.com/english/2015-06/12/c_134321139.htm

http://goodvisionforlife.com.au/better-vision/digital-devices/

http://www.quickanddirtytips.com/health-fitness/healthy-eating/farm-raised-vs-wild-caught-fish